Phenomenon

Other Books by John Michael Greer

Atlantis: Ancient Legacy, Hidden Prophecy
Encyclopedia of Natural Magic
Inside a Magical Lodge: Group Ritual in the Western Tradition
Monsters: An Investigator's Guide to Magical Beings
Natural Magic: Potions and Powers from the Magical Garden
The New Encyclopedia of the Occult

About the Author

A student of magic and the unexplained for more than thirty years and the author of more than a dozen books, including the award-winning *New Encyclopedia of the Occult*, John Michael Greer has earned a reputation as one of the most original writers in the occult field today. His background combines academic study in the history of ideas with training and initiation in several occult and Druid orders. He lives in the mountains of southern Oregon with his wife, Sara.

Many of Llewellyn's authors have websites with additional information and resources. For more information, please visit our website at http://www.llewellyn.com.

FORTY-FIVE

John Michael Greer

Phenomenon

Fact, Fantasy and Disinformation

Llewellyn Publications
Woodbury, Minnesota

First Edition
First Printing, 2009

Book design Steffani Sawyer
Editing by Brett Fechheimer
Cover design by Kevin R. Brown

Llewellyn is a registered trademark of Llewellyn Worldwide, Ltd.

Library of Congress Cataloging-in-Publication Data
Greer, John Michael.
  The UFO phenomenon : fact, fantasy and disinformation / John Michael Greer. — 1st ed.
      p.   cm.
  Includes bibliographical references and index.
  ISBN 978-0-7387-1319-9
  1. Unidentified flying objects—History. I. Title.
  TL789.G7455 2009
  001.942—dc22
                                                                    2008040890

Llewellyn Publications
A Division of Llewellyn Worldwide, Ltd.
2143 Wooddale Drive, Dept. 978-0-7387-1319-9
Woodbury, Minnesota 55125-2989, U.S.A.
www.llewellyn.com

Printed in the United States of America

 Printed in the United States of America on recycled paper comprised of 15 percent post-consumer waste

contents

acknowledgments

No author writes a book by himself, and this exploration of the UFO phenomenon has depended more than most of my other works on the assistance of others. Heading the list of those who deserve thanks are Jordan Pease, who gave me free run of his extraordinary collection of rare UFO books; David Larson, who lent me rare contactee classics from the 1950s and shared his recollections of the space program that gave the UFO phenomenon so much of its cultural context; David Spangler, who helped me understand the contactee and New Age scene in which he played so significant a part; and Erskine Payton, talk show host extraordinaire, whose identification of an alien goddess as one of Dean Martin's Ding-a-Lings will doubtless give us something else to talk about on a future show. The staff of the Rogue Valley Metaphysical Library, Southern Oregon University's Hannon Library, and the Ashland, Oregon, public library were consistently helpful, and Elysia Gallo of Llewellyn Publications played her usual enthusiastic part in helping to get this project into print.

Some of those mentioned may not be especially pleased with the results of all this work. My research started out within the familiar opposition between those who believe that UFOs are spacecraft from other planets and those who believe UFOs do not exist at all, but it soon left that conflict behind to pursue stranger and more rewarding topics—the nature of apparitions, the history of American secret aerospace projects, the mythology of progress, and the role of popular culture in defining experienced reality, to name only a few.

The result is not the book I intended to write about UFOs, though it turned into the only one I could write on that subject. It challenges many of the most basic assumptions of both sides in the ongoing quarrel, and attempts to restate the unanswered questions surrounding the UFO phenomenon in ways that allow them to be dealt with and solved. Whether or not that solution turns out to be correct, my hope is that the explorations and redefinitions attempted here at least cast a new light on one of the abiding mysteries of the twentieth century.

introduction
The UFO Mystery

I n many ways, the best way to approach the subject of this book is to glance at the gray silhouette in the upper right-hand corner of this page. If you're like most people in the world today, you recognized it immediately as an image of an unidentified flying object, or UFO. During the second half of the twentieth century, this image leapt from obscurity to become one of the most widely recognized visual icons in modern culture. As instantly recognizable and fraught with meanings as the swastika or the Christian cross, it carries an additional burden of mystery and controversy. Some people have questioned whether Jesus of Nazareth was ever a living human being, but nobody doubts the existence of the Christian church, and Adolf Hitler and his Nazi party made their appalling reality all too evident within living memory.

UFOs are different. Around half of all Americans believe that they exist, according to a variety of recent polls, and about half insist that they do not exist. After sixty years of confusion and controversy, claims and counterclaims, hoaxes, delusions, and honest reports of strange things in the air, nobody has yet been able to build a case for their existence or nonexistence convincing to those not already committed to one belief or the other. Yet these mysterious objects, whether or not they exist in any physical sense, have become a massive reality in the world of our collective imagination.

This reality surfaces in small ways as well as obvious ones. Go to the nearest large grocery store, for example, and you'll most likely have a close encounter with at least one flying saucer. It might be the one hovering on the labels of UFO Brand sponges and scrubbing pads—"cleaning products that are out of this world"[1]—or those on the box of UFOs breakfast cereal, surrounding the smiling face of a green-skinned alien. Stop in the greeting-card section and you'll likely be able to buy a humorous birthday card with a joke revolving around flying saucers or alien abduction. Glance over the toys, and you'll probably find a brightly colored flying saucer or two hanging among the dolls and toy cars. Go home and turn on the television, and if you can find an old science fiction movie or an episode of one of the SF series of yester-year, your chances of spotting saucers on the screen are pretty good.

Now it's true that the same sort of presence surrounds many other entities whose nonexistence is accepted by everybody. An image of Santa Claus or the Easter Bunny, for example, is just as recognizable as that of a flying saucer, and at the right time of year could be found even more easily in the same grocery store. Part of the difference, of course, is that nobody claims to have seen Santa Claus or the Easter Bunny, at least to any listener much past kindergarten age, while people—tens of thousands of them—do claim to have seen UFOs.

Yet there's another side to the UFO phenomenon that sets it apart at least as forcefully. Santa Claus and the Easter Bunny are relics of folk beliefs centuries old, long since stripped of the meanings that once made them powerful symbols. Few people nowadays recall the northern European shamanic traditions that gave Santa's clothing the color of the northern world's most widely used hallucinogenic mush-room,[2] along with his reindeer and nocturnal flights near the winter

---

1. See http://www.ufobrand.com.

2. This is *Amanita muscaria*, which has a red skin spotted with white and a fringe of white gills. See Renterghem 1995 for a discussion of Santa's shamanic roots.

solstice. In the same way, the robust sexual symbolism of rabbits and roosters that once surrounded the spring equinox, and passed over to Easter with the coming of Christianity, has been watered down into the pastel cuteness of bunnies and chicks in modern Easter imagery.

Once again, though, UFOs are different. The fabric of meanings and beliefs that have grown up around them in the years since 1947, when the UFO phenomenon first exploded into public awareness, draws on issues that are still very much with us today. For many people, whether or not they believe in their physical existence, UFOs have become a central element in attempts to make sense of some of the biggest questions of our time—the future of industrial society, the relationship between citizens and their government, the nature of scientific evidence, and the origin and destiny of humanity, to name just a few. Beliefs about Santa Claus don't lead people to devote their lives to researching a mystery, accuse their government of conspiracy, question their entire view of reality, or commit mass suicide. Beliefs about UFOs do.

TABLE 1
The late J. Allen Hynek, one of America's most distinguished UFO researchers and the founder of CUFOS (Center for UFO Studies), devised the standard system for classifying UFO sightings; this was expanded in the late 1980s to provide a category for abductions. The expanded system is given below.
NL: Nocturnal light—a glowing object seen at night from more than 300 meters away DD: Daylight disk—a UFO seen in the daytime from more than 300 meters away CE-1: Close encounter of the first kind—a UFO seen from less than 300 meters away CE-2: Close encounter of the second kind—a UFO that leaves physical traces CE-3: Close encounter of the third kind—an encounter with UFO occupants CE-4: Close encounter of the fourth kind—the abduction of a human by UFO occupants

All these complexities unfold from the simple if awkward fact that people all over the world have seen things in the sky that they cannot explain in terms acceptable to the modern scientific worldview. A glance at a typical sighting will highlight some of the issues involved, and start the process of unraveling the UFO mystery.

Anatomy of a Sighting

The evening of Monday, January 6, 1969, was cool and clear in the small town of Leary, Georgia. By 7:15 PM, as a cluster of men in business suits gathered in front of the town swimming pool, a skyful of bright stars blazed overhead, veiled here and there by a few scattered clouds. The men in suits paid little attention to the stars; members of the local Lions Club, which met in the pool building, they puffed on cigarettes and shook hands with the district governor of the club, who had driven down to Leary for his official visit that night. Then somebody pointed to a bright light hovering in the western sky—a light that appeared to be moving toward them.[3]

Bluish at first, the light turned red as it approached the startled club members. At its closest approach, it seemed to be perhaps a few hundred yards away, and appeared as large and bright as the moon. It stopped, moved a short distance away, came close again, and then flew off into the distance and vanished. "It was the darnedest thing I've ever seen," the district governor commented some years later. "We watched it for ten minutes, but none of us could figure out what it was."

The club members filed into the pool building a few minutes later, held their meeting, took in a speech by the district governor, and went home for the night. Nothing else unusual happened. In the terminology of UFO investigators, it was one more classic close encounter of the first kind, like some hundreds of thousands recorded since the beginning of the UFO controversy in 1947. The entire sighting would likely have been forgotten forever, except that the district governor visiting the club on that January evening was a peanut farmer and Georgia politician named Jimmy Carter, who was inaugurated Presi-

---

3. I have used the account in Sheaffer 1981, 4–12, as the basis for this and the following four paragraphs.

dent of the United States almost exactly eight years after the night he watched a UFO in Georgia's skies.

The publicity that surged around the sighting once Carter became a national figure guaranteed that an investigation would follow. More precisely, there were two investigations—one by a believer in the theory that UFOs come from another planet, the other by a believer in the theory that UFOs do not exist. The first investigation was by Hayden Hewes of the International UFO Bureau, and consisted simply of sending Carter a form, which he obligingly filled out and returned. Without further ado, the light was identified as an extraterrestrial craft. Thereafter the Carter sighting routinely appeared in one set of UFO-related publications as a classic case of a close encounter with an alien spaceship.

The second investigation was by Robert Sheaffer of the Committee for Scientific Investigation of Claims of the Paranormal (CSICOP), one of the major UFO-debunking organizations. Sheaffer tracked down the date and time of the sighting, determined that the planet Venus had been more or less in the same region of the sky where the witnesses had seen the light, and announced that the case was closed—Carter had mistaken a planet for a UFO. Thereafter the Carter sighting routinely appeared in a different set of UFO-related publications as a classic case of simple misperception of a known and entirely natural object.

These two investigations and their results were just as typical as the sighting itself, and just as inconclusive. Both of them satisfied the expectations of the audiences for which they were written, and neither one offered anything to quell the reasonable doubts of people outside those audiences. The claim that the light observed by Carter and his fellow Lions must have been an alien spacecraft, on the one hand, only makes sense to those who already believe that unusual lights in the sky must, by definition, be starships from another world. Nothing in the light's appearance or behavior justifies that assumption; all the evidence shows is that the witnesses watched an odd light in the sky that none of them were able to identify.

At the same time, the claim that the light in the sky must have been the planet Venus is nearly as unsatisfactory. Most people have watched Venus rising before the sun or setting after it. Very few, at least without chemical help, have observed it change color from bluish to red, expand to the apparent size of a full moon, and maneuver back and forth through the sky. If the same ten witnesses testified that they saw a dump truck go rumbling down the street in front of them, Sheaffer would have a hard time convincing a jury that they actually saw a child's tricycle sitting in a yard at the end of the block, after all, and it's reasonable to suggest that the same logic applies here.

As for Sheaffer's claim that since Venus was in the same general region of the sky, the light must have been Venus, this is a circular argument that assumes what it claims to prove. If something strange hovered in the sky that evening, Carter and the other witnesses could reasonably be excused for not noticing a planet off in the background. If the light actually was the planet Venus, on the other hand, some explanation has to be given for the hallucination that affected the members of the Leary Lions Club that night. The small business owners and middle-class retirees who make up the bulk of Lions Club members are arguably not the world's most hallucination-prone population. Insisting that this particular group must have hallucinated the light's changes in position and size because the Venus theory requires such a supposition, again, assumes what it claims to prove.

Both investigations, in other words, started from a preconceived agenda—one, that UFOs must be alien spacecraft; the other, that UFOs must be hoaxes, delusions, or misidentifications of natural phenomena—and both investigations, in fine displays of circular reasoning, found exactly what they expected to find. Start with a different set of presuppositions and pursue them in the same way, and it would be just as possible to "prove" anything you like about the curious light Jimmy Carter and his fellow Lions saw in the Georgia sky. A few UFO researchers have found their own reasons to support various alternative theories, and a few—a very few—have tried to approach the phenomenon from a less doctrinaire standpoint. On the whole, though, our culture's collective discussion about UFOs has been dominated by the same two theories that found their own preferred answers to the Carter sighting.

A War of Hypotheses

What makes the role of these two theories about UFOs so fascinating is that for most people, in or out of the various communities concerned with UFOs, they aren't theories at all. It has become a staple belief in popular culture that unidentified objects seen in the sky must be alien spacecraft from a distant planet, if they exist at all. For decades now it's been common to find terms such as "pro-UFO" or "UFO believer" used for people who accept the claim that UFOs must be extraterrestrial spaceships, and terms such as "anti-UFO" or "UFO skeptic" for those who insist that UFOs must be some combination of hoaxes, hallucinations, and misperceptions of perfectly ordinary objects.

It should be obvious that a very large number of factors could cause people—the members of the Leary Lions Club or anyone else—to see something in the sky they cannot identify. It should be equally obvious that the phrase *unidentified flying object* means what it says—an object in the air that the observers cannot identify—and nothing more, and that any theory about what the object might be is something separate from the experience itself. The fact that neither of these things is obvious at all in today's UFO debates is one of the most interesting and least discussed dimensions of the whole phenomenon. As Thomas Bullard has pointed out in a cogent article, the experiential dimension of UFOs—the unidentified lights and objects seen in the skies by hundreds of thousands of people over the last six decades and more—has long since been pushed off center stage by the myths, stories, and assumptions that have made the UFO one of the most recognizable cultural icons on Earth.[4]

It's unlikely that one book can bring clarity to a tangle this dense, but the effort has to be made. In this book, therefore, terms like "UFO believer" and "UFO skeptic" will occur only in quotations. The theory that people who see UFOs have spotted alien spacecraft from distant planets will be called the *extraterrestrial hypothesis* or ETH, the term that has most often been used for it in the small minority of books that have explored other options. The theory that people who claim

---

4. Bullard 2000.

to see UFOs are reporting hoaxes, delusions, or misidentifications of ordinary phenomena will be called the *null hypothesis* or NH; this term has been used a few times in UFO-related publications, notably by NH believer Robert Sheaffer in his debunking volume *The UFO Verdict*. There are, as it happens, a number of other hypotheses about the origins and nature of UFOs, and they will also be discussed in this book.

The dominance of the extraterrestrial and null hypotheses in the UFO debate has resulted in remarkable distortions in the way UFO experiences are collected, interpreted, and used. Both sides collect evidence that supports their point of view as ammunition for the struggle against the other side, and devalue everything else. Thus it's common to find believers in the extraterrestrial hypothesis claiming that a "large and consistent body of UFO evidence . . . almost shouts 'extraterrestrial technology,'"[5] while believers in the null hypothesis insist that the evidence clearly shows that UFOs do not exist.[6] As a result, dimensions of the phenomenon that don't fit either set of presuppositions fall through the cracks.

This distorting effect has had a particularly potent influence on the way the history of the UFO phenomenon has been portrayed. David Jacobs' 1974 doctoral dissertation, *The UFO Controversy in America*, for many years the only serious attempt at a historical study of the phenomenon, managed to leave out many of the most influential figures of the early years of UFO studies—Charles Fort, Raymond Palmer, and Meade Layne, among others—whose roles in the controversy, as we will see, cast an uncomfortable light on the origins of the extraterrestrial hypothesis Jacobs' work supports.[7] Equally drastic distortions of history can be found in books supporting the null hypothesis.

For this reason our investigation will start by tracing UFOs back through time. When did people first start seeing UFOs of the sort reported by modern witnesses, and what did they think about the things that they saw? The answers redefine the UFO phenomenon in unexpected ways.

---

5. Donderi 2000, 56.

6. Sheaffer 1981, 197–213.

7. Keel 1989, 145, discusses the revisionist dimension of Jacobs' history.

Part One

Tracking the Phenomenon

A procession of the damned.

By the damned, I mean the excluded.

We shall have a procession of the data that Science has excluded.

Battalions of the accursed, captained by pallid data that I have exhumed, will march. You'll read them—or they'll march. Some of them livid and some of them fiery and some of them rotten . . . the naive and the pedantic and the bizarre and the grotesque and the sincere and the insincere, the profound and the puerile.
—Charles Fort, *The Book of the Damned*

The White Rabbit put on his spectacles. "Where shall I begin, please your Majesty?" he asked.

"Begin at the beginning," the King said, very gravely, "and go on until you come to the end: then stop."
—Lewis Carroll, *Alice's Adventures in Wonderland*

one

Before the Saucers Came, Prehistory–1947

Most popular histories of the UFO phenomenon trace its origins to 1947, when pilot Kenneth Arnold spotted nine unidentified objects in the air near Mount Rainier. More historically literate researchers connect the phenomenon to the "ghost rockets" tracked over Sweden in 1946, the "foo fighters" encountered by pilots of both sides in the Second World War, and the phantom airships sighted in American airspace in 1896–1897 and 1909 and in Britain's skies between 1909 and 1912. All these are important precursors to the contemporary UFO mystery. Still, like UFOs themselves, they need to be placed in a much wider historical context.

When a defender of the extraterrestrial hypothesis comments that "to all appearances, the UFO phenomenon is a recent historical occurrence, apparently no more than two centuries old,"[8] he is, in fact, quite simply wrong. Since the beginning of recorded history, people have seen strange things in the sky much like the ones that have been central to the UFO phenomenon since 1947. Consider the following sighting from Japan. A luminous object described as resembling an

---

8. Clark 2000, 122.

"earthenware vessel" was sighted around midnight in Kii Province; it flew out from behind Mount Fukuhara in the northeast, turned in midair, and passed out of sight due south. A perfectly ordinary UFO sighting—except that this one happened on the night of October 27, 1180.[9]

Such sightings are far from rare in old chronicles. To cite only a few examples, the great Roman historian Livy describes a sighting of a "shield in the sky" near the town of Arpi in Book XXII of his *Histories*. Sightings of a similar flying shield were chronicled by Pliny in Book II, chapter 24 of his *Natural History*. Holinshed's *Chronicle of England* describes a flaming wheel seen in the sky by many people in the winter of 1394, while Pedro Sarmiento, a Spanish sea captain of the Age of Discovery, sighted a shield-shaped object in the skies above the Straits of Magellan in 1580.[10] This brief list could be expanded many times over from nearly any historical chronicle from the ancient or medieval worlds.

During the Renaissance and early modern periods, an entire literature on "prodigies"—unexplained phenomena of various kinds—had a wide popularity, not least because strange events were anything but uncommon. As Pierre Boaistuau, one author in this genre, commented in his *History of Prodigies* in 1560: "The face of heaven has so often been disfigured by bearded, hairy comets, torches, flames, columns, spears, shields, dragons, duplicate moons, suns, and other similar things, that if one wanted to tell in an orderly fashion those that have happened since the birth of Jesus Christ only, and inquire into the causes of their origin, the lifetime of a single man would not be enough."[11]

Boaistuau's shields and duplicate moons would doubtless be called UFOs if they appeared in today's skies. The raw diversity of his descriptions and those of other writers on prodigies, though, points up a crucial fact about the UFO phenomenon: it is far more diverse

---

9. Cited in Vallee 1969, 5.

10. See the useful list in Hurley 2003.

11. Ibid., 7.

than most of the theories that have been proposed to explain it. In order to put the phenomenon into its proper context, it's necessary to take a wider view and include the whole range of weird phenomena that have been sighted in the skies down through the centuries.

The list of "flying shields" given above, in fact, could equally well be used as an example of a bad habit common to all sides of the contemporary UFO controversy—the habit of picking through diverse data to select out only those examples that support an existing theory. The same books of prodigies that yield ancient, medieval, and Renaissance flying-saucer sightings also record reports of aerial objects that looked like dragons, swords, fighting armies, sailing ships, and many stranger things. If the "flying shields" are admitted as evidence, and they should be, the dragons cannot be excluded.

Dragons and their like are hard to force-fit into the mold of the extraterrestrial hypothesis, and of course this is why they have so little place in today's discussion. Still, many of these aerial apparitions echo elements of today's UFO phenomenon in surprising ways. People in early medieval Europe, for example, were quite familiar with the idea of nonhuman beings who traveled through the air and abducted human beings for their own sinister purposes. These entities belonged to the Wild Hunt, a spectral army that rode phantom horses (the most advanced transportation technology of the time) through the night skies. The Wild Hunt was not just folklore; there are people living today in southern Germany and the northern cantons of Switzerland, where many old beliefs still linger, who claim to have seen it in their youth.

Another class of legendary beings in European folklore also have more than a little relevance to the modern UFO phenomenon. These are hovering nocturnal lights of varying colors and brightnesses, most often seen near wetlands. In Britain, they have comfortable folk names such as Kit wi'th' Canstick, Will o' the Wisp, and Jack o' Lantern—a "canstick" is a candlestick, a wisp was a twist of dry straw dipped in oil and lit for temporary illumination, and Jack with his lantern was a spirit long before his name became attached to the hollow, candle-bearing pumpkins that imitate his presence in late October nowadays.

These have sometimes been explained by modern scientists as bursts of methane—that is, swamp gas—that spontaneously ignite, but this phenomenon does not produce the effect described by medieval and modern witnesses alike: a hovering ball of light, anything from a few inches to a few feet in diameter, that drifts through the night air for minutes at a time.

In eastern Africa, unusual lights moving through the night sky are a known phenomenon, though there they are attributed to the activities of witches. These lights are not just folklore, either. British anthropologist Philip Mayer, who did extensive fieldwork among a Kenyan tribe, the Gusii, had this to say about them:

> *I have seen among the Gusii at night lights moving near my camp, lights that died down and flared up again exactly as the witchcraft myth alleges. Gusii say that witches produce this effect by raising and lowering the lids of covered fire-pots which they carry with them.*[12]

No less an anthropologist than E. E. Evans-Pritchard, whose 1937 book *Witchcraft and Oracles among the Azande* ranks as a classic scientific explication of witchcraft beliefs, confessed to having seen the same mysterious lights that Mayer observed and that the Azande, like the Gusii, attributed to flying witches.

Since the dawn of recorded history, in fact, human beings have been seeing weird things moving through the air, and those things have usually had a very close resemblance to the hopes, fears, and speculations of those who saw them. It was probably inevitable, then, that with the arrival of an age in which people focused their hopes, fears, and speculations on machines, people would start to see machines in the skies instead.

Airships, Foo Fighters, and Ghost Rockets

On the evening of April 19, 1897, two residents of the town of Beaumont, Texas—J. B. Ligon, the local agent for the Magnolia Brewery, and his son Charles—observed lights moving around in a neighbor's

---

12. Quoted in Harpur 1994, 6.

pasture a few hundred yards from their home and went to investigate. They found four men standing next to a grounded airship, who asked them for two buckets of water. The Ligons provided the water, and then questioned one of the men, who gave his name as Wilson. The airship was one of four, Wilson told them, with propellers and wings powered by electricity; they had been made in secrecy in a small Iowa town, and Wilson and his crew were returning there after a flight to the Gulf of Mexico. After the conversation, the men entered the airship and flew away.[13]

This was only one of dozens of airship sightings in twenty American states in 1896 and 1897. Several thousand witnesses in all spotted airships that appeared to consist of a long, cigar-shaped body with a gondola slung below it and some combination of propellers and flapping wings giving it motive power. The majority of these sightings involved airships moving past at a great height, but some came close enough to the ground to allow witnesses to hear voices and see people aboard the craft, and a few, like the one sighted by the Ligons, involved landings and contact between witnesses and the airships' occupants.

What makes these airship sightings a mystery is that in 1896 and 1897, no one anywhere on Earth had yet flown an airship that could do what the mystery airships were said to do. The best dirigible up to that time, built by Charles Renard and A. C. Krebs in France and flight-tested in Paris in 1884, could reach speeds of thirteen miles an hour, but could carry little more than its own pilot and had a maximum range of not much over a mile. The first really successful airship in the world was created by Alberto Santos-Dumont in France in 1898, and proved itself by rounding the Eiffel Tower in a seven-mile flight in 1901. The first successful airship in America, the *California Arrow* built by Thomas Baldwin, had its maiden flight in 1904.

While working airships were barely on the drawing boards in 1897, on the other hand, the idea of air travel had become close to a national obsession. In America, more than anywhere else in the industrial world, the belief that technological progress was as inevitable as

---

13.   Jacobs 1975, 12; see also *Houston Post*, April 21, 1897, 2.

it was beneficent had become a faith of religious intensity, and the dream of flying machines occupied a special place in that faith. Many Americans believed that sometime soon, the dramatic advances in transportation technology that yielded railroads and steamships would be more than matched by the conquest of the air, and a great deal of national pride focused on the hope that American inventors would lead the rest of the world in air travel. The airship sightings of 1896 and 1897 thus fed on, and fed, passionate hopes and expectations throughout the country.

The success of balloon flight, then nearly a century old, made the airship appear to be the most likely candidate for a successful air-travel technology, and speculative visions of a dirigible-filled future pervaded the popular press of the time. Many people in the last years of the nineteenth century believed that heavier-than-air craft would never fly; Carl Jung was among them, and commented ruefully on his youthful certainties in his 1958 book on flying saucers.[14] As late as the first decade of the twentieth century, when the Wright brothers' first airplanes had already shown the potential of heavier-than-air craft, science fiction stories by writers such as H. G. Wells and E. M. Forster still assumed that airships rather than airplanes would prove to be the wave of the future.

Yet dirigibles, despite their apparent promise, turned out to be a blind alley. The craft Americans in 1896 and 1897 saw cruising through the sky or coming to rest in pastures and woodlots across much of the country, in other words, were the aircraft Americans expected to see in the near future, rather than the ones Americans would actually see when the age of air travel finally dawned. More curiously still, the flapping wings and big fanlike propellers that seemed to drive the mystery airships across the sky would have been completely incapable of doing so—similar designs were tried repeatedly by airship inventors, and failed dismally—but they copied, down to fine details, the images of future airships in the popular literature of the late nineteenth century.

---

14. Jung 1978, 136.

Whatever the source of the mystery airships, they vanished toward the end of 1897. Aside from a repeat performance by phantom airships in New England in 1909, unknown aerial craft made only very occasional appearances in American skies thereafter until 1947. Overseas, by contrast, unidentified flying objects of various sorts enlivened the news at intervals straight through the intervening years. Airships appeared over Britain in 1909 and 1910, and again in 1912; by this time dirigibles had become a reality, but these sightings stubbornly failed to match the activities of any of the dirigibles known to exist in or near Britain during those years.

Another round of unexplained aerial sightings took place in Sweden and Norway in the years just before the Second World War. During the late 1930s, hundreds of witnesses sighted unmarked gray aircraft in Scandinavian airspace. Some of these craft, according to the descriptions, were larger than anything currently flying—one sported eight propellers—and engaged in impossibly risky maneuvers such as shutting off their engines and gliding in a descending spiral during severe snowstorms. The Swedish and Norwegian air forces tried and failed to find any firm evidence for their existence.

During the war years, these sightings stopped, but the end of hostilities brought these aerial phantoms back at once. This time the witnesses spotted "ghost rockets"—wingless, cylindrical flying craft moving at high speeds. More than two thousand sightings of these objects were reported in 1946. Speculation at the time focused on the possibility that the Russians were testing captured German V-2 rockets, but no evidence to support this claim ever surfaced, even when Russian military files became available after the fall of the Soviet Union.

Between these two Scandinavian flaps,[15] another set of puzzling aerial phenomena had scientists, pilots, and military officials scratching their heads all over the world. The "foo fighters," balls of light that played tag with aircraft, were sighted in every theater of the Second World War and by all sides in the conflict. They appeared to be balls of colored light a foot or so in diameter that appeared suddenly and

---

15. A *flap*, in UFO parlance, is a cluster of sightings in time—usually a period of several months to two years—during which sighting reports rise far above ordinary levels.

followed aircraft for up to forty minutes. They were sighted in daytime as well as at night, in a wide range of weather conditions, and were photographed more than once.[16] They first appeared in 1940, were sighted by pilots of all the warring powers in the years that followed, and remained active until the end of the war, when they went back to wherever aerial phantoms go in their off hours.

It's worth noting that nearly all the people who spotted these unidentified flying objects of the pre-1947 era assumed that they came from elsewhere on Earth. The phantom airships of the 1890s were widely thought to be the secret project of some clever inventor, while the Scandinavian ghost craft and the "foo fighters" were assumed to be secret military technology wielded by some hostile power. Still, a few voices during the 1896–1897 American airship flap proposed a different source for the unknown craft sighted in the skies. They argued that the airships must have come from Mars.[17]

Other Worlds Than Ours

The idea that intelligent beings might inhabit other worlds, in fact, has been in circulation in the Western world for more than two thousand years.[18] Ancient Greek philosophers such as Democritus of Abdera (c. 460–370 BCE) and Epicurus (341–270 BCE) argued that inhabited worlds existed all through an infinite cosmos. Renowned medieval scholars such as Albertus Magnus (c. 1193–1280) and Thomas Aquinas (1224–1274) debated the question of intelligent life on other worlds, and Etienne Tempier, bishop of Paris, ruled in 1277 that it counted as an article of Christian faith that God could make as many inhabited worlds as he wanted to. Nicholas of Cusa (1401–1464), Giordano Bruno (1548–1600), and Johannes Kepler (1571–1630) were among many important intellectual figures in the Renaissance who suggested that intelligent beings lived on other planets.

The emergence of modern scientific thought brought the question of extraterrestrial life to the forefront of many minds. One of the

---

16. See Hurley 2003, 154, for one such photo.

17. Jacobs 1975, 28–29.

18. I have relied on Crowe 1986 and Dick 1982 for the following survey.

top literary bestsellers of 1686 was *Conversations on the Plurality of Worlds* by Bernard le Bovier de Fontenelle (1657–1757), six charming dialogues between a philosopher and a noblewoman that presented cogent arguments for intelligent life on other worlds. In his dialogues Fontenelle took a step very few had taken before him, and argued that not only the planets around our own sun but the unseen worlds circling other suns might be inhabited with intelligent beings. Many later writers followed his lead, arguing that human beings were only one of countless species of intelligent life in the universe. This sort of thinking was particularly popular in America, where the famous Puritan clergyman Cotton Mather (1663–1728) was one of many intellectuals who argued that the universe contained countless other inhabited worlds.[19]

To many of these thinkers, it seemed obvious that many, perhaps all, of the other species in the cosmos were more intelligent than we are. Their argument was founded on the concept of the Great Chain of Being—the belief, all but universally held until the late nineteenth century, that the world of nature formed a spectrum of intelligence and being, in which every point along the spectrum from God down to raw matter had its necessary occupant.[20] In its classic form, as taught in every school in the Western world in the Middle Ages and Renaissance, the Great Chain of Being had humanity as its middle link. Other living things cascaded downward from there, with apes just a step below human beings, monkeys below apes, and so on, all the way down to the simplest living creatures and the realm of nonliving matter below them. Above humanity, in mirror image, stood the realm of disembodied intelligences: spirits, angels, and archangels, rising up rank on rank to the foot of the throne of God.

The coming of the scientific revolution in the seventeenth century strengthened the lower half of this sequence, by revealing the many biological similarities that linked humanity to its animal relatives, but it lopped off the upper half of the Great Chain of Being by

---

19. Crowe 1986, 106–7.

20. Lovejoy 1936 is the classic study of this concept.

making talk of angels and spirits unfashionable. Speculations about extraterrestrial life filled the resulting gap. If intelligent beings wiser and better than humanity dwelt elsewhere in the cosmos, the Great Chain was still complete even though not all its links could be seen from the limited perspective of Earth. Benjamin Franklin spoke for many eighteenth-century thinkers when he asserted that "there are an infinite number of worlds under the Divine Government, and if this [world of ours] was annihilated it would scarcely be missed in the Universe."[21] With the coming of the industrial revolution and the emergence of today's ideas about progress, this belief in alien beings more intelligent than humanity inevitably changed into a belief that inhabitants of other worlds must be far in advance of humanity in a strictly technological sense.

By Franklin's time, meanwhile, a new revolution as dramatic as the one launched by Copernicus two-and-a-half centuries earlier was brewing. As the second half of the eighteenth century dawned, philosophers proposed the daring theory that the Milky Way—that uneven band of light that sprawls across Earth's skies—was a vast disk of stars, and certain odd milky patches of light called nebulae were other disks of the same kind. It took until 1920 for the second half of their conceptual leap to find conclusive proof, but long before that happened, the vision of a cosmos vast enough to contain countless galaxies had already seized the collective imagination of the Western world. It became something close to an article of faith among educated people that so immense a universe could not have been created for the benefit of human beings alone. Though some writers, notably William Whewell (1794–1866), argued against the existence of extraterrestrial life on religious grounds, the consensus of the times stood against them.

Belief in the existence of alien life became so widespread in the early nineteenth century that when a New York journalist named Richard Adams Locke (1800–1871) wrote a satire on the wilder speculative literature about life on other worlds, and had it published in

---

21. Cited in Crowe 1986, 109.

1835 in the pages of the New York *Sun*, people across America and in many other corners of the world took it seriously. Locke's satire claimed that the astronomer Sir John Herschel, equipped with a massive new telescope, had spotted life on the moon. The earth's satellite, he announced in breathless prose, was inhabited by giant tailless beavers who lived in huts, and bat-winged humanoids covered in copper-colored hair. Bizarre though all this was, people accepted it as fact, and for some weeks the discovery of life on the moon was hailed as one of the great scientific triumphs of the age. Only when Locke let it be known that he had invented the whole thing did his "moon hoax" lose scientific credibility.[22]

The idea that beings from other worlds might travel through the cosmos also played a role in these early accounts of an inhabited universe. Most of the early speculations about space flight—including the earliest of all, a pair of fictional moon voyages written by the Greek philosopher Lucian of Samosata (c. 120–c. 200 CE)—focused on travel between the earth and other planets and satellites in our solar system. One of the philosophers who introduced the idea of galaxies, Johann Heinrich Lambert (1728–1777), was among the first to break from this model, proposing in 1761 that alien beings could travel from solar system to solar system by riding comets.[23] Aware of the vast time scale that interstellar travel by comet would take, he imagined life forms for whom thousands of Earth's years counted as a few days.

It took more than a century and a half, the evolution of a faith in technological progress as intense as any religion, and the birth of the new literary genre of science fiction, before anyone else would follow in Lambert's imaginative footsteps and picture journeys through the spaces between the stars. When those spaceflights of the imagination finally took off, the long history of speculation about life on other worlds guaranteed them an eager audience. Still, it took another movement in popular culture to make a sizeable portion of that audience susceptible to claims that voyages between the stars were already

---

22. See the discussion of Locke's work in Crowe 1986, 202–15.

23. Crowe 1986, 57.

taking place. Among the most influential figures in that movement was a plump, bespectacled man with a walrus mustache—a man named Charles Hoy Fort.

A Procession of the Damned

During the first three decades of the twentieth century, New York City won its reputation as one of the world's great cities, the cultural capital of the New World, and one of the planet's primary seeding grounds for new literary, artistic, and social initiatives. Literary soirees at the Algonquin Hotel and world-famous art exhibitions such as the Armory show in 1913 added to a cultural ambience that attracted the talented and the curious from around the world. Amid all the bustle and hype, though, perhaps the most revolutionary venture of those years took place in a quiet reading room in the New York Public Library, where Charles Fort could be found every working day amid stacks of old scientific journals, taking careful notes.

For so revolutionary a thinker, Fort (1874–1932) led a remarkably quiet life. Born and raised in a wealthy family in Albany, New York, he left home in his teens, traveled around the world on a shoestring, married his grandfather's cook, and then settled down to a career in journalism in New York City, where he spent the rest of his life. When he was forty-two, he inherited enough money to quit the newspaper business and spend the rest of his life pursuing an extraordinary research program into the nature of reality itself.

During his years as a newspaperman, Fort watched the pendulum of scientific opinion swing back and forth on subject after subject, and saw how scientists trumpeted their successes, forgot about their failures, and stuffed round pegs into square holes when a preferred theory demanded it. A favorite example of his was the flurry of self-congratulation that followed the discovery of Neptune in 1846, following predictions made by the astronomer Urbain Leverrier. As Fort pointed out, though, Leverrier was only one voice in the scientific community of his time; other astronomers, on equally good grounds, predicted that there were two planets beyond Uranus, or none at all, and so no matter what showed up in the telescope, scientists would have been just as quick to trumpet the results as proof of their own infallibility. Fort wrote wryly: "One planet was found—so calculated Leverrier, in his profound meditations. Suppose two had been found—confirmation of the brilliant calculations by Hansen. None—the opinion of the great astronomer, Sir George Airy."[24]

This skepticism drove Fort's great project. For twenty-seven years he scoured the best scientific journals of his time for facts that didn't fit. He documented fish and raw meat falling from the skies, planets observed by astronomers where no planets could be found before or since, mysterious appearances and disappearances, strange lights and objects in the sky, and more, all recorded by eminent scientists and sober witnesses and many backed up by physical evidence, and all, in Fort's terminology, "damned"—condemned to the limbo of the unrecognized and unproven by a scientific community unwilling to admit the existence of any phenomenon it couldn't understand. In four sprawling books—*The Book of the Damned* (1919), *New Lands* (1923), *Lo!* (1931), and *Wild Talents* (1932)—he marshalled a procession of the damned in support of the claim that the science of his time knew less about the world than it supposed.

This claim had become a significant force in popular culture in the Western world around the time Fort was born. In 1877, Helena Blavatsky's first major book, *Isis Unveiled*, launched occultism into the popular imagination as an alternative to orthodox religion and accepted scientific thought alike, and in the process sparked a flurry of alternative theories about the nature of reality and the shape of human history. In 1882, Ignatius Donnelly resurrected the old legend of Atlantis in the first of a series of books that challenged many of the everyday assumptions of his time. Both these books first saw print in America, and in their wake, rejected knowledge and alternative visions found a wider audience in America than anywhere else. It was thus probably inevitable that Fort, who consolidated this earlier work into a theory of universal skepticism that rejected dogmas of every kind, would appear in the New World as well.

---

24. Fort 1974, 318.

Phenomena of the kind that would later be called UFOs play a prominent role in Fort's four tomes. Examples tumble out of his pages: a large luminous body shaped like a square table, hovering motionless over the town of Niagara Falls on November 13, 1833, reported in the *American Journal of Science*;[25] a glowing green cigar shape, sighted from the Royal Observatory at Greenwich and many other places in Britain and Holland, that crossed the sky at a measured pace on the night of November 17, 1882;[26] an airship sighted by thousands of spectators in the skies above Chicago on the evening of April 11, 1897, at a time when no successful airship had yet flown anywhere in North America;[27] a procession of lights moving slowly over Toronto on the night of February 9, 1913;[28] and hundreds more.

Fort himself suggested that these lights might be piloted craft from outer space. He made this suggestion in the same wry spirit that led him to suggest that portions of outer space were full of some gelatinous substance that occasionally fell to Earth, and that teleportation might play an important factor in the life cycle of eels. He proposed these and many sillier theories to highlight the equal absurdity of claims made by reputable scientists, and repeatedly stated that he believed his own theories no more than he believed theirs. In the long run, though, it may not have mattered; Fort's claims planted a seed that would sprout more than a decade after his death.

Fort's legacy proved unexpectedly durable, not least because his books found an audience among a wide range of alternative thinkers in the early twentieth century. Among the most influential was Tiffany Thayer, who founded the Fortean Society to carry on Fort's work in 1932. (True to form, Fort himself refused to join the society named after him, and had to be tricked into attending its inaugural banquet.) Thayer was an ardent conservative who hated Franklin Roosevelt and insisted that the New Deal and everything related to it was a vast

---

25. Fort 1974, 287.
26. Ibid., 293–94.
27. Ibid., 469.
28. Ibid., 516–17.

conspiracy, and under his leadership the Fortean Society moved away from Fort's own gentle skepticism toward a strident intolerance for disagreement that would later be faithfully duplicated in many corners of the UFO debate. By the late 1940s, the Fortean Society had some fifteen hundred members spread across the United States and several other countries, and its members were well positioned to take the role of experts when flying saucers appeared in America's skies.

The Impact of Science Fiction

Still, the Fortean Society was far from alone in its enthusiasm for alternative realities and visions of interplanetary flight. The first decades of the twentieth century also saw science fiction find a permanent home in the world of popular culture via the thriving pulp-magazine industry. Named for the cheap paper that filled the space between their garishly printed covers, the pulps descended from the Victorian penny dreadfuls, with the same blend of lurid topics, loud advertising, and dubious quality that made their nineteenth-century equivalents so profitable. American pulps ranged across the spectrum of popular genres—Westerns, romances, mysteries, two-fisted adventure stories, and more—but the gaudiest of all were devoted to science fiction.[29]

Scientifiction, as it was often called in those days, had a complex pedigree all its own. Historians of the genre have traced it back to any number of sources, but most agree that nineteenth-century writers in Europe and America, who began to explore the literary possibilities of science and technology, laid the foundations for the growth of science fiction. Somewhere between the 1819 publication of Mary Shelley's *Frankenstein* and the breakthrough success of Jules Verne's *From the Earth to the Moon* in 1865, science fiction found its voice as a literature exploring the future of technological progress. Most nineteenth-century works of science fiction, however, counted as serious literature, and some of the most significant literary voices around the beginning of the twentieth century tried their hand at it. At the hands of the pulp industry, though, science fiction traded the salon for the gutter, and

---

29.   Goulart 1972 is the best guide to the pulps.

for much of the first half of the twentieth century few authors who valued a literary reputation would touch it.

This plunge into the depths of popular culture had immense consequences. Despite its perennial claims to importance, serious literature rarely has a major impact on society. Its readership is simply too small and, in most cases, too well educated to slip into the uncritical enthusiasm that shapes the imagination of an age. Most often it turns out to be the popular literature—the reading material of housewives, factory workers, and schoolchildren—that moves into the crawlspaces of culture where the future takes shape. By shedding its literary credentials and wrapping itself in the gaudy finery of the pulp magazines, science fiction came to draw on powerful forces rooted deeply in the collective imagination of the modern industrial world.

The German historian Oswald Spengler (1880–1936) pointed out most of a century ago just how central the concept of infinite space is to the modern Western vision of reality.[30] That concept was unthinkable to most cultures of the past; to the ancient Greeks, for example, the unlimited (*apeiron*) was the opposite of existence, and the ancient Greek language had no term at all for "space" in our modern sense of the word. To the modern mind, by contrast, anything less than infinity seems claustrophobically small, and onto the blank screen of infinite space, the modern imagination projects all those dreams, fantasies, and fears other cultures assign to some more obviously metaphysical realm. Drawing on this vision of space, and on the passionate modern belief in the goodness and necessity of progress, science fiction in its pulp days transformed itself from a somewhat esoteric literary genre to a folk mythology that still shapes most of our thinking about the future today.

Among the dominant figures in this transformation was the pulp editor Raymond A. Palmer (1910–1977).[31] Crippled by a truck accident in childhood, Palmer took refuge from a difficult life in the colorful alternate reality of science fiction. By the late 1920s he was a

---

30. See Spengler 1962, especially 41–69.

31. I have drawn extensively on Keel 1989 for Palmer's biography and work.

leading figure in the newborn subculture of science fiction fandom; in 1930, he launched the first known fanzine (amateur science fiction magazine), *The Comet*, and published his first science fiction story; by 1933 he had organized the first literary prize for American science fiction, the Jules Verne award. In 1938, when the Ziff-Davis publishing chain acquired the failing SF pulp *Amazing Stories* from its founder and needed a new editor, they chose Palmer for the position.

Palmer's own writing was unburdened by the least trace of talent, and the writers he recruited to fill the pages of *Amazing Stories* at a penny a word were generally worse. What made him a brilliant success as a pulp editor was an infallible ear for the lowest common denominator of taste. While other pulps pushed the boundaries of science fiction and launched some of the genre's best authors on their careers, Palmer pandered shamelessly to the interests of his adolescent male audience with interchangeable adventure tales about brawny raygun-packing heroes, nubile damsels in distress, and hideous monsters from space. Science fiction fans groaned and highbrow editors sneered, but Palmer turned *Amazing Stories* into one of the most successful of the SF pulps, with a circulation dwarfing most of its competitors. In 1939 the Ziff-Davis chain rewarded him with the editorship of a second magazine, *Fantastic Adventures*, covering the fantasy end of the pulp spectrum.

To keep his audience happy, Palmer hired some of the best illustrators in the field to produce eye-catching covers for his magazines, and in the process helped create imagery that would take on radically new meanings in the decades that followed. He was far from the first or the only pulp editor to make a contribution here. The cover of the December 1915 issue of *The Electrical Experimenter*—despite the title, this was a science fiction magazine edited by SF pulp pioneer Hugo Gernsback—featured the first of countless disk-shaped flying craft in pulp cover art, for example, and such staples of later UFO imagery as flying saucers, alien abduction, and underground bases are as common in other pulps as in *Amazing Stories* or *Fantastic Adventures*.

The flying disk, in particular, took on a dominant role in science fiction iconography early on. So inevitable did disk-shaped aircraft seem to the popular imagination of the 1930s that when the innovative architect Frank Lloyd Wright set out to design a city of the future in 1934—this was the famous Broadacre City project, a core inspiration for decades of urban planners—his sketches of the city show flying saucers coursing through the air above Broadacre City's slender towers and green vistas, the inevitable aircraft for a future society.[32]

Still, Palmer's own interests were shifting away from science fiction, toward the alternative realities that Charles Fort had championed not long before. The arrival of a letter signed "S. Shaver" at Palmer's offices in 1943 gave him a chance to bring these interests to center stage. The letter announced the discovery of an ancient language called Mantong that proved the reality of the Atlantis legend. Palmer handed the letter to associate editor Howard Browne, who read the first few pages and tossed it into the trash. Palmer grinned, fished it out, and ran it in the letters column of *Amazing Stories*. Readers liked it, and so Palmer wrote to the author for more material. He got back a nearly incoherent ten-thousand-word letter entitled "A Warning to Future Man" by one Richard S. Shaver.

Shaver, a Pennsylvania welder, explained that several years back, he began hearing voices in his head while operating his welding equipment. The voices revealed to him the existence of an underground world of abandoned tunnels built by the ancient Lemurians, who fled beneath Earth's surface to escape the destructive radiations of a sun gone mad. Later on, the Lemurians fled into space, leaving the tunnels and huge caches of their technology to a race of malignant dwarfs called *deros*—*de*trimental *ro*bots in Mantong—who used Lemurian telaug (telepathic augmentation) machines and sex-stim rays to torment the hapless surface dwellers. Shaver claimed he was in contact with the deros' opposite numbers, the *teros* (in*te*grative *ro*bots), and had a sexual liaison with a tero named Nydia. Palmer took all this, rewrote it into a 31,000-word novella titled *I Remember Lemuria!*, and ran it in the March 1945 issue of *Amazing Stories*.[33]

---

32. See, for instance, Pfeiffer and Nordland 1988, 90–91.

33. *I Remember Lemuria!* has been reprinted in all its glory in Childress and Shaver 1999.

The response was so positive that the Ziff-Davis chain—still suffering under the constraints of wartime paper rationing—had to divert paper from other magazines to keep up with demand for the issue. Palmer quickly got more material from Shaver and rewrote it for publication. Browne described it as "the sickest crap I'd run into,"[34] but *Amazing Stories*' circulation doubled over the next four months and reached the astonishing total of 250,000 copies a month by the end of 1945.

Meanwhile, thousands of letters poured through Palmer's mail slot each month, most of them from people who wanted to share their own experiences with the deros. The letters column of *Amazing Stories* when the "Shaver Mystery" was at its height, in fact, reads like a preview of the UFO phenomenon, full of credible witnesses sighting strange aerial craft and relating close encounters with sinister, dwarf-like nonhumans obsessed with human sexuality and reproduction. Palmer and his stable of writers filled in the blanks with stories like "Earth Slaves to Space" (*Amazing Stories*, September 1946), a tale of aliens descending to Earth to abduct human beings. The lead story in the following issue of *Amazing Stories*, "The Green Man" by Harold M. Sherman, prefigured the UFO phenomenon even more closely, portraying the arrival of a superhumanly wise alien just in time to save the earth from nuclear holocaust.

The Shaver Mystery continued to build momentum all through 1946 and the first half of 1947, and Palmer finally decided to devote an entire issue of *Amazing Stories* to Shaver's theories and the public response to them. That issue saw print in June 1947, and was still on the newsstands on the day that Kenneth Arnold climbed aboard his plane and took off on a flight into UFO legend.

Waiting for the Space Brothers

There were plenty of people in America who were tuning into the same imagery Palmer was marketing just then, and many of them had nothing to do with the pulp science fiction industry at all. Harold Sherman's story "The Green Man," in fact, formed a bridge between two

---

34. Cited in Keel 1989, 142.

communities that shared a common vision of the possibility of salvation from space. Sherman, who went on to become a popular writer in the field of psychic phenomena, had a substantial background in the popular occult movements of the early twentieth century, and his "Green Man" story drew on a personal visionary experience. In 1945, while living in Chicago, he had a vision of the imminent mass arrival of alien starships in Earth's skies.

These ideas drew on a poorly chronicled but highly influential body of teachings and imagery in American alternative culture—a tradition that would have an immense influence on the UFO phenomenon when it arrived.

All over America, between the end of the Civil War and the end of the Second World War, familiar religious forms based on Bible narratives and Christian theological concepts gradually gave way among large segments of the population to new forms and imagery that seemed more relevant to an age of science and the growing popular faith that technological progress would become the key to Utopia. Long before Sherman's time, this sea change in popular religion had begun to draw on ideas about life on other planets, and people who once turned their eyes to heaven in prayer began to look toward outer space instead.

An astonishing range of influences flowed into these new religions of space. One of the most important was the Spiritualist movement. Spiritualism was born in 1848 when three teenage girls, the Fox sisters, announced that they had found a way to communicate with the dead. By the end of that year the girls, their story, and the messages they apparently brought from the dead formed the storm center of a hurricane of media stories, new religious visions, and accusations of fraud. By 1850 hundreds of other people claimed to be able to communicate with the dead by going into trance, borrowing techniques from Mesmerism, the most popular of the alternative health systems of the time.

Spiritualist mediums and their followers founded churches and religious communes, published hundreds of books detailing their communications with the "Other Side," and for a time—especially in the aftermath of the Civil War, when countless grieving families on both sides of the Mason-Dixon line hoped for firm evidence of life after death—counted as one of the larger religious movements in the country. As Spiritualism matured, however, its practitioners found that they needed something more appealing than private messages from dead relatives to attract audiences. As the nineteenth century drew on, mediums began to pass on teachings from spirits who claimed to rank well above the ordinary dead.

This process went into overdrive as another influence on the later religions of space, the spread of knowledge about Asian religions, spread through American culture. From the New England Transcendentalists on, American alternative thinkers have found Asian philosophy and religion a potent source of inspiration. By the second half of the nineteenth century it was possible for an educated person in most parts of America to get access to fairly accurate data about Hindu, Buddhist, and Zoroastrian thought.

The Scottish Rite of Freemasonry, headed from 1859 to 1891 by the scholar and mystic Albert Pike, played a crucial role in this process by including detailed and relatively accurate material on Eastern religions in its rituals and publications, above all Pike's encyclopedic *Morals and Dogma of the Ancient and Accepted Scottish Rite* (1871). In an age when most of the leading male figures in American public life belonged to Freemasonry, and the Scottish Rite held undisputed pride of place among Masonic orders, Pike's advocacy of comparative religious study spread Asian teachings far and wide.

The rising popularity of Eastern teachings also helped the birth of the Theosophical Society, founded in 1875 in New York City by the expatriate Russian mystic Helena Petrovna Blavatsky and longtime American occultist Henry Steel Olcott. Theosophy claimed to teach the wisdom of the East, but drew heavily on the philosophical end of Spiritualism and the secretive occult traditions of the Western world.

As an organized movement, Theosophy went through more than its share of booms and busts, but it had an overwhelming impact on the collective imagination of the Western world for a century after its founding. The teachings presented in Blavatsky's masterpiece, *The Secret Doctrine* (1888), remained central to most American alternative faiths for a century and still have influence today—the contemporary New Age movement draws more ideas from Theosophy than from any other source. Among Blavatsky's innovations was a vision of the cosmos in which souls pass from planet to planet in the course of their evolution. Where Blavatsky led, most American alternative groups inevitably followed.

Out beyond the walls of Masonic lodges and Theosophical lecture halls, in the terra incognita of the American soul where so many new religious impulses have had their origin, these same influences blended and fused with more traditional religious ideas in ways that had dramatic impacts on the future. The war between biblical Christianity and materialist science, a raging cultural conflict all through the late nineteenth and early twentieth centuries, helped drive this process in important ways. By the dawn of the UFO era, many Americans had listened to enough of the arguments of science to find belief in the literal truth of the Bible insupportable, while absorbing enough of the arguments of religion to find the scientific faith in pure materialism just as impossible to accept. Any third alternative that could claim a position in between was thus guaranteed an eager audience.

Among the most influential of these alternatives was *Oahspe*, an alternative Bible published in 1882 by John Ballou Newbrough.[35] Born in 1828, Newbrough embraced Spiritualism early in his adult life,[36] and became a medium using automatic writing—a common Spiritualist practice in which the medium's hand, holding a pen, moves and writes without the intervention of the medium's conscious mind. In 1881, after a series of visions, Newbrough purchased a typewriter and spent an hour each morning allowing the spirits to type through him. The result was *Oahspe, A New Bible, in the Words of Jehovih and His Angel Ambassadors*, a hefty tome proclaiming a new gospel to the world.

---

35. For *Oahspe*, see Gardner 1995, 161–78, and Newbrough 1950.

36. Professional debunker Martin Gardner claimed that Newbrough was raised in a Spiritualist family—a remarkable trick, since Spiritualism did not come into existence until Newbrough turned twenty. Such errors of fact are embarrassingly common in the debunking literature. See Gardner 2003, 101.

Like many channeled works, *Oahspe* defies easy characterization. Written in the style of the King James Bible, it combines Christian imagery with ideas borrowed from many other religions; Adam, Eve, and Jesus all appear in its pages, but so do Apollo, Thor, the Buddha, and the Zoroastrian supreme god Ormuzd. What sets it apart most strikingly from the religious visions of a previous century, though, is the way it locates its theology in outer space. Its angels and gods live on countless planets scattered across the infinite reaches of Etherea, Newbrough's term for interstellar space, and travel from world to world in Etherean vessels that range from little scout craft to vast mother ships the size of a planet.

Newbrough's new revelation never attracted a huge following, but it found readers throughout the alternative scene, and for more than three quarters of a century it had a potent influence on the far ends of the American religious imagination. In its wake, and as often as not under its influence, hundreds of other alternative religious movements in America embraced the same fusion of traditional religious imagery with popular adaptations of scientific ideas about outer space.

By the early twentieth century these same ideas had begun to shape popular culture in unexpected ways. Once again, the pulp industry provides a useful gauge of the tidal shifts in the collective imagination that laid the groundwork for the UFO phenomenon. In the 1920s, for example, two of the most popular and influential writers in the pulp industry were Robert Howard and H. P. Lovecraft. Howard was the creator of Conan the Barbarian and a galaxy of less famous heroes, and kept *Weird Tales* and several other pulps supplied with brash and violent accounts of adventure in forgotten ages of the past. Few of his readers today realize that all these tales are set in the universe of Helena Blavatsky's *The Secret Doctrine*, a worldview intimately familiar to most of his readers.

Lovecraft, though he was among Howard's closest friends and sold his stories to the same pulp magazines that featured Conan's brawny exploits, wrote at the other end of the pulp spectrum. As one of the most original authors of twentieth-century horror literature, Lovecraft took the same Theosophical imagery Howard used and turned it on its head, creating a fictional universe where vast cosmic intelligences, older than humanity and utterly evil, lurk just beyond the limits of our awareness, waiting for the moment when "the stars are right" and their ancient dominion over the earth will be restored. Lovecraft's literature of cosmic paranoia found eager readers throughout the pulp community, and played an important role in creating a subculture in which Richard Shaver's accounts of deros in Lemurian caves could be taken seriously.

All this fed back into the alternative spiritual scene by making the idea of contact with other worlds believable to a large fraction of Americans. By the 1930s, the leadership of one of the most popular alternative spiritual movements in America—the I AM Activity, an offshoot of Theosophy—claimed to be in contact with advanced beings from the planet Venus. Meanwhile, the Native American spirit guides popular among mediums in the first years of the century were falling out of fashion in favor of alien intelligences. One example out of hundreds was San Diego medium Mark Probert, whose communications from an alien being calling himself E Yada Da Shi'ite, the emissary of the interplanetary High Council, attracted the interest of a circle of students headed by the veteran occultist Meade Layne.[37]

Like most channeled material before and since, Probert's communications consisted of long discussions of cosmology and alternative science mixed with moral and spiritual advice. Starting in early 1946, however, E Yada Da Shi'ite swerved into the same new theme Harold Sherman caught in his story "The Green Man"—the imminent arrival of extraterrestrial craft in Earth's skies. Layne's group, the Borderland Sciences Research Foundation, had a private newsletter with nationwide distribution, and Layne himself, a longtime member of the Hermetic Order of the Golden Dawn, had connections with occult lodges around the country. Through these channels, word of the approaching visitation spread quickly.

All through the American alternative spirituality scene, eyes began to turn upward, waiting for signs to appear in the heavens. Not long after, Kenneth Arnold spotted nine strange craft over the Cascade Mountains. The UFO phenomenon had arrived.

---

37. See Layne 1950 and Reeve 1957.

two

A Mystery in the Skies, 1947–1966

On the afternoon of Tuesday, June 24, 1947, a private pilot and businessman named Kenneth Arnold took off from the Shelton, Washington, city airport in his red and white Callair monoplane and headed east, toward the southern Cascade Mountains. Arnold, who had a part-time position with the Forest Service alongside a prosperous fire-control business, was taking part in the hunt for a downed plane near the 14,000-foot volcanic cone of Mount Rainier. Conditions could not have been better for the search: perfect summer weather, with smooth air and unlimited visibility.[38]

About three minutes after he reached cruising altitude at 9,200 feet, Arnold's attention was caught by a bright flash to his north. He glanced that way and saw what looked like nine unusual aircraft headed south, across his flight path, at what appeared to be a very high speed. In view of what came later, it's worth mentioning that the craft looked nothing like the "generic UFO" that hovers in the collective imagination of the world today. Arnold described them as crescent

---

38. For Arnold's sighting, see Arnold and Palmer 1952 and Peebles 1994, 8–10.

shapes about fifty feet long, forty-five feet wide, and only three feet thick, with blunt points in the center of the aft end. As they flew, they dipped from side to side, hugging the terrain and weaving between mountain peaks, and sunlight flashed off their mirror-bright hulls; that was the source of the flash that first caught his attention.

When he landed at Yakima, Washington, ninety minutes later to refuel his plane, Arnold mentioned his sighting to several other pilots. One of them suggested that he might have seen guided missiles from the military base at Moses Lake in central Washington. Arnold flew on to Pendleton, Oregon, later in the afternoon, and found a small crowd waiting for him. Word of his sighting had gone ahead of him.

He tried to report it to the local FBI office, but the office had already closed for the evening, so he talked to journalists from the Pendleton newspaper instead. Trying to explain the way the objects dipped and veered, Arnold described them as flying "like a saucer if you skip it across water." One of the reporters, Bill Becquette, turned that description into the phrase "saucer-like" in the story he sent out onto the Associated Press newswire, and some unknown assistant editor twisted Becquette's phrase into "flying saucer."

The story broke the next morning in newspapers across the country. Within a few days, other people were reporting unknown objects in the skies that the media instantly equated with Arnold's encounter. Thus on July 4, for example, witnesses in Portland, Oregon—among them policemen and harbor patrolmen—spotted flying disks "shaped like chrome hubcaps" flying at high speed over the city. The same evening, the crew of a United Air Lines flight from Boise to Seattle spotted nine more flying disks, and a Coast Guard publicity officer living in Seattle's Lake City neighborhood snapped two clear photos of a flying disk in the sky above his home; the photo appeared on page 1 of the *Seattle Post-Intelligencer* the next morning.

Meanwhile the Army Air Corps had entered the fray with a press release announcing that the flying disks weren't American secret weapons, and speculating that the sightings were due to the sun reflecting on low clouds, meteors, or large flat hailstones.[39] Meteorologists quoted by scores of newspapers dismissed these explanations as nonsense.

On July 7, the *Post-Intelligencer* gave banner headlines to claims that the flying disks had landed somewhere in Idaho, while the *San Francisco Chronicle*'s front page blared FLYING SAUCERS SEEN IN MOST STATES NOW. The seventh of July was a banner day for sightings; in Seattle, for example, twenty-one people reported seeing silvery disks high in the air. The following day, though the *Post-Intelligencer* missed it, newspapers elsewhere carried an even more sensational story: the Army Air Corps public relations officer at Roswell Field in New Mexico reported that one of the flying disks had crashed at a nearby ranch, and fragments had been recovered.[40]

The ninth of July, though, brought anticlimax. Brigadier General Roger A. Ramey, the Roswell Field commander, announced that the fragments belonged to an American military balloon. Pictures released to the media showed Ramey and Major Jesse Marcel, the intelligence officer at Roswell Field, displaying chunks of tinfoil, wood, and paper. The Roswell crash vanished from the media. Over the following weeks, so did the flying disks; sightings peaked around the time of the Roswell report and then declined steadily, and newspapers lost interest. By the beginning of August, the great 1947 UFO wave had ended.

The Narrative Takes Shape

The broader impact of the sightings, though, had barely begun. In a society madly in love with all things technological, the idea of mysterious disk-shaped craft in the sky was far too enchanting to fade away, and American popular culture leapt aboard the flying saucers with enthusiasm even before the flap ended. The same newspapers that blared news of sightings around the country also carried advertisements for freshly invented flying saucer cocktails, flying saucer sundaes, flying saucer sandwiches, flying saucer burgers, and a song titled "The Flying Saucer Blues." On July 12, milliner Frank Barell of San

---

39. See, for example, the *New York Times*, July 4, 1947, 26.

40. See Saler, Ziegler, and Moore 1997 for a documented account of the original Roswell reports.

Francisco announced his latest design—the Flying Saucer Chapeau, a disk-shaped hat for ladies with a white chiffon contrail meant to drape around the shoulders.[41]

In these first days of the phenomenon, though, nothing like a popular consensus yet existed about the nature of the silvery dots and disks sighted in American skies. The Port Arthur, Texas *News* was one among countless voices of opinion to mirror this uncertainty. On July 10, 1947, the *News* announced a contest, offering twenty-five dollars for the best letter to the editor explaining what the saucers actually were:

> *How do YOU explain the "flying saucers?"*
> *Are they real—or are the reports of them as phony as a counterfeit dime?*
> *Are the Russians sending them over? Are they missiles from Mars? Is the Moon chunking things at us on account of that radar-gram we sent her a year or so ago?*
> *Or is the whole business a product of the silly summer season?*[42]

As this article suggests, one of the most widespread theories at the time was that the saucers were some sort of Russian secret weapon. Many people in the late 1940s feared that the Soviet Union might achieve some breakthrough in advance of the Western powers. Russian military technology at the time was competitive with the best the West had to offer, and coming achievements from Russia's first successful nuclear test in 1949 to its breathtaking leap into space following Sputnik 1's launch in 1957 showed that Western worries about Soviet scientific prowess were by no means unreasonable.

Another popular theory at the time argued that the saucers were a secret American military technology not yet ready for deployment, wrapped in the same secrecy that kept the Manhattan Project out of sight until Hiroshima made further concealment a moot point. The

---

41. Like all researchers into the history of the phenomenon, I am indebted to the UFOs in Popular Culture website (http://www.ufopop.com) for documenting the extraordinary spread of flying saucers into the public imagination. Examples cited in this section are all from this source.

42. *Port Arthur News*, July 10, 1947.

occultist Manly Palmer Hall was one of many voices pointing out that the Russians would hardly choose to test some exotic new technology in American airspace, where a single mistake could give the Soviet Union's worst enemy access to its secret weapon.[43] Hall himself argued that the saucers were almost certainly an American invention, and he became the first of several generations of pundits to set themselves up for public embarrassment by claiming that the secret behind the saucers would soon be revealed by the U.S. government.

Hall's conclusions, however, were not generally shared by the occultists of his time. Much more typical was Meade Layne, whose remarkable anticipations of the UFO phenomenon were mentioned in chapter 1. Layne and his Borderland Sciences Research Foundation studied the reports of flying saucers closely, and came to the conclusion that the "ships" were not, in fact, material craft from physical planets. In his mimeographed pamphlet on the subject, *The Ether Ship Mystery and its Solution* (1950), Layne argued that the flying saucers were *etheric* in nature—that is, composed of the subtle substance midway between mind and matter that has long been one of the central arcana of occult tradition—and were built and manned by beings of the etheric plane, the Ethereans of *Oahspe*.[44]

Down in the subterranean spaces of popular culture, though, none of these speculations found listeners. The cheap magazines and comic books that framed the fears and fantasies of the rising postwar generation treated the identification of UFOs as alien spacecraft as a foregone conclusion. The faith in unlimited technological progress that ran through American society at all levels made the idea of space travel seem inevitable—and if we were going there, it made perfect sense to readers of science fiction that alien beings from Mars or elsewhere might have gotten there a bit ahead of humanity.

These certainties predetermined the response of pulp culture. With Raymond Palmer's magazines predictably in the lead, the pulp industry jumped onto the flying saucer bandwagon the moment it

43. Hall 1950.

44. Layne 1950, see especially 2–6.

appeared, defined it as an alien visitation, and began flooding the newsstands at once with gaudy images of disk-shaped craft from other worlds. Their speculations and stories continued to prefigure the future of the phenomenon to an astonishing extent.

Consider the back cover of the November 1947 issue of *Fantastic Adventures*, Palmer's fantasy magazine. It featured a flotilla of golden saucers above the New York skyline, and the words: "Will the ancient gods of Egypt and other lost civilizations come back to Earth in time to avert an atom war? Is the Eye of Horus still watching us? See the story on page 170!" In 1947 this was the plot of a forgettable science fiction short story; less than a decade later contactees presented it as prophecy; another few decades, and ideas such as this would be taken seriously over large sections of the modern industrial world.

Reading the enthusiastic response of his audience with character-istic skill, Palmer started planning an entire issue of *Amazing Stories* devoted to UFOs for 1948. After the controversies surrounding the Shaver Mystery, though, his superiors in the Ziff-Davis chain decided that enough was enough, and told him to drop the project; they may, as Palmer always claimed later, have been encouraged to do so by a visit from uniformed Air Force officers. Unfazed, Palmer raised capi-tal from friends and launched his own magazine, *FATE*, dedicated to "true stories of the mysterious and unknown." In the context of the time, that meant flying saucers above all else.

The first issue of *FATE* came out in the spring of 1948, with Ken-neth Arnold's account of his sighting as the lead article and an art-ist's rendition of his encounter on the front cover. Many of Palmer's regular authors contributed to the new venture—Harold Sherman of "Green Man" fame had a piece on Mark Twain's psychic life in that first issue—and it soon became clear that Palmer had a roaring suc-cess on his hands. He launched a second magazine, *Mystic*, later that year, then changed its name to *Search* and used it to publish letters and articles that were too much even for *FATE's* omnivorous read-ers. In 1949, after several more quarrels with his bosses at Ziff-Davis, he resigned as editor of *Amazing Stories* and *Fantastic Adventures* to devote his time to his own pulp empire.

The pulp industry and its audience quickly became a springboard from which the extraterrestrial hypothesis leapt into mainstream American culture with remarkable speed. In 1948 newspaper comic-strip hero Buck Rogers faced disk-riding beings from a distant planet in "The Adventure of the Flying Saucers." In 1950 Li'l Abner, the hero of Al Capp's hugely popular daily comic of that name, caught a ride in a flying saucer piloted by a three-headed Martian. Fans of both strips could buy cardboard "flying disks" (the Frisbee® had not yet taken over that market) that could be cut out, assembled, and flown with a flick of the wrist.

Around this same time, Hollywood caught the extraterrestrial wave. The first movie about flying saucers was the 1949 serial *Bruce Gentry: Daredevil of the Skies*, in which the saucers were a secret weapon wielded by terrestrial villains; the same plot shaped 1950's *The Flying Saucer*, in which an earthly disk-shaped airplane attacks the Panama Canal. The same year, however, saw the release of *Flying Disc Man from Mars*, which set the tone for dozens of B-movie sequels featuring hostile aliens invading Earth in flying saucers.

The year 1951, in turn, saw the release of *The Day the Earth Stood Still*, which even now ranks as one of the best UFO movies ever made. Its portrayal of a wise alien emissary descending to Earth to warn its inhabitants about the dangers of nuclear war set off echoes in the collective imagination that remain present today. While it was based on a science fiction story dating from before Harold Sherman's "The Green Man," it borrowed Sherman's idea that alien technology could shut off human electrical equipment. It's worth noting that in 1951, no one had yet reported this effect in an actual UFO sighting, but that time was not far off.

By 1952 even the normally sedate world of children's literature had its own close encounters with the unfolding phenomenon. Stella Clair's *Susie Saucer and Ronnie Rocket*, illustrated by Edward Andrewes, took aim at the preschool set, while Louis Slobodkin's best-selling *The Space Ship Under the Apple Tree*—the space ship in question was, of course, a flying saucer—appealed to their older brothers and sisters. The same year saw Glencoe Models come out with the first model kit of a UFO, a stylish disk with tail fins, rocket engines, and a bubble canopy through which its pointed-eared alien pilot could enjoy earthly scenery.

This constant drumbeat of UFO appearances in popular culture proved to be prophetic. In 1952, the flying saucers came back in force, and what had looked like a minor postwar fad turned into a serious issue in the eyes of many Americans.

The Invasion from Space

In retrospect, one of the most remarkable things about the period between 1947 and 1952 was the relative scarcity of UFO sightings during those years. A few striking and heavily publicized cases caught the public's attention, but on the whole the skies had fewer unknown objects in them than they would have for many years thereafter. Even so, one important case—the Mantell encounter of 1948—played a critical role in shaping one of the enduring themes of the emerging UFO narrative.

On January 8, 1948, civilian and military witnesses spotted an unknown craft shaped like an ice cream cone high over Godman Airfield in Kentucky.[45] A flight of four Kentucky National Guard F-51 fighters was scrambled to investigate. The flight leader, Captain Thomas Mantell, attempted to get close to the craft. "It appears to be a metallic object," he told the Godman tower over the radio, "tremendous in size . . . directly ahead and slightly above . . . I'm trying to close in for a better look." Those were his last recorded words.

A few hours later, his body was found in the wreckage of his plane in a field not far from Fort Knox. An inquiry showed that he had flown high enough to black out from lack of oxygen and lost control of his aircraft. The Air Force claimed that the "metallic object" Mantell had been chasing was the planet Venus, a claim that had to be retracted when journalists found out that Venus had been nowhere in the sky at that time.

Not until three years later did the Navy admit that the object had been an experimental test in the then-secret Skyhook balloon pro-

---

45. See Good 1988, 146, for the Mantell case.

gram. The Skyhook balloons were designed to rise into the upper atmosphere, higher than any airplane then in service could fly. They were made of polyethylene plastic that looked metallic under some light conditions and, when their upper ends reflected sunlight, resembled a giant ice cream cone with a red top.

The Air Force's attempt to blame Venus for Mantell's death, though, remained a live issue in the newborn UFO investigation community, and played a massive role in launching the theory that the Air Force was covering up evidence relating to UFOs. Admittedly the Air Force itself did a great deal to further this theory. Two weeks after Mantell's death, in response to growing pressure from the media and Congress, the Air Force launched an inquiry into the UFO phenomenon under the code name Project Sign. Most of a year later, on December, 16, 1948, Project Sign was replaced by Project Grudge, which earned its name by insisting that all UFO sightings resulted from hoaxes, hallucinations, and misidentifications, even though project staff could not find any natural explanation for 23 percent of the sightings collected.[46] In April 1952, Grudge gave way to Project Blue Book, which would manage the Air Force's response to the phenomenon for most of two decades.

The odd thing about the Air Force's handling of the UFO phenomenon all through this period was that its behavior seemed completely at odds with its stated intentions—a point not lost on psychologist Carl Jung, who commented on it in his book on the flying saucer myth, though it escaped most other researchers. Far from reducing public interest in UFOs, the Air Force's ham-handed and unconvincing explanations gave the phenomenon far more credibility than it could have obtained on its own. Many people who might otherwise have ignored the entire issue drew the conclusion that the Air Force had to be hiding something.

This conviction took on strength even as the number of sightings continued to decline. It found its first major proponent in Donald Keyhoe, a retired Marine Corps officer turned writer who published an

---

46. Thompson 1991, 8.

incendiary article on the UFO phenomenon in the January 1950 issue of *True* magazine. Keyhoe drew on Charles Fort's speculations as well as the 1947 flap to back up an argument that the earth had been under observation by alien beings from another planet for at least 175 years. He insisted that the Air Force was sitting on the evidence that would prove this claim. Later in the same year he turned the article into a popular book, *Flying Saucers Are Real*, which sold half a million copies.

Journalist Frank Scully joined the fray at the same time with an equally inflammatory book titled *Behind the Flying Saucers*, claiming that the Air Force not only knew about the extraterrestrial origin of the saucers but had three recovered saucers in its possession, from a crash near Aztec, New Mexico. Scully's information came from Silas M. Newton and Leo A. GeBauer, two professional con men for whom flying saucer stories were a sideline; their main business was the sale of fraudulent oil leases and worthless "magnetic oil-detecting machines." The samples of saucer hull they provided to investigators turned out to be ordinary pot metal, and the rest of their claims were solidly discredited by investigative journalist J. P. Cahn in a 1952 article. The Aztec crash thereupon vanished from UFO discussions.[47] The image of crashed saucers in Air Force custody proved too appealing to abandon, however, and many of the details of Scully's account surfaced years later in versions of the Roswell case.

These broadsides did not go unanswered. In short order, *Time* published an article claiming that all UFO sightings were Skyhook balloons, *U.S. News & World Report* insisted they were secret technologies operated by the Navy, and *Cosmopolitan* featured a blistering article describing anyone who claimed to see a flying saucer as a bona fide member of the lunatic fringe. At a time when sightings of unusual objects in the sky were at their post-1947 nadir, these arguments seemed to have force.

The year 1952 brought a shift in the debate, however. In its April 7 issue that year, *Life*, one of the most popular magazines of the time, headlined an article "Have We Visitors from Space?" Produced with

---

47. Cahn 1952. See also Cahn 1956 and Peebles 1994, 67–71.

the assistance of Project Blue Book, the *Life* article featured two distinguished scientists who supported the extraterrestrial hypothesis, and oriented the entire debate toward the idea that the saucers must be craft from other planets. The Air Force uncharacteristically refused to criticize the *Life* article, stating only that the article's data was accurate but its conclusions were its own.

The spring of 1952 also saw the founding of the Aerial Phenomena Research Organization (APRO) by Coral and James Lorenzen of Sturgeon Bay, Wisconsin. Focusing its efforts on collecting data on reported UFO sightings, APRO quickly evolved from an informal network to one of the largest UFO research organizations, with a monthly newsletter and several hundred members around the country and the world.

At this same time, as if on cue, the flying saucers came back with a vengeance.[48] April 1952 was a busy month for sightings, with ninety-nine reports received by Project Blue Book staff. Seventy-nine more arrived in May, 149 in June, and no fewer than 862 in the two peak months of July and August. One of them was the Nash-Fortenberry sighting of July 14, 1952, generally considered one of the classic UFO sightings of all time.

William Nash and William Fortenberry were the pilot and co-pilot, respectively, of a Pan Am DC-4 airliner on its way from New York to Miami. According to their accounts, at 8:12 PM, while they were flying at eight thousand feet over Chesapeake Bay near Norfolk, Virginia, they saw a line of six glowing red disks ahead and to the right of the plane, about two thousand feet above the ground. The disks flew toward the plane at high speed and turned sharply. Then, joined by two more disks, they zoomed off to the west and vanished from sight. Several other witnesses on the ground near Norfolk claimed to see flying disks about the same time.

This was the prologue to even more dramatic sightings to come. On the nights of July 19 and July 26, clusters of moving lights appeared

---

48. See any of the standard histories of the UFO phenomenon, such as Jacobs 1975 or Clark 2000, for the 1952 flap. For the Nash-Fortenberry sighting, see Nash and Fortenberry 1952 and Tulien 2002.

over Washington, D.C., where they were watched by hundreds of spectators. Radar operators at one of the city's airports tracked something in the air, news cameras snapped pictures of the lights, and the Air Force reported that fighter jets were scrambled but never got close enough to fire on the unidentified craft. After the event, however, the Air Force insisted that the sightings had been caused by a temperature inversion that reflected lights from the ground and caused false targets on radar.

Witnesses and news media alike rejected this explanation with a fine display of scorn. All over the country, thousands of witnesses were comparing their own experiences to the dubious explanations offered by the Air Force, and coming to their own conclusions—or, more precisely, the conclusions that had been prepared for them by popular culture. Nobody at the time seems to have wondered if the Air Force's hamhanded mismanagement of the UFO situation might have concealed an agenda of its own.

The extraordinary "Flatwoods Monster" close encounter of September 1952 set the seal on the busiest year in UFO history. After a series of reports from eastern states of fireballs in the night sky, seven witnesses in the small town of Flatwoods, West Virginia, saw one plunge to Earth in the woods nearby. They went to investigate and reported encountering a ten-foot-tall creature with glowing eyes, surrounded by an overpowering stench. The "Monster" closely echoed folklore accounts, found all over the American South, about humanlike or apelike monsters of the Bigfoot or "skunk ape" variety. Only the most dedicated students of Fortean lore, however, drew these connections. To most of the American public, the eerie entity sighted at Flatwoods could only have come from outer space.

Messages from Clarion

That conviction was soon reinforced from an unlikely angle. In the midst of the 1952 flap, a fifty-two-page book appeared in alternative spirituality bookstores across America. Released by the New Age Publishing Company in Los Angeles, *I Rode a Flying Saucer* by George

Van Tassel heralded a new twist in the evolving UFO narrative—the emergence of the contactees.

Van Tassel was a professional pilot with twenty years of experience testing aircraft for the Douglas and Lockheed corporations. He was also a longtime participant in the California occult scene, and headed an organization called the College of Universal Wisdom. After the Second World War, he purchased a private airport at Giant Rock, near Yucca Valley, California, intending to start a restaurant and tavern there. According to *I Rode a Flying Saucer*, though, he soon started to receive telepathic messages from outer space, a process that culminated in a series of physical encounters with flying saucers and their occupants.

Van Tassel's book caused a sensation in alternative circles but failed to find a wider audience; that destiny was reserved for the next contactee to break into print. Polish-American writer George Adamski was an unsuccessful science fiction author and, like Van Tassel, a minor celebrity in the California alternative spirituality scene. As the founder and head of an occult society called the Royal Order of Tibet, he was a familiar figure in lecture halls and radio programs in the Los Angeles area in the 1920s and 1930s. On November 20, 1952, Adamski claimed he went into the desert with several companions, including the occult writer George Hunt Williamson, in the hope of seeing a flying saucer.

The results surpassed his expectations. After watching two UFOs in the skies, Adamski said, he saw a saucer on the ground and encountered its pilot. Through telepathy and gestures, the alien—who was blond, humanlike, and dressed in a brown uniform—told Adamski that he had come from Venus to warn humanity of the danger of nuclear war. The similarity of Adamski's account to the plot line of *The Day the Earth Stood Still* did nothing to blunt his impact on an eager public. By 1955 Adamski had two best-selling books in print, chronicling his further adventures with the flying saucers and their occupants, and was busy on lecture tours throughout the United States, Europe, and Latin America.

Well before that point was reached, others were hurrying to climb aboard the contactee bandwagon. Another Californian, auto mechanic Truman Bethurum, published a book entitled *Aboard a Flying Saucer* in 1954, describing his encounters with a UFO and its gorgeous female captain, Aura Rhanes. Daniel Fry, Orfeo Angelucci, Howard Menger, and several others followed suit over the next few years, helping to build a booming subculture of UFO enthusiasts whose interest in the phenomenon centered on the contactees and their messages. Many of the members of this subculture came to it from occult circles and brought their ideas with them, providing the growing UFO scene with a ready-made cosmology and worldview.[49]

The most important writer in the field during the 1950s was George Hunt Williamson, who came to the study of UFOs from a longtime involvement in the occult. Williamson had been an active member of Soulcraft, an occult society founded by American fascist and occultist William Dudley Pelley, who claimed his own telepathic contacts with aliens in a book published in 1950. A close friend of George Adamski, Williamson also had connections with Van Tassel and with Meade Layne's Borderland Sciences Research Association, and drew heavily on these sources to write books that were required reading in the contactee circles of the 1950s and 1960s. Most of the ideas circulated by ancient astronaut theorists and alternative thinkers from the 1970s right up to the present decade can be found in detail in such Williamson classics as *Other Tongues, Other Flesh* (1953) and *Secret Places of the Lion* (1956).

The hope of an imminent mass landing of flying saucers was high. In 1953, the International Flying Saucer Bureau (IFSB)—one of the very first UFO organizations in North America—organized a "World Contact Day."[50] IFSB had been founded in 1952 by occultist and science fiction fan Albert K. Bender, and managed to bridge the gap between the contactee community and the small circles of scientific UFO researchers; its honorary board of directors included Ray-

---

49. See Reeve and Reeve 1957 for a participant's view of the contactee movement.

50. Bender 1963, 82–84.

mond Palmer and Meade Layne, on the one hand, and Coral Lorenzen of APRO on the other. The goal of C-Day—March 15, 1953—was to contact the UFOs by mass telepathy.

At exactly 11 PM Greenwich Mean Time, members of the IFSB all over the world concentrated on a message to the saucer pilots that began: "Calling occupants of interplanetary craft!" (Some twenty years later this message was put to music by an obscure Canadian band called Klaatu and became their only hit, one of the surprise musical success stories of 1976.) The Bureau hoped that "a sudden flurry of saucer sightings . . . or even a saucer landing" would follow and show that the message had been received. They were disappointed, but the aftermath of C-Day proved oddly prophetic.

Four months afterward, IFSB founder Bender announced that he had solved the riddle of the flying saucers and would reveal the secret in the next issue of the IFSB newsletter. Instead, the next newsletter announced that the IFSB was closing its doors and the secret would not be revealed. Gray Barker, a saucer enthusiast from West Virginia who headed IFSB's research department, published the lurid *They Knew Too Much About Flying Saucers* (1956), claiming that Bender had been frightened into silence by three mysterious men in black. A decade after the IFSB's sudden demise, Bender himself published *Flying Saucers and the Three Men* (1963), expanding on the story of the men in black and describing his own repeated experiences with alien beings who abducted him several times and subjected him to bizarre medical treatment. Bender was ahead of his time; a quarter century later, his claims would be mirrored in two of the UFO phenomenon's most influential bestsellers, but in the early 1960s even the contactee scene dismissed his claims as bad science fiction.

The sheer scale of the contactee movement of the 1950s and 1960s has routinely been underestimated or ignored by historians of the UFO phenomenon. While no meaningful research on membership numbers seems to have been done then or later, the evidence suggests that from the middle of the 1950s well into the next decade, the contactee community accounted for the vast majority of people interested in UFOs. During these years, for all practical purposes, the contactee community *was* the UFO community, and the handful of researchers who tried to carry out scientific research into the phenomenon were a fringe movement within a fringe movement, ignored by all sides in the debates that were springing up around the phenomenon.

Thus in the middle years of the decade, when APRO had a few hundred members and had to rely on volunteer labor for most of its functions, the contactee movement supported its own lecture circuit, a lively publishing trade that produced dozens of books a year, and an assortment of monthly and quarterly newsletters such as Van Tassel's *Proceedings of the College of Eternal Wisdom*. Annual festivals at the Giant Rock airport drew crowds in the thousands, and many thousands who never made the pilgrimage to Giant Rock joined the local contactee groups that sprang up in most American cities.

Contactee beliefs and teachings also inevitably found their way into Raymond Palmer's magazines, filling the pages of *FATE*, *Search*, and a later journal titled *Flying Saucers*—for more than a decade after its founding in 1957, the most widely circulated UFO magazine in the world—with accounts of alien contact and messages from the wise beings Adamski named the Space Brothers. As the sales of contactee literature increased, Palmer established a mail-order business that for many years had a better selection of UFO books than any other firm in America. He also published three editions of *Oahspe*, and publicized Newbrough's opus enthusiastically in the pages of his magazines.

From 1955 on, however, *Oahspe* shared space in the contactee circuit with another work of the same kind, the even more massive *Urantia Book*, which was received in trance by an anonymous channeler in the 1920s and 1930s and remained in manuscript form for some two decades before finally seeing print.[51] Like *Oahspe*, the *Urantia Book* combined biblical narratives with extraterrestrial settings, and packed its angels and archangels aboard starships for journeys across interstellar space.

---

51. See Gardner 1995 for a competently researched study of the *Urantia Book* marred by the author's angry polemics against his subject.

Still, communications with the Space Brothers were by no means reserved for a few celebrities or specially gifted channelers. By the second half of the 1950s, most American cities of any size had at least one contactee group focusing on a local medium who claimed to be in contact with alien intelligences, and passed on messages about spiritual development and the imminent landing of the saucers. One group located in the Chicago area made the news briefly in 1954 when its leader, a housewife turned channeler named Dorothy Martin, announced that her alien teachers from the planet Clarion had warned that the eastern half of the United States would be destroyed by floods on December 21.[52]

This prophecy brought the group to the attention of sociologists at the University of Minnesota, who placed several researchers in Martin's group and watched the group dynamics as the predicted date came and went. The result was a classic sociological study, *When Prophecy Fails*, in which Martin appears as "Marion Keech." What the sociologists did not anticipate was that several participants in the Martin group would go on to become significant figures in later versions of the contactee community.

Martin herself traveled to Peru, where she became a leading figure at the Abbey of the Seven Rays, an unsuccessful attempt to create an international contactee center near the shores of Lake Titicaca. She returned to the United States in 1961 and spent the rest of her life teaching New Age philosophy under the name of Sister Thedra. Charles and Lillian Laughead ("Thomas and Daisy Armstrong" in *When Prophecy Fails*), two other members of the circle, also took part in the Peruvian adventure. After its failure, they went to Mexico, where they played a major role in introducing Dr. Andrija Puharich to the contactee movement.[53]

Puharich was one of the researchers who helped create parapsychology—the scientific study of psychic powers—out of the less rigorous "psychical research" of the late nineteenth and early twentieth centuries.

---

52. See Festinger, Riecken, and Schachter 1956 for the history of the Martin group.

53. See Picknett and Prince 1999, 162–88 and 220–25, for Puharich and his interactions with the Laugheads.

Beginning in 1948, he ran a parapsychological research center, the Round Table Foundation of Glen Cove, Maine, which tested some of the most popular mediums and psychics of the time. On the last day of 1952 one of his test subjects, Dr. D. G. Vinod, went into trance and passed on a communication from "the Nine," who claimed to be the nine principles or forces of God. After meeting the Laugheads, though, Puharich came to believe that the nine were extraterrestrial intelligences, and through Puharich and his associates the basic ideas of the contactee movement began to spread all through avant-garde intellectual circles, with important results over the decades to come.

The Extraterrestrial Ascendancy

The contactee movement had a surprisingly widespread impact on popular culture during the 1950s and 1960s. In terms of the UFO phenomenon, though, its most significant effect was the impetus it gave to the belief that UFOs were by definition spacecraft from another planet, piloted by beings who had progressed far beyond earthly humanity. The contactees thus completed the work begun by Raymond Palmer and his fellow pulp publishers. By the middle years of the 1950s, the extraterrestrial hypothesis, very much a minority opinion at the time of the original 1947 flap, had become the default explanation for unexplained things seen above the earth's surface. While the contactee organizations and more respectable UFO research groups such as APRO agreed on little else about the phenomenon, they both assumed as a matter of course that UFOs must come from outer space.

Ironically, even those people who rejected the whole thing as nonsense—and most people in 1950s and 1960s America did just that—usually equated UFOs and extraterrestrial spacecraft as readily as Donald Keyhoe or George Adamski did; they simply insisted that spacecraft from other planets didn't exist, and so UFOs didn't exist either. Very few people took an active role in arguing this position during the years in question, however. The one significant exception was Harvard astronomer Donald Menzel, whose first book defending the null hypothesis came out in 1953 and, rewritten with the help of coauthor Lyle G. Bord, saw print again in 1963.

Menzel's assault on the extraterrestrial hypothesis relied largely on far-fetched arguments involving atmospheric optics, few of which found support even within the scientific community. It allowed people who already wanted to disbelieve in the existence of UFOs to justify their position, but made few converts outside the ranks of the convinced. The irony, a rich one, is that most of the flurry of books published in support of the extraterrestrial hypothesis during these years preached to the converted in their own camp in exactly the same way.

A dissonant note, however, came from the far side of the Atlantic. During the last years of his life, the brilliant Swiss psychologist Carl Jung (1878–1961) became fascinated by reports of the UFO phenomenon coming from America, and collected information on them from every source he could find. The possibility of visits from other worlds, however, seemed far less central to him than the psychological dimension of the phenomenon. In his 1958 book on the subject, *Flying Saucers: A Modern Myth of Things Seen in the Skies*, he drew a crucial distinction between the physical reality of UFOs—whatever that turned out to be—and the rich and complex mythology that was springing up around them.[54]

About UFOs as a physical reality, Jung stressed, almost nothing was known for sure. About UFOs as a mirror of human psychological needs, fears, and desires, on the other hand, quite a bit more could be said, and he pointed out how flying saucers filled a long-recognized void in the modern psyche. People raised to believe in science rather than spirituality could no longer approach the old spiritual symbols with open minds, so the saviors, angels, and devils of traditional faith had to dress up in spacesuits to appeal to a contemporary audience. In the depths of the Cold War, with the threat of nuclear war between Russia and the United States on everyone's mind, the same emotional needs that drove belief in the imminence of the Second Coming in previous periods had reached fever pitch. Enter the flying saucers.

---

54. Jung 1978, 107–9.

Jung's perceptive view of the UFO phenomenon, however, zoomed right over the heads of all sides of the emerging UFO debate. The *APRO Bulletin* even published an article claiming that Jung had affirmed the physical reality of UFOs—a claim Jung rebuffed at once in a statement to the press.[55] It took another decade of UFO sightings, and a steady rise in the strangeness of the phenomenon itself, to bring his insights at least briefly to center stage.

While all these debates were ongoing, another set of crucial events was unfolding, though it would be years before anybody recognized its relevance to the UFO controversy. In 1954, Lockheed Aviation's secret aircraft production unit—the legendary Skunk Works—received a contract to build the first of a series of revolutionary new surveillance planes for the CIA. The U-2, as it was named, combined glider wings with a new high-performance engine that allowed it to fly above 60,000 feet, high above the reach of hostile fighters or anti-aircraft missiles.

Designed and built in total secrecy, the U-2 needed an isolated location for its test flights and pilot training exercises. In January 1955, a few months before the first U-2 was scheduled for its first flights, chief test pilot Tony LeVier and crew chief Dorsey Kammerier located the perfect location for the secret base: the dry bed of Groom Lake, Nevada, a spot surrounded by mountains on federal land in the middle of the Nevada desert. Decades later, it would become known as Area 51.

Toward the Sputnik Years

In the last years of the 1950s, the minority of UFO enthusiasts whose reading centered on the *APRO Bulletin* and its equivalents rather than Raymond Palmer's more colorful periodicals could have used the encouragement that an endorsement by someone of Jung's stature would have brought. They were a very small group at the time, wedged between the ebullience of the contactee community and the inertia of government and scientific institutions, and largely ignored

---

55. Jung 1978, 136–37.

by both.[56] Under the circumstances, the work they performed was impressive in its quality and breadth. Soon after its founding, APRO found its element in collecting reports of UFO sightings, and played a central role in bringing accounts of UFOs from Latin America and Europe to the attention of investigators in the United States. APRO founder and president Coral Lorenzen turned the best of these collections into a series of books attempting to prove that something unexplained—and by implication, something extraterrestrial—was present in Earth's skies.

More of the limelight, though, went to Donald Keyhoe, the retired Marine whose 1950 article played so crucial a role in launching the controversy in the first place. Keyhoe was a voice in the wilderness until 1957, when he was invited to take charge of a faltering UFO organization, the National Investigations Committee on Aerial Phenomena (NICAP), that had been founded the year before by physicist Townsend Brown. Keyhoe quickly turned NICAP into a platform for his own agenda, an appeal to Congress to hold public hearings on the phenomenon and make the Air Force release the evidence of extraterrestrial contact Keyhoe was certain it was hiding from the public.

Meanwhile, the UFO phenomenon itself went on from strength to strength.[57] The record numbers of sightings in the peak months of 1952 were never equalled afterward and 1953 saw a slump in reports, but 1954 was another busy year, and 1957—the year Keyhoe became head of NICAP and Palmer launched *Flying Saucers*—turned out to be even busier, with 1006 reports submitted to Operation Blue Book. The year had another claim to fame, though; October 4 saw the launch of Sputnik 1, the first artificial satellite in history, into low Earth orbit.

The response in the United States to Sputnik's triumph can be fairly described as stark panic. The idea that the Soviet Union had beaten America into space was unpalatable enough, but the Soviet follow-up, the larger and much more ambitious Sputnik 2, which carried

---

56. I have used Jacobs 1975, Keel 1989, and Dolan 2002 as the basis for the history of the mainstream UFO organizations given in this section.

57. Dolan 2002 provides a thorough if credulous account of UFO sightings during this period.

the first living animal into space, was worse; and with the embarrassing failure of the first American attempt to respond—Vanguard, which blew up on the launch pad on December 6, 1957—the United States' humiliation was complete. Curiously enough, the rate of UFO sightings in American skies soared immediately after Sputnik and remained very high until the end of the year.

The next year brought a sharp drop in American reports. The focus of the phenomenon, however, moved overseas, with major flaps in France and Brazil in 1957 and across most of South America in 1958. With the beginning of the next decade, UFOs became a worldwide phenomenon. Only the Communist countries—who repeatedly denounced UFOs and everything associated with them as a capitalist plot—failed to report any UFO activities at all in the early 1960s. From the end of 1958 to the beginning of 1964, while NICAP continued to call for congressional investigations, APRO and most of the smaller UFO organizations concentrated on investigating the handful of American sightings and circulating details of the far more interesting activities of UFOs overseas.

With 1964, though, the phenomenon returned to American skies in force, and in a crucial incident, to American soil as well. This latter incident was the Socorro, New Mexico, close encounter of April 24, 1964. According to dozens of published accounts, Sergeant Lonnie Zamora of the Socorro police department was chasing a speeding car at 5:45 PM when he saw a "flame in the sky" and heard a loud roaring sound. Thinking that a dynamite shack on a nearby hill might have exploded, he abandoned his pursuit and drove toward the shack.

Parking his squad car well away from the shack's site, he walked the rest of the way up the hill and saw an egg-shaped craft resting on four legs, with two "children" in white coveralls by it. When they noticed Zamora, the "children" hurried inside the craft, which took off with a roar and a burst of flame as Zamora ran back to his car, and flew away toward the southwest. Later examination of the site showed irregularly spaced depressions in the ground that might have been from the craft's landing gear. Curiously, nobody else in the area—and there were a number of other potential witnesses—reported anything unusual that afternoon.

The next year saw another widely cited case, the Kecksburg crash of December 9, 1965.[58] That evening something hurtled eastward through the skies above Ontario, Michigan, and Ohio, before finally crashing to Earth at 4:47 PM near the small town of Kecksburg, Pennsylvania. Several firefighters who went to investigate, thinking that a plane had crashed, found an acorn-shaped metal object between nine and twelve feet in diameter. The area was sealed off by military personnel later the same evening, the object was loaded atop a flatbed truck and driven to Wright-Patterson Air Force Base, and military and government authorities quickly announced that the object had been a meteor.

UFO researchers came to the conclusion that it must have been an alien spacecraft. At a time when the United States and the Soviet Union both had active space programs that included a great many secret dimensions, including spy satellites and antisatellite weapons, and the Air Force had an ongoing program titled Project Moon Dust to pick up any Soviet space equipment that fell outside of Eastern Bloc territory, this conclusion required something of a leap of logic. Still, that was a leap many people were prepared to make at the time.

Both Socorro and Kecksburg quickly entered the canon of classic UFO cases and are still regularly cited by believers in the extraterrestrial hypothesis as evidence for the arrival of visitors from space. At the time, though, these were only two among many hundreds of sightings. Between 1964 and 1968, the United States rarely went without a flurry of UFO sightings for long, and sightings in other countries rose to record levels. All over the world, unusual lights at high altitude were spotted by thousands of witnesses, and rumors of landings by strange creatures in disk-shaped spacecraft filled the local media. By the second half of the 1960s, UFOs had become an unavoidable cultural presence in most countries around the world.

---

58. See Dolan 2002, 294–96.

One of the most remarkable of the overseas cases began in 1965. In that year Fernando Sesma, a contactee in Spain, began receiving messages from extraterrestrials who claimed to come from a distant planet named Ummo—or, as it is always written in the UFO literature, UMMO.[59] Sesma's method for receiving these communications was unusual in contactee circles, then or later; the visitors from UMMO mailed him packages through the Spanish postal service, containing long disquisitions on Ummian philosophy and science. Some of these messages were marked with a distinctive symbol,)+(, made by typing a plus sign between two parentheses.

The next year, the same symbol vaulted onto the front pages of UFO periodicals around the world. On February 6, 1966, a dozen witnesses in Aluche, Spain, claimed to have sighted a flying saucer with the UMMO symbol on its underside. Photographs duly appeared, showing a white disk with the black symbol. Another sighting occurred on June 1 of the same year at San José de Valderas, and afterward metal cylinders containing rolls of silvery plastic were found near the place of the sighting. For a short time it looked as though the phenomenon had finally provided the perfect case—multiple witnesses, photographs, and physical traces, all from a single sighting.

As UFO investigators began to research these events, though, the mirage of UMMO began to unravel. Though the photos had supposedly been taken by several different witnesses, analysis showed they had all been taken by the same camera, at the same angle and distance, using the same kind of film. The silvery plastic in the metal cylinders turned out to be a wholly terrestrial product manufactured by the DuPont company. Close study of the UMMO documents revealed obvious scientific mistakes.

To their credit, the great majority of UFO investigators responded to these discoveries by dismissing the case as a hoax, though a minority continued to believe in the reality of the visitors from UMMO. Many years later, a man named José Luis Peña admitted to having

---

59. For more on the UMMO case, see Vallee 1979 and Carballal 2006.

concocted the whole series of events as an elaborate prank.[60] The near-success of the UMMO hoax was made possible by two factors. The first was the flurry of unusual lights and objects sighted by credible witnesses in Europe and elsewhere at that time; the second was the huge amount of media publicity given to any story concerning UFOs all through the same years.

The Swamp Gas Incident

While these events unfolded, the attitude of the U.S. Air Force and other government agencies toward the UFO phenomenon had taken a sharp turn toward the negative. By the beginning of the 1957 wave, the relative openness of the early days of Project Blue Book gave way to a systematic effort to downplay the entire phenomenon and dismiss as many reports as possible, whether or not the dismissals made sense.

Consider the following case, by no means atypical during the great UFO wave of the 1960s. On the night of August 2–3, 1965, many thousands of witnesses across the American heartland in a band from South Dakota to Texas observed formations of brilliant lights moving through the night air, changing their apparent size, speed, and color as they flew. Reports from state police across the affected area claimed that the objects were tracked on civilian and military radars. The officials at Project Blue Book collected the reports, and stated that the witnesses had simply misinterpreted the four brightest stars in the constellation Orion. This explanation had to be withdrawn shortly afterwards when the press pointed out that Orion was below the horizon at that time of year, and a new explanation blaming the planet Jupiter was quickly issued.[61]

What made these dubious claims all the more curious is that the Air Force itself showed every sign of intense interest in the supposedly nonexistent phenomenon. Many of the most colorful UFO reports came out of the Air Force and other branches of the military, often by unofficial leaks to media personalities interested in UFOs such as

---

60. See the interview with Peña in Carballal 2006.

61. Dolan 2002, 285–86.

Mutual Radio broadcaster Frank Edwards and investigative journalist Dorothy Kilgallen. Among the reports passed onto the media by this roundabout route were claims that Air Force fighter jets were constantly being scrambled to intercept UFOs but never managed to get near them. Those who doubted the Air Force's honesty could also point to the draconian JANAP (Joint Army-Navy-Air Force Publication) 146, issued in December 1953, which made public reporting of any UFO sighting by military personnel and several categories of civilians, including commercial airline pilots, a federal crime under the Espionage Act, carrying the penalty of a one- to ten-year prison term or a $10,000 fine. All this convinced many Americans that the Air Force must be hiding something.

It's difficult, in fact, to imagine any strategy more likely to turn the UFO phenomenon into a cause célèbre than the one the Air Force pursued. Every time Air Force investigators proclaimed a case solved on dubious grounds like the ones just listed, that act added to the list of witnesses who found that their experiences simply didn't jibe with the official explanations, and the even larger number of ordinary Americans who had never seen a UFO but found that the Air Force's claims were harder to believe than the claim that UFOs might be coming from other planets. The constant flow of leaks from anonymous military sources, claiming that UFOs were being tracked and chased by the Air Force, only added to this conviction.

As the pace of UFO sightings increased through the great 1960s wave, the cognitive dissonance between sightings and explanations built toward an explosion. Changes in media coverage of UFO sightings trace the shift. Newspaper stories from the beginning of the decade typically treated the entire phenomenon as a subject for satire or scorn, but by 1965 the tone had changed. An editorial in the *Fort Worth Star-Telegram* was typical:

> *They can stop kidding us now about there being no such thing as "flying saucers." Too many people of obviously sound mind saw and reported independently from too many separate localities. Their descriptions of what they saw are too similar*

to one another and too unlike any familiar object. It is becoming clear to many that the air force explanations succeed only in making the air force look ridiculous.[62]

The flashpoint finally arrived in the early spring of 1966. On March 14 of that year, witnesses across three counties in western Michigan, including police officers, spotted brightly lit objects maneuvering overhead before dawn. March 20 brought reports from a farmer near Ann Arbor that a pyramid-shaped object festooned with lights landed in one of his fields and then took off again. More than fifty witnesses, once again including police officers, gathered to watch the same object dancing through the night air. The finale came the next night, when eighty-seven college students at Hillsdale College, along with the college dean, watched a luminous object shaped like a football zigzagging near a college dormitory for some four hours, before it vanished in a nearby marsh.

These sightings got nationwide media coverage, and Project Blue Book was forced to respond. Astronomer J. Allen Hynek, at that time the chief scientific adviser to the project, was sent to investigate. He found himself in the midst of something not far from mass hysteria, with every light in the sky from crop dusters to bright stars automatically being reported as UFOs. Four days after the last sighting, Hynek went in front of the microphones at a hastily called press conference and explained that some of the sightings might have been caused by methane produced by rotting plant matter in the marsh near the campus, which could spontaneously ignite and produce weird light effects. The phrase he used, to his lasting regret, was *swamp gas.*

The media grabbed hold of the phrase, and filled headlines all over America with the claim that the Air Force had declared the sightings to be swamp gas. Hynek tried to clarify his position in the days that followed, and found that neither the media nor the Air Force was interested in his attempts. The media had a story that would sell papers, and Hynek's superiors at Project Blue Book announced that

---

62. Cited in Dolan 2002, 290.

they were satisfied with Hynek's explanation and classified the Michigan sightings as solved.

For many people, and not only in western Michigan, this was the last straw. People from the area of the sightings bombarded Michigan congressman Gerald R. Ford with a deluge of angry letters and phone calls. Ford responded by going onto the floor of the House of Representatives and calling for a congressional investigation of the UFO phenomenon. So many other representatives were getting the same message from their constituents that hearings actually took place.

The House Armed Services Committee held a one-day open session on April 5, 1966, and ended it by calling on the Air Force to launch an independent scientific study of the UFO phenomenon under the direction of an American university. After nearly two decades of hammering on the doors in vain, the UFO phenomenon would finally get its day in court.

three

Waiting for First Contact, 1966–1987

I t took the Air Force months and a good deal of legwork to find a
university willing to take on the UFO study. Most scientists in relevant disciplines had no interest in a subject that, from their perspective, had been tarred with the stigma of irrationality by its association
with pulp science fiction and the contactee community, and most university administrations had, if anything, even less willingness to get
tangled up in the potential controversy. The University of Colorado
finally accepted the project on October 6, 1966, and assembled a team
headed by Dr. Edward Condon, a widely respected physicist who was
the former head of the National Bureau of Standards, and university
administrator Robert Low.[63]

The initial reaction from the UFO research organizations was
cautious but favorable. During the first months of the study, most of
the major civilian UFO researchers in the country made their way to
Boulder, Colorado, to make the case for the extraterrestrial hypothesis.
Among them was J. Allen Hynek, who was in the process of leaving

---

63. I have used Dolan 2002 and Peebles 1994 extensively for the chronology of the Condon
     Committee.

Project Blue Book in the aftermath of the swamp gas incident, and was beginning to carve out a niche for himself as an independent UFO researcher. Hynek presented his case on November 11, 1966; James McDonald, an atmospheric physicist at the University of Arizona and the most significant scientist in the extraterrestrial camp, briefed project staff members on November 22; Donald Keyhoe arrived on November 28. APRO sent some two hundred and fifty UFO reports to Boulder in the last months of 1966. For a short time, many believers in the extraterrestrial hypothesis thought they had reason to believe their case would get a fair hearing.

This initial optimism did not survive long. The loss of confidence in the committee was almost entirely due to Condon himself, who made little attempt to conceal his distaste for the entire subject and his conviction that UFOs did not exist. His comments during a speech in January 1967 were typical: "'It is my inclination right now to recommend that the government get out of this business. My attitude right now is that there's nothing to it.' With a smile he added, 'But I'm not supposed to reach a conclusion for another year.'"[64] When he read these remarks, Keyhoe decided to pull NICAP's support from the study, and had to be talked into continuing to send UFO reports to Boulder. By the middle of 1967, after more comments by Condon and the discovery that the committee staff had no interest in researching sightings, most of the civilian UFO research community were backing away from the Condon Committee, convinced that it was simply another attempt to sweep the phenomenon under the rug.

The Condon Debacle

The irony is that they were quite correct in that suspicion. A memo written by Robert Low to his superiors in the university administration in August 1966, months before the committee began its work, set out its strategy in advance:

> Our study would be conducted almost exclusively by non-believers who, although they couldn't possibly prove a negative

---

64. Quoted in Peebles 1994, 175–76.

result, could and probably would add an impressive body of evidence that there is no reality to the observations. The trick would be, I think, to describe the project so that, to the public, it would appear to be a totally objective study but, to the scientific community, would present the image of a group of nonbelievers trying their best to be objective but having an almost zero expectation of finding a saucer.[65]

In July 1967 one of the project staff members, Roy Craig, stumbled across this memo while searching through office files, and circulated it among the other project staff. Most of the staff members by this time were convinced that, in the words of project member David Saunders, "we were involved in a whitewash noninvestigation, probably aimed at getting the Air Force off a public relations hook."[66] The Low memo, however, was the last straw. In November, Saunders passed it secretly to Donald Keyhoe, who had already withdrawn NICAP's support from the committee in September after another public denunciation by Condon of the subject he was supposed to be studying. By February of 1968 the committee staff was in open revolt against Condon and Low, who responded by firing Saunders and Norman Levine, the two most outspoken of the rebels. The committee's secretary, Mary Lou Armstrong, resigned later the same month, as did another member of the staff.

By this time the committee's problems were becoming public knowledge, and the media pounced on the story. John Fuller's April 27, 1968, *Look* article, "The Flying Saucer Fiasco," covered the project's dirty laundry in embarrassing detail, sparking articles in the popular press and hearings before the Science and Astronautics committee of the House of Representatives. Undeterred, Condon hired a new team to write the final report for the study, which was released to the Air Force on October 31, 1968, and saw print in January of the following year.

The Condon Report was an odd document in many ways. The first two sections, as well as the conclusions, recommendations, and the

---

65. Quoted in Peebles 1994, 180.
66. Quoted in Dolan 2002, 330.

project summary, were written by Condon himself and were relentlessly and predictably negative:

> Our general conclusion is that nothing has come from the study of UFOs in the past 21 years that has added to scientific knowledge. Careful consideration of the record as it is available to us leads us to conclude that further extensive study of UFOs probably cannot be justified in the expectation that science will be advanced thereby.[67]

The bulk of the report—the summaries of evidence and the fifty-nine case studies of UFO sightings—struggled hard to back up this conclusion, but with limited success. Many of the explanations offered in the summaries of evidence were almost comical in their eagerness to find a natural explanation at all costs. The account of one 1954 sighting by the crew of a commercial airline and a military pilot featured the remarkable conclusion: "This unusual sighting should therefore be assigned to the category of some almost certainly natural phenomenon which is so rare that it apparently has never been reported before or since."[68] Despite the team's efforts, however, nearly a third of the case studies had to be classified as unknown.

The media had a field day with the Condon Report. Most news stories treated Condon's conclusions as the solution to the mystery, though a noticeable minority gave voice to the doubts many people felt about official culture's easy dismissal of the phenomenon. One much-reprinted editorial cartoon showed Condon himself being abducted by a pair of little green men. As they dragged him to a waiting saucer, a colleague called out helpfully, "Try telling them that they don't exist, Dr. Condon."

Still, the release of the Condon Report marked a major turning point in the history of the UFO phenomenon. Project Blue Book was terminated later the same year, and for the first time since 1948 there was no official U.S. government body to which citizens could report

---

67. Condon 1969, 1.

68. Quoted in Dolan 2002, 355.

UFO sightings. The hope of congressional investigations that had kept the respectable wing of the UFO community going for more than a decade faded out after the Condon Report, though some groups continued to go through the motions of trying to attract interest from government and the scientific community.

The fate of NICAP, the largest of the civilian UFO research groups of the 1960s and the one that had always been most vocal in its insistence on an Air Force coverup and its calls for a congressional investigation, was a bellwether for the movement as a whole. At a meeting of NICAP's board on December 3, 1969, the board members forced Donald Keyhoe to resign as the organization's director. Once Keyhoe and his longtime assistant Gordon Lore, Jr., were out of the way, the board brought in a new administration notable less for its interest in UFOs than for its close connections to the U.S. intelligence community.[69]

The new leadership forbade any criticism of U.S. government policy concerning UFOs, got rid of the investigating subcommittees that did much of the organization's work on the local level, and turned NICAP into a "sighting collection center." Most of its active members left in the years that followed, joining new UFO research organizations such as the Mutual UFO Network (MUFON), founded by Motorola executive Walter Andrus in 1969. In 1973, as NICAP spiraled downhill, J. Allen Hynek—by this time a significant figure on the extraterrestrial side of the UFO controversy—founded another UFO organization, the Center for UFO Studies (CUFOS), which drew even more of NICAP's former members away. The husk of NICAP survived a few more years and then quietly imploded.

An even more tragic denouement waited for Dr. James McDonald, whose attempts to influence the Condon Committee were only a small part of his advocacy for the extraterrestrial hypothesis. In the late 1960s McDonald was the most prominent professional scientist to support the ETH, and he clashed repeatedly with Philip Klass, the editor of *Aviation Week* and *Space Technology* and a leading proponent

---

69. Dolan 2002, 364–65.

of the null hypothesis. Klass retaliated with a campaign of harassment that targeted McDonald's professional standing and research funding. In 1971, with his career and reputation in ruins and his marriage disintegrating, McDonald committed suicide.[70]

Phoenix from the Ashes

Still, those who expected the UFO movement to fade away in the wake of the Condon Report were in for a surprise. In the decade or so following the report's release, belief in the physical reality and extraterrestrial origin of UFOs moved out of the fringes and into the cultural mainstream in America and most other Western countries.

Popular culture, which played such a massive role in shaping the UFO phenomenon, had an even larger role in preserving it at this juncture in its history. During the very years that the Condon Committee spent poring over the phenomenon, for example, TV programs on all American channels based their plots on the core beliefs of the very same extraterrestrial hypothesis that the committee report rejected so flatly—and the cultural dominance of the United States at the time guaranteed that these same shows appeared on television screens around the noncommunist world in the years that followed.

ABC's leading science fiction show at the time was *The Invaders*, starring Roy Thinnes as an engineer who was trying to warn a disbelieving world about aliens landing in flying saucers to pursue a plan of world conquest. Ironically, one of the show's episodes featured a Condon-like committee with an alien staff member who biased the investigation toward the null hypothesis to cover up the secret invasion. CBS wound up the successful three-year run of the situation comedy *My Favorite Martian* in 1966, featuring a Martian visitor to Earth, and the year before had launched the equally popular *Lost in Space*, featuring a saucer-shaped spacecraft sent from a polluted and resource-short Earth to find another planet for humanity to colonize. NBC had the most innovative and, at the time, the least commercially successful of the three, *Star Trek*, which touched on most of the

---

70. Druffel 2003 is the only detailed biography of McDonald published to date.

themes of the decade's UFO mythology and even had one episode— "Tomorrow is Yesterday," which first aired on January 26, 1967—based on the 1948 Mantell sighting, with the U.S.S. Enterprise playing the role of the UFO.

These were only the tip of a much larger iceberg of UFO-related popular culture that flooded every level of society in the late 1960s. In the books, comics, and Saturday morning cartoon shows that catered to children at the time, flying saucers crewed by aliens from distant planets had an inescapable presence. The American tabloid press, which emerged from the background static of low-end journalism in those years, had already begun its love affair with the UFO phenomenon and turned out colorful flying saucer stories in issue after issue. Meanwhile the durable Ray Palmer, who sold *FATE* to his partners in 1958, continued to crank out issues of half a dozen pulp magazines dedicated at least in part to the UFO phenomenon until his death in 1977, blending the flying saucer mythology with the hollow earth, further Shaver revelations, and anything else that caught his omnivorous interest.

These same patterns had echoes much further up the cultural pyramid of the time. The Sixties saw science fiction emerge from its long exile in pulp culture to become the serious literary genre it had been in the days of H. G. Wells. Alongside it, every form of imaginative literature found new respectability in a world that no longer seemed to be playing by familiar rules. In the phantasmagoria of the Sixties, a generation that drew much of its cosmology from J. R. R. Tolkien's fantasies of Middle-Earth when it wasn't imbibing Carlos Castaneda's allegedly factual tales of magic in the Mexican desert[71] found it easy to believe that aliens from outer space made at least as much sense as anything else.

The 1960 publication of *Le Matin des Magiciens*, by Louis Pauwels and Jacques Bergier, released three years later in English translation, set the seal on these transformations. A bestseller in several languages, *The Morning of the Magicians* drew on the writings of Charles Fort,

---

71. See Thompson 1971 for Tolkien's role as a source of the Sixties worldview, and de Mille 1980 for a discussion of Castaneda's role as a counterculture guru.

most of a century of popular occult literature, and a collection of titillating rumors about the involvement of Nazi Germany in arcane traditions and hidden sciences to level a challenge at the most basic assumptions of scientific materialism. Its phenomenal success guaranteed that the same cheap paperback format would welcome countless similar titles in the following decades.

Plenty of factors fed into the wave of changes that reshaped the popular imagination of the Western world toward the end of the Sixties, but one immense factor has not always been given the importance it deserves. On July 20, 1969, Neil Armstrong climbed out of a hatch on the Apollo 11 lander and became the first human being to leave footprints on the soil of another world. As blurry images broadcast from the moon via NASA's Houston Control appeared on television sets around the world, people who had dismissed science fiction out of hand found themselves staring the fantastic in the face. In the light of Apollo's resounding triumph, the vision of a future of infinite progress among the stars that powered so much of science fiction, and played such an important role in the collective imagination of the industrial world, seemed on the verge of inevitable fulfillment.

Yet America in the Seventies followed up the technical triumphs of the Apollo program with the final debacle in Vietnam, the oil crisis of 1973, and the implosion of the Nixon presidency in the Watergate scandal. Among the lasting legacies of Apollo was a question on many minds—"If we can put a man on the moon, why can't we . . . ?" At the moment that the dream of perpetual progress seemed to have become a reality, each passing day seemed to call it more deeply into question. The decade of the 1970s saw the first widespread awakening of popular concern about the environment and the popularity of books such as *The Limits to Growth*, which argued that the entire basis for the dream had been a delusion from the start. In such times alternative visions of reality find many takers.

The twin national traumas of defeat in Vietnam and the Watergate scandal also had a huge if delayed impact on the UFO phenomenon, as on every other aspect of American popular culture. In their aftermath, as the barriers of government secrecy faltered for a time,

Americans were horrified to discover how many of the seemingly preposterous claims made by political radicals in the previous decade were simple fact, and how many of the plausible denials offered up by government and the media during the same period were bald-faced lies.

Despite years of official denials, the United States had in fact been fighting secret wars across half of southeast Asia, overthrowing governments throughout the Third World, spying systematically on its own citizens, and sabotaging domestic political movements of left and right with complete disregard for its own constitution. All this gave the claims of a government coverup hiding the truth about UFOs an enormous boost. If the U.S. government could conceal the bombing of Cambodia and FBI spying on domestic dissidents, UFO activists argued plausibly, why couldn't it be hiding crashed saucers at Wright-Patterson Air Force Base?

Yet these same years saw another significant change in the UFO phenomenon itself. After 1974, sightings of UFOs in North America dwindled steadily, and the vast majority of those that were reported were plain nocturnal lights at high altitudes. The silvery spheres that were seen by so many people in the 1950s, and played such a large role in gaining a public presence for the UFO phenomenon, vanished completely, and close encounters of the first and second kinds—those involving landings and physical traces—became very rare. None of this had the slightest effect on the popularity of the extraterrestrial hypothesis. As Curtis Peebles points out, "The flying saucer myth had become separated from the flying saucer itself."[72]

The end of the mass saucer sightings of the 1960s left a void, but nature—and especially human nature—abhors a vacuum. Before long, a new flurry of strange phenomena, some real, others imaginary, found themselves drawn into the widening spiral of the UFO phenomenon. Among the most troubling were the mutilated corpses of livestock that began to surface at the end of the 1960s, and sparked a full-blown panic in the following decade.

---

72. Peebles 1994, 325.

Cattle Mutilations

There is a certain ghoulish humor in the name of the first reported victim of cattle mutilation: Snippy. She was an Appaloosa mare, not a cow, but her fate—literally "snipped" by persons or nonpersons unknown—played the same role in the popular imagination of the cattle mutilation panic that Kenneth Arnold's original sighting over Mount Rainier played in the wider UFO phenomenon.[73]

Snippy belonged to Mrs. Nellie Lewis of Alamosa, Colorado, who was fascinated by UFOs. Lewis' eighty-seven-year-old mother had seen something in the sky on September 7, 1967, about the time Snippy disappeared, though she wasn't wearing her glasses and so could not say for sure that the object was a flying saucer. A month later, Snippy's corpse turned up. An Associated Press bulletin on October 5 announced breathlessly that the horse had been entirely skinned and drained of blood, and that the place where the corpse was found showed high radioactivity and signs that some heavy object had landed and taken off.

None of this, as it happens, was true. Photos of Snippy's body show that the head and neck, not the whole body, had been stripped of skin and flesh; the same photos show no signs of the supposed heavy object, and the site had been checked by a Forest Service employee with a Geiger counter and showed no signs of unusual radioactivity. Furthermore, a veterinary physician from Colorado State University found signs of an infection in the animal's hindlimb that would have been severe enough to incapacitate it, and the stripping of the head and neck was exactly the sort of thing scavengers such as coyotes do to carrion.

These corrections, though, failed to make any impact on the public imagination. Far more influential was a nationally syndicated newspaper story, "Snippy's Death Just Chapter in Stellar Rustling," by journalist and UFO researcher John Keel. Keel's story alleged that Snippy was merely one of hundreds of mutilated animals associated

---

73. For Snippy and the cattle mutilation panic generally, see Kagan and Summers 1983 and Thompson 1991, 127–32.

with UFO sightings. At the time, this was a wild exaggeration—there were only a handful of cases in the UFO literature at that time that could be described in these terms—but it had its effect.

Other reports of mutilated livestock began to appear thereafter, first in a trickle and eventually in a flood. By 1974, ranchers and farmers across the American West were convinced that some mysterious force was slaughtering and mutilating their cattle. The September 30, 1974, issue of *Newsweek* featured a story titled "The Midnight Marauder" about the mutilation epidemic, describing posses of heavily armed local men staking out hilltops and watching through the night, hoping to deter the mutilators. Still, the bodies kept appearing—hundreds of them each year, in a region extending from Texas north to South Dakota and from Iowa west as far as Idaho. The vast majority were cows, found dead on the ground with soft tissues—eyes, tongues, ears, sex organs, and anuses—removed, and no sign of blood anywhere around.

All this made great news copy, and helped feed a paranoid streak in the UFO movement that would have dramatic results a decade later. Despite all the media furor, though, the cattle mutilations were much less mysterious than they appeared. Veterinary pathologists pointed out again and again, to no avail, that scavengers finding a dead cow normally eat exactly the tissues found missing in mutilated cattle, that animals more than a few hours dead don't bleed because the blood coagulates after death, and that wounds made in a corpse in dry air shrink in a way that makes them look cleaner and more precise than they originally were. Reports of mutilated cattle came almost entirely from small ranches with inexperienced owners; professional ranching operations rarely reported anything of the kind, and many experienced cattlemen dismissed the entire thing as nonsense. Nor did the death rate among cattle increase significantly during the years when mutilation reports peaked.[74]

---

74. See Kagan and Summers 1983 for these points.

What was going on, in fact, was a classic rumor panic, of the sort studied at length by sociologists.[75] A rumor panic begins with a shocking claim about an unsuspected threat to something that symbolizes one or more of the primary values of a culture. The claim needs no evidence to support it; if it touches the raw nerve of a culture's unspoken fears, it can easily find or manufacture its own evidence, and anyone who asks hard questions about that evidence can count on being labeled hopelessly naive if not actually in league with the enemy. Like other modern American rumor panics—the Communist infiltration panic of the late 1940s and early 1950s, say, or the Satanic ritual abuse panic of the 1980s—the cattle mutilation panic quickly collected a support system of amateur investigators whose methods focused on proving what they knew to be true, rather than testing their own theories against the facts on the ground. The result in each case was a torrent of misinformation that fed the panic in a self-reinforcing cycle.

What distinguished the cattle mutilation panic from the others just cited is that it was drawn into the UFO controversy, and turned into a source of support for the extraterrestrial hypothesis. UFOs were far from the only suspects proposed for the apparent epidemic of mutilated cattle. Secret government programs and Satanic cultists—two other hot-button topics at the time—were also blamed for the phenomenon, and stories supporting these claims played just as large a role in the panic as those backing the alien origin of the cattle mutilators. In fact, the black helicopters that later became a staple image of evil on the fringes of American politics got their start from a handful of reported sightings that circulated among mutilation researchers. Still, as time passed and corpses mounted up, the theory that UFOs were responsible elbowed the other hypotheses out of the way, and many believers in the extraterrestrial hypothesis adopted the cattle mutilation epidemic as another set of evidence supporting the theory of alien contact.

---

75. Victor 1993 has a useful discussion of rumor panics.

The juxtaposition of flying saucers and dead cows, however, posed a strong challenge to those members of the UFO community—very much in the majority in the 1970s—who thought of aliens in a positive light. For many, it was hard to imagine enlightened Space Brothers or superhumanly intelligent galactic explorers taking a break from their other projects to drain the blood from cows in Wyoming. The interface between UFOs and cattle mutilation was thus left to the further reaches of the UFO community, where it began laying the groundwork for the more sinister vision of alien contact that would rise to dominate the UFO controversy a decade later.

A typical example of the way cattle mutilation was embraced on the fringes of the UFO research community can be found in the books and videos of Linda Moulton Howe, who began studying cattle mutilations from a UFO perspective in the late 1970s and released a series of popular documentaries and books in the 1980s and 1990s. Howe's book *An Alien Harvest*, packed with large color photos of mutilated cows, claims that she was taken into confidence by a government agent and shown secret documents proving, at least to her satisfaction, that aliens from a distant planet were killing and mutilating cattle to provide themselves with raw material for genetic-engineering experiments crucial to the survival of their species.[76]

It is unfortunately almost needless to say that Howe presented no evidence for these claims, other than the very ambiguous evidence provided by rotting cow carcasses. Nor did she, or for that matter many other UFO researchers, notice that all these claims could be found in popular culture going back decades into the past. During the middle years of the 1970s, for example, when cattle mutilation reports were at their height, television watchers in many parts of America could tune into broadcasts of the British TV show *UFO*, which featured a dying race of aliens whose bid for survival involved abducting, killing, and mutilating human beings so their organs could be transplanted into alien bodies. This was not a new theme in science fiction—equivalent stories had appeared in the pulps decades before—but it was new

---

76. Howe 1989.

to the UFO scene in the 1970s. A decade later, it would seize center stage.

The Rise of Alternative Culture

Behind the cattle mutilation panic, and for that matter the growing acceptance of the extraterrestrial hypothesis, lay an eagerness to embrace ideas rejected by the accepted worldview of modern science that spread through much of the industrial world during the 1970s and 1980s. The rebirth of evangelical Protestantism as a major social force, decades after it had been banished to the cultural fringes, was one marker of this trend, but far from the only one.

Another, even more striking, was the explosive growth of books on alternative culture as a mainstream publishing trend. As late as the mid-1960s, most books on UFOs, ritual magic, Fortean phenomena, and the like came from small publishers specializing in fringe topics. The huge success of bestsellers such as *The Morning of the Magicians* and Carlos Castaneda's *The Teachings of Don Juan* changed all that. Mass-market paperback houses soon recognized that books promoting alternative ideas in science, health, and spirituality could make them a great deal of money. Writers who wanted an audience for radical ideas found that their opportunities had ballooned almost beyond imagining.

Inevitably, much of the flood of intellectual heresy that resulted was long on claims but short on evidence, and a significant amount of it created mysteries out of thin air. The Bermuda Triangle was a classic example. Two books by popular writers in the alternative press of the 1960s, Vincent Gaddis' 1965 *Invisible Horizons* and Charles Berlitz's 1968 *Limbo of the Lost*, claimed that an unaccountably large number of ships and planes had mysteriously vanished without a trace over a triangular region of ocean near Bermuda. The same claims were rehashed and embellished by close to a dozen writers over the following decade.

Investigators who took the time to review the original evidence found nothing out of the ordinary—just the toll of sunken ships and crashed airplanes normal for an area of ocean that size—and many of the details that made the Triangle look mysterious had been invented out of whole cloth.[77] None of this kept the Bermuda Triangle from finding a home among the popular beliefs of the 1970s, or from being recruited by the UFO community as another form of proof that something literally out of this world was hovering in Earth's skies.

Another popular set of claims that surfaced at the same time claimed that astronauts from other worlds had been responsible for the creation of ancient human cultures and of *Homo sapiens* itself. These ideas had a long prehistory in the contactee movement; George Hunt Williamson's seminal *Other Tongues, Other Flesh* (1953) centered on the same idea, and key writers from the early phase of the UFO controversy such as Brinsley Le Poer Trench and Desmond Leslie had dilated on it at some length. The mass-market publication of Erich von Däniken's *Chariots of the Gods?* in 1970 launched these same ideas into the wider public, with dramatic results.

Chariots of the Gods? and its five sequels went on to rack up total sales above fifty million copies by the end of the century. Scientific critics pointed out that many of Däniken's claims were based on inaccurate information about history, and many of his arguments were impressively circular. UFO researchers from the scientific wing of the movement backed these criticisms, distancing themselves from Däniken's claims as forcefully as they had backed away from the contactees of the 1950s. None of these critiques slowed the popular acceptance of Däniken's theories, any more than disapproval from NICAP and APRO slowed the spread of contactee beliefs, and for the same reason: the rejected beliefs in question had a large and enthusiastic constituency of their own.

The same climate of ideas had a potent influence on narratives more directly linked to the UFO phenomenon as well. A prime beneficiary of this process was the long-forgotten claim that a flying saucer had crashed near Roswell, New Mexico, during the original 1947 UFO wave. The same Charles Berlitz who helped put the Bermuda Triangle on the map, together with UFO researchers William Moore

---

77. Kusche 1975.

and Stanton Friedman, published *The Roswell Incident* in 1980. This book combined material from the actual events of the first days of July 1947 with some elements borrowed from Frank Scully's discredited Aztec crash, and others that Berlitz and his co-authors apparently made up.[78] These difficulties did not prevent *The Roswell Incident* from becoming a potent influence on later UFO writings.

By the time *The Roswell Incident* appeared, for that matter, nearly any set of ideas that could present itself as an alternative to the status quo was guaranteed an audience. If it managed to touch on emotionally appealing themes, it also stood a good chance of attracting a great deal of money, even from some of the more mainstream institutions of Western culture. In the late 1970s and early 1980s, for example, the CIA put millions of dollars into testing the ability of psychics to carry on extrasensory espionage, while Fortune 500 corporations hired psychologists from the human potential movement to start encounter groups for middle management, and millions of ordinary Americans invested substantial sums in seminars in mass-marketed mysticism offered by groups such as Transcendental Meditation and est.

The contactee scene of the 1950s had played a significant role in setting the stage for all this. Some of the most influential figures in the alternative scene in these latter decades had been active in contactee circles for decades. George King, a former London taxi driver turned voice of the Interplanetary Parliament and head of the Aetherius Society, and Ruth Norman, founder of the religion of Unarius ("Universal Articulate Interdimensional Understanding of Science"), whose followers believed her to be the Archangel Uriel, are among the better known examples. The colorful habits and improbable claims of these and similar figures irritated the more scientific UFO researchers, but opened the way for less obviously exotic beliefs to find their way into the mainstream.

An influential example of this latter process at work can be traced in the career of Dr. Andrija Puharich, the parapsychologist whose interactions with the contactee movement were mentioned in chapter

---

78. See, for example, Saler, Ziegler, and Moore 1997, 12–19.

2. Puharich spent the 1950s and 1960s at the cutting edge of alternative thought, studying shamanism with Hawaiian kahunas and investigating the Brazilian "psychic surgeon" Arigó (José Pedro de Freitas), whose medical treatments were guided by information he received in trance states. In 1970 Puharich heard of a young Israeli mentalist named Uri Geller, who was making a name for himself in the nightclub circuit in Israel. Puharich visited the future psychic superstar and hypnotized him several times in an attempt to find out the source of Geller's powers.[79]

Though Puharich had professional training as a hypnotist, accounts of these sessions make it clear that Puharich violated standard hypnotic practice in several ways, most strikingly by asking a series of leading questions focusing on his own beliefs in alien intelligences and "the Nine." Geller obligingly responded to Puharich's prompting with a story about a childhood UFO encounter and a trance communication from a "conscious computer" orbiting the earth on a spacecraft named Spectra.

In 1972 Puharich brought Geller to the United States to be tested at the Stanford Research Institute (SRI) labs near Palo Alto. At that time SRI was earning a reputation on the cutting edge of parapsychology; less widely known, but rather more lucrative, was its involvement in secret research programs for the CIA and the Defense Department. During these tests, Geller once again channeled the computer on board Spectra, announcing that flying saucers would soon land en masse, and claiming that he and Puharich had both been selected by the aliens to prepare humanity for the landing.

The next year, however, the aliens found their plans disrupted when Geller's appearance on *Dimbleby's Talk-In* on British television made him the psychic equivalent of a rock star overnight. Geller parted company with Puharich soon afterwards. Undaunted, Puharich found another medium who would pass on messages from "the Nine," and he continued to play his role as the *éminence grise* of the contactee movement. His sponsorship of Geller, however, helped give

---

79. For Puharich and Geller, see Picknett and Prince 1999, 169–73.

the emerging rejected-knowledge movement one of its first popular figureheads and helped seed the popular imagination with ideas that would have potent cultural influences later on.

Alongside these longtime figures in the movement were a new generation of contactees such as Eduard "Billy" Meier, a Swiss farmer whose claims became the subject of a lavishly produced 1979 book, *Spaceships from the Pleiades*.[80] According to Meier, his contacts with spiritually advanced beings from the Pleiades began in 1975 and involved hundreds of UFO sightings and conversations with aliens. As evidence he offered photos of Pleiadian "beamships" and blurry pictures of Semjasa, the female leader of the Pleiadean expedition, as well as a great deal of religious teaching of the usual contactee type.

Analysis of the beamship photos showed them to be clever fakes, and pictures of one of Meier's Pleiadian contacts have an unnerving resemblance to television screenshots of American actress Darleen Carr in her appearances in *The Dean Martin Show*, on which she played one of the Ding-a-Ling Sisters. His claims were nonetheless widely accepted in alternative circles in Europe and the United States, and Shirley MacLaine, doyenne of American New Age circles, donated a substantial sum to support Meier's Semjase Silver Star Center.

To an extent few people realized, in fact, the New Age movement that grabbed so many headlines during these decades was simply the contactee movement with a new label and a slightly different focus. Under the banner of the New Age, the old claims about a mass landing of flying saucers had been reshaped into a subtler form; the new version suggested that a transformation in consciousness then under way would do the saucers' work for them. Books such as Marilyn Ferguson's *The Aquarian Conspiracy* (1980) and Theodore Roszak's *Person/Planet* (1978) celebrated the imminent arrival of a new era of human potential and garnered substantial sales. In their wake, ideas once confined to the contactee circuit spread throughout popular culture.

---

80. See Kinder 1987 for a thoughtful study of the Meier affair; Stevens, Elders, and Elders 1979 for Meier's side of the story; and Korff 1996 for a critical examination. I am indebted to Erskine Payton for pointing me to the Ding-a-Ling dimension of Meier's claims.

Challenging the Extraterrestrials

A cultural ferment on this scale guaranteed that a great deal of pro-foundly creative work would be done. It also guaranteed at least as large a helping of delusion and self-serving fraud. The UFO scene itself was far from immune to either of these. Some of the delusions and frauds have already been mentioned, but the creative work also deserves attention. Moving away from the stalemate between the extraterrestrial and null hypotheses, a number of innovative UFO researchers began to ask hard questions about the basic assumptions underlying current attempts to make sense of the phenomenon. The most influential of these "New Wave" ufologists, Jacques Vallee and John Keel, argued forcefully that UFOs could not be pigeonholed into the slots reserved for them by all sides in the debate since 1947.

The works produced by these two writers could hardly be more different. Vallee, a successful computer scientist who worked closely with J. Allen Hynek for many years, provided a series of incisive analy-ses of the phenomenon that made it clear the old assumptions could no longer be justified. His *Passport to Magonia* (1969) showed that UFO sightings could not be separated in any meaningful sense from accounts of apparitions and spiritual beings in the past. His more troubling *Messengers of Deception* (1979) broke even further from the ufological mainstream, tracing the uncomfortable links that united UFO sightings with alternative religious movements and military intelligence, and proposing that UFOs might be used—and indeed might have been manufactured—as a way of shaping public opinion, by governments, secret societies affiliated with the occult, or some entirely nonhuman presence.

Keel, a veteran journalist and former pulp writer who had covered any number of oddball beats since the Korean War, presented the same challenging insights in a different way. His best book, *The Mothman Prophecies* (1975), left analysis at the door in order to launch the reader on a harrowing plunge into the dark heart of the UFO phenomenon, with all the folklore elements, hallucinatory experiences, and paranor-mal dimensions most mainstream UFO researchers edited out of their accounts. In sketching the weird events that foreshadowed the 1967 collapse of the Silver Bridge at Point Pleasant, West Virginia—events that included UFO sightings, Men in Black, and a bizarre winged humanoid figure the press labeled "Mothman"—Keel showed that the neat explanatory category of "visitors from space" had long since failed to keep pace with the phenomenon it claimed to describe. He argued instead that the UFO phenomenon, and a great many other strange occurrences, were manifestations of a "superspectrum," a level of reality outside the world of ordinary human experience.

A great many UFO researchers remained firmly committed to the extraterrestrial hypothesis and rejected the new "ultraterrestrial" hypothesis (the word was Keel's), often with some heat. Still, Keel, Vallee, and other writers who adopted the same approach found an eager audience for their ideas among a younger generation of UFO fans and the general public. Few recent eras have had so passionate a desire for wonders, and the ultraterrestrial hypothesis—with all its implications of unknown realities and paranormal forces—satisfied that desire much more thoroughly than the extraterrestrial hypothesis could. To the *Star Wars* generation of the 1970s, who grew up with astronauts on the evening news and science fiction in high school English classes, the idea of spaceships zooming through Earth's skies simply wasn't that exciting any more.

For a time, the New Wave seemed likely to sweep everything before it and redefine the entire UFO phenomenon as a single element in a much wider pattern of alternative realities. By the end of the 1980s, though, the extraterrestrial hypothesis reemerged triumphant. Many factors contributed to this reversal, but one of the most important was also one of the most richly ironic: the appetite for wonders that inspired so much innovative thinking in the 1970s generated its own nemesis, in the form of an opposition movement that resembled nothing so much as the UFO movement itself.

The defining moment in this turn of events was the birth of the Committee for Scientific Investigation of Claims of the Paranormal (CSICOP) in 1976. CSICOP was the brainchild of Paul Kurtz, a professor of philosophy at the State University of New York in Buffalo and a leading figure in the American Humanist Association. The year before CSICOP's founding, Kurtz reacted to the rising popularity of occult beliefs by helping to formulate a manifesto entitled "Objections to Astrology," getting 186 prominent scientists and scholars to sign it, and releasing it to the media.[81] Encouraged by the response, Kurtz arranged a special conference of the American Humanist Association on April 30 and May 1, 1976, to launch a new organization intended to oppose occultism and other nonscientific ways of thinking.

CSICOP, the result of this initiative, succeeded in attracting most of the prominent American critics of occultism, parapsychology, and similar topics dear to the alternative culture of the time, from scientists Carl Sagan and Marcello Truzzi to science fiction writer Isaac Asimov and stage magician James "The Amazing" Randi; UFO debunker Philip Klass was another founding member. More important was its success in attracting a wider following among people outside the worlds of scholarship or the media, a move that provided it with a source of funding through membership dues and a network of amateur investigators who applied the CSICOP belief system to reports of unexplained phenomena in their own areas.

If this sounds like a description of a UFO research organization, it should. To a remarkable extent, CSICOP evolved into a mirror image of the UFO groups it opposed so strenuously. Like the UFO groups, its membership soon sorted itself out into a core of public figures eager for media attention, a wider circle of investigators who did not always have the professional qualifications to back up their claims of expertise, and a broad base of ordinary members who paid their dues, received their newsletters, and circulated the organization's ideas among their own social circles. Like the UFO groups, too, it pursued a strategy centered on investigating reports of strange phenomena and publicizing the results of those investigations when they supported the organization's agenda. For that matter, debunkers such as Philip Klass and James Oberg became as much a part of the UFO movement as

---

81.   See Bok, Kurtz, and Jerome 1975. Neither Kurtz nor the other contributors to this paper appear to have taken the time to learn anything about astrology before critiquing it, and the many inaccuracies that resulted have been much cited by astrologers ever since as evidence that the scientific rejection of astrology is based on prejudice rather than evidence.

their opponents, and used essentially the same strategies as the partisans of extraterrestrial contact to promote their own viewpoints and assail the alternatives.

The first years of CSICOP's history were enlivened by internal disputes centering on the organization's agenda and its sometimes problematic relationship to matters of fact. Marcello Truzzi, one of the founding members, departed after less than a year, accusing Kurtz and other members of the organization of a "pseudoskepticism" that put defending current scientific beliefs ahead of objective assessment of the evidence. The year 1978 saw another explosion when CSICOP executive committee member Dennis Rawlins pointed out that a CSICOP study of Michel Gauquelin's "Mars Effect," a phenomenon that offered some support to astrology, had massaged the data to get the desired negative result; not long afterwards, via a series of events that have remained a subject of controversy ever since, Rawlins was ejected from the executive committee and either left or was thrown out of the organization.[82] The aftermath of these struggles saw CSICOP complete its transformation into an advocacy group supporting a closely defined set of acceptable beliefs about the causes of apparently paranormal events, in another close parallel to the UFO organizations.

These ironies came full circle in the years that followed, as a movement largely inspired by CSICOP, and enthusiastically adopting the angry and contemptuous rhetoric that pervaded CSICOP publications, became an unwitting source of support for believers in the extraterrestrial hypothesis and many other alternative worldviews. From the late 1970s onward, people who came forward to report a UFO sighting in most parts of the United States could count on the appearance of a local "skeptic" who, much more often than not, accused witnesses of dishonesty or gross ignorance, and presented explanations for the sighting that begged more questions than they answered. The same witnesses could also very often count on the appearance of a local UFO researcher who treated them with courtesy, took their report seriously, and placed it in a framework—the extraterrestrial

---

82. For the Rawlins controversy, see Rawlins 1981 and Kamann 1982.

hypothesis—that made sense of the sighting in the context of widely held popular beliefs. It should come as no surprise that the supportive approach of the UFO investigators helped encourage belief in the ETH, just as the arrogance and hostility of so many self-proclaimed skeptics closed many minds to the possibility that less exotic explanations for UFO sightings might be worth considering.

The Extraterrestrials Triumph

Still, it was once again popular culture that cast the deciding vote. Movies and fiction all through the UFO era gave aliens an ambivalent status—UFO movies covered the gamut from the extraterrestrial horrors of *The Thing* and *Alien* to the saintly Klaatu of *The Day the Earth Stood Still* or the cloying cuteness of the title character in *E. T.: The Extraterrestrial*—but the countless stories about monsters from outer space that filled the pulp magazines in the preceding decades left deep traces in the collective imagination.

In his 1958 book on the phenomenon, Carl Jung noted that the emotions surrounding UFOs in the previous decade had shifted decisively from hope to fear, as people contemplated the possibility of alien invasion.[83] It's thus no surprise that flying saucer films from the beginning of the genre in 1950 up into the 1970s gave more space to hostile aliens than to friendly ones, with potent effects on the collective imagination. It's symptomatic of the times that a popular book on survival techniques published in 1967 included a brief paragraph about self-defense against aliens from flying saucers.[84]

Television followed the same pattern with even less originality. The aliens of the ABC-TV series *The Invaders* or the British series *UFO* were a threat, pure and simple, invading Earth from a distant, dying world to find a new home for their species, in the one program, or to harvest human organs to repair their bodies in the other. CBS's *Lost in Space*, the most popular science fiction series of its time, stood the same story on its head without challenging any of its assumptions;

---

83. Jung 1978, 61.

84. Greenbank 1967, 34.

its saucer-shaped spacecraft took off from a polluted and overcrowded Earth in 1997 on a mission to find a new home for humanity among the stars. What the inhabitants of that new home might think of such an invasion by humans from space was left mostly to the imagination, but could not have been far back in the minds of many of the program's viewers.

This set of themes shifted unexpectedly in the 1970s and 1980s, though, as the media refocused on positive images of aliens. A single storyline—a lone extraterrestrial stranded on Earth, recruiting help from sympathetic earthlings while dodging sinister government agents and arrogant skeptics in a quest to return home—turned into one of the most consistently lucrative movie plots of the period. Compare Spielberg's *E. T.* with the otherwise forgettable 1978 Disney vehicle *The Cat from Outer Space* or 1984's *Starman*, say, and you'll find the same basic theme repeated with only the slightest variation. Those themes spoke powerfully to a time of widespread alienation, when many people in America and elsewhere felt as though they had suddenly arrived on a strange planet.

The space monsters of previous decades never abandoned the field completely, of course. Ridley Scott's phenomenally successful horror-SF film *Alien* (1979) featured the ugliest extraterrestrial yet to grace the silver screen, while the 1983 American TV miniseries *V* provided a glimpse at the future of UFO mythology with its tale of shapeshifting, bloodthirsty alien reptiles in red jumpsuits who come to Earth in flying saucers and take over the planet by using mind-control technology on political leaders.

Still, the most influential UFO film of all time—Steven Spielberg's special-effects extravaganza *Close Encounters of the Third Kind*—probably played the largest role of all in bringing the extraterrestrial hypothesis back to center stage. In Spielberg's vision, UFOs were nuts-and-bolts alien spacecraft, and the stranger aspects of the phenomenon simply proved how advanced alien technology had to be. There was a fine irony in this, since one of the movie's characters—a French UFO researcher played by François Truffaut—was modeled on influential ETH challenger Jacques Vallee.

Close Encounters of the Third Kind borrowed materials from most areas of contemporary UFO myth, though it left cattle mutilation strictly alone. The Bermuda Triangle, though, was fair game, and one of the supposed disappearances that had been adopted into the Triangle mythos fed into a plot twist that had the aliens taking groups of human beings for a ride to the stars. This theme fed into one of the most powerful elements to emerge in the UFO phenomenon in the 1980s—the belief that aliens aboard flying saucers were abducting large numbers of human beings for purposes of their own.

Abducted by Aliens

Like so many other elements of the UFO phenomenon, the abduction narrative has a complicated prehistory. Stories of abductions that include most of the details in current accounts of the phenomenon appeared in science fiction stories starting with the pulps. French sociologist Bertrand Méheust took the time to search through most of a century of science fiction and found hundreds of stories that used alien abduction as a central motif between 1880 and 1940; in the usual way, these presented the core themes of today's narrative in detail.

One frequently cited example, Ege Tilms' 1934 story "Hodomur, Man of Infinity," combined alien abduction and missing time—the phenomenon, frequently reported by abductees, of losing hours when only minutes seemed to pass by—with curiously flattened areas in wheat fields, foreshadowing the crop circles of the 1990s.[85] The abduction scene in Albert Bender's *Flying Saucers and the Three Men* (1963), among the first appearances of the theme in UFO literature, borrowed many of these same ideas from science fiction and helped place them in the collective imagination of the UFO community.

Still, like the UFO phenomenon itself or the cattle mutilation panic of the 1970s, the alien abduction narrative had its real beginning in a single highly publicized case, the equivalent of Kenneth Arnold's sighting or the gruesome fate of Snippy the horse. Sometime after 10:30 on the night of September 19, 1961, Barney and Betty Hill spotted a

---

85. See Thompson 1991, 67–68.

glowing object, like an airplane fuselage without wings, above them in the sky as they drove on Route 3 near Lancaster, New Hampshire.[86] The object appeared to follow them, and finally came within a few hundred feet of their car. Barney pulled over and walked toward it, then came pelting back after seeing strange faces staring down at him from portholes in the side of the object.

According to the Hills' later accounts, he tried to drive away, but a beeping sound that seemed to come from the car's trunk made them sink into a strange drowsy state. Two more sets of beeps sounded, and then all at once the Hills found themselves thirty-five miles farther down the road, with no idea how they got there.

In the days that followed, Betty became convinced that something extraordinary had happened during the encounter. She read Donald Keyhoe's *The Flying Saucer Conspiracy*, and began to have dreams in which she was taken on board a flying saucer, which she recounted to her husband. She contacted UFO researchers, and while describing the events of the sighting to them, the Hills realized that the trip had taken two hours longer than it should have. The researchers urged them to be hypnotized in the hope of figuring out what had happened during the interval of "missing time."

A referral brought them to Dr. Benjamin Simon, a respected Boston psychiatrist, who hypnotized the Hills separately on several sessions and regressed them to the time of the UFO sighting. Under hypnosis, Barney described looking up into the portholes of the craft and seeing figures that reminded him of Nazis. His account went on to describe being captured by the "Nazis," taken aboard their craft, and subjected to a physical examination; he had been so terrified the whole time, he said, that he had rarely opened his eyes. Betty also described being taken into the craft and put through a medical examination; on her way out she was shown a chart of dots joined by lines, and her captors explained that this diagram showed where they were from. After being returned to their car, Betty said, they had watched

---

86. See Fuller 1968 for the classic account of the Hill abduction.

the UFO glow brightly and then rise up into the air, taking the form of a glowing orange ball.

During 1962, this account began to circulate among believers of the extraterrestrial hypothesis as an accurate and credible account of activities by the crew of an alien starship. Dr. Simon himself disagreed. As an experienced professional hypnotist, he knew that hypnotic recall reliably includes large amounts of fantasy and unconscious content— a point we'll cover in more detail in chapter 7—and his best assessment was that the "abduction" was a vivid dream rather than an actual event.[87] This view failed to have any impact in the face of the popular faith in extraterrestrial UFOs or the common belief, as inaccurate as it is widespread, that hypnotic regression plays back an exact recording of events in the past.

For all that, it took a long time for the Hills' experience to have much of an impact outside a narrow segment of the UFO community. The case first surfaced at a time when NICAP, the most prestigious of the "respectable" UFO groups, refused to deal with any sighting report that involved UFO occupants for fear of being too closely identified with the contactees. What brought the case to national attention, as with so much else in UFO history, was its transformation into a media phenomenon.

This was the work of journalist John Fuller. Fuller had become interested in the UFO phenomenon a few years earlier after a series of remarkable sightings of glowing aerial objects in the town of Seacoast, New Hampshire, in 1965. His lively and intensely readable book on the subject, *Incident at Exeter* (1966), became a bestseller, and the Hill case was an obvious subject for a sequel. *The Interrupted Journey* saw print in 1968 and eclipsed its predecessor, becoming one of the most influential UFO books of the decade and receiving seven offers for movie rights. A TV movie titled *The UFO Incident*, starring James Earl Jones, duly appeared on NBC on October 20, 1975. Many of the details of the original abduction were changed in the movie—notably, the aliens Betty Hill described, who had black hair and Jimmy Durante

---

87. Peebles 1994, 226.

noses, were replaced by spindly, hairless, gray-skinned creatures with bulbous heads and huge slanted eyes—but the basic plot of Fuller's book remained central.

Responses from the other side of the controversy followed. CSICOP member Robert Sheaffer, then just beginning to make a name for himself among defenders of the null hypothesis, published an article the next year insisting that the Hills had mistaken the planet Jupiter for a flying saucer.[88] This claim found little acceptance outside the ranks of those already committed to the null hypothesis, not least because the only evidence Sheaffer offered for his theory was the fact that Jupiter was more or less in the right part of the sky that night. Plenty of UFO enthusiasts also knew that the Air Force had originally blamed the 1948 Mantell sighting on the planet Venus, too, only to have Mantell's UFO identified later on as a secret Skyhook balloon test, and a growing number were aware that null hypothesis proponents had been calling on planets to explain unidentified aerial objects since the days of the 1896 airship sightings.

By the time Sheaffer published his claims, though, even a more convincing explanation would likely have had little effect. In the crawlspaces of the collective imagination, the abduction narrative had taken what would become its classic shape. At the same time, the UFO phenomenon itself had begun to shift in unexpected ways.

Black Triangles

On the evening of March 17, 1983, a truck driver named William Durkin was driving west on Interstate 84 in New York's Hudson River valley.[89] Around 8:30 PM, as he passed through Brewster, he noted a cluster of lights in the air moving toward the highway from the south. The cars around him began driving erratically as other drivers tried to get a view, and drivers in the oncoming lanes pulled over to the shoulder so they could climb out and look.

---

88. Sheaffer 1976.

89. The Durkin sighting is summarized here from Hynek, Imbrogno, and Pratt 1998, 23–24.

At first Durkin thought the lights belonged to an airliner flying too close to the ground, but after a few moments he realized that it was moving too slowly to be any kind of conventional aircraft. It looked like a huge black boomerang as long as a football field, decorated with many-colored lights. Finally he pulled over and got out of his car, just as the craft passed overhead. He could see a structure of dark pipes connecting the lights together, but heard nothing. The craft moved a short distance away, and then shone a beam of white light straight down onto a truck, whose startled driver stayed motionless while the light shone but sped away as soon as it was turned off. After a short time the craft flew slowly out of sight to the northeast.

Durkin was one of more than a hundred witnesses who saw the "Westchester boomerang" on the night of March 17, and one of several thousands who saw it in action over the months that followed.[90] The description was always the same—a huge boomerang or blunt-nosed triangle colored flat black, sporting dozens of multicolored lights, and moving at not much more than a walking pace a few hundred feet above the ground. Some witnesses, like Durkin, claimed that it was completely silent, while others reported hearing a very quiet engine noise when the craft was directly above them. A few others noted what looked like a metal framework underneath the black shape, holding the lights in position. The craft was never seen landing, and only a few witnesses saw it do anything but drift slowly across the sky at night, flashing lights down at intervals on the startled witnesses below.

Local newspapers gave the sightings banner headlines—HUN-DREDS CLAIM TO HAVE SEEN UFO, for example, blared the Westchester-Rockland *Daily Item* on the morning of March 26, 1983, after a particularly active night—but the rest of the media never picked the story up at all. After one brief and curious gaffe—the county sheriff's department responded to calls reporting one sighting by saying that a local military base was testing a new aircraft, then denied saying anything of the kind—local police announced that the "boomerang" was a group of ultralight aircraft flying illegally at night,

---

90. See Hynek, Imbrogno, and Pratt 1998 for a thorough survey.

while local air traffic control personnel denied seeing anything out of the ordinary at all. The boomerang, whatever it might have been, kept appearing at intervals all through the spring, summer, and early autumn of 1983. It took the winter off, but appeared again in late March of 1984 and paraded through the skies again until the end of October. After that, sightings dropped off sharply, and the mass sightings of the 1983–1984 flap became a thing of the past.

Investigators from CUFOS, by that time the most prominent of the UFO organizations, interviewed witnesses, collected reports, and announced that the "Westchester boomerang" was a bona fide alien spacecraft, another piece of evidence for the arrival of aliens from space. Debunkers mostly repeated the police insistence that the lights were simply pranksters in ultralights flying in close formation. By that time, the Hobson's choice between the extraterrestrial hypothesis and the null hypothesis had become so firmly entrenched that very few people considered the possibility that certain well-known earthly technologies could easily have put the boomerang into the air.

Over the years that followed, black boomerangs and triangles began to crop up elsewhere in America, and throughout the world. By the end of the decade, they had been seen over most of North America and more than a dozen countries on other continents. They never succeeded in displacing the flying saucer as the core cultural icon of the UFO, but they gave a potent new shape to the deep-rooted fears that began to cluster around the UFO phenomenon as the 1980s drew toward their end. As UFO enthusiasts looked up hopefully at the stars, remembering the luminous spacecraft of *Close Encounters of the Third Kind* and dreaming of first contact, a far more sinister vision of human-alien interaction was moving in toward the mainstream of the UFO phenomenon.

four

Shadows of Dreamland, 1987–Present

The alien face on the cover of Whitley Strieber's best-selling book *Communion*, with its tiny mouth and huge almond-shaped eyes, has become one of the most widely recognized icons of the UFO phenomenon, second only to the flying saucer itself. Woven around it is one of the most distinctive elements of the latest phase of the UFO phenomenon, the narrative of alien abduction. According to this narrative, a central purpose—perhaps *the* central purpose—behind the secret visits of extraterrestrials to Earth involves the nocturnal kidnapping of thousands, perhaps millions, of human beings, so they can be subjected to painful medical procedures for reasons that are central to much of the current UFO debate.

As described in chapter 3, the abduction narrative crystallized around media portrayals of the Barney and Betty Hill case, but it did not emerge as a dominant theme in the UFO phenomenon until the 1980s. That has to be understood in its own historical context. Even with the mass sightings of black triangles added in, UFO sightings in the United States were far less common in the 1980s than they had been before 1974. The "Billy" Meier affair, which promised so much at the beginning of the decade, had foundered in charges of fraud and faked photographs, and the cattle mutilation panic of the 1970s had become an embarrassment as evidence piled up against claims that anything out of the ordinary was happening in American pastures. Most aspects of the phenomenon seemed to be at a standstill, and UFO investigators who did not focus on abductions spent much of their time rehashing old cases.

This made research into abduction reports irresistibly compelling to many people in the UFO community. Retellings of the Barney and Betty Hill case in UFO literature lent credibility to the abduction narrative, and hypnosis gave investigators a tool that proved remarkably successful at eliciting vivid, colorful, and consistent abduction accounts. During the 1970s, a handful of pioneering researchers pursued this approach by hypnotizing people who reported experiences like the Hill encounter—sightings of UFOs at close range accompanied by missing time—and found that nearly every one of these witnesses produced an account of being taken aboard the UFO, examined, and returned. By the early 1980s, researchers were hypnotizing people who had never seen a UFO or noticed a missing time experience, but simply worried that something odd had happened to them at some point in the past. These, too, produced accounts of being abducted by UFO occupants.[91]

Budd Hopkins, a New York artist turned UFO investigator, became one of the leading figures in the abduction field with the publication of his 1983 book *Missing Time*, which relied entirely on the results of hypnotic recall. Hopkins and other abduction researchers argued that the abductees that had been discovered so far might be only the tip of a huge iceberg. There might, they suggested, be millions of "silent abductees" scattered around the world, regularly visited by the same dwarfish gray aliens that starred in *The UFO Incident* and *Close Encounters of the Third Kind*. That was where the abduction narrative stood at the beginning of 1986, when a writer named Whitley Strieber contacted Hopkins with a classic abduction account.

---

91. For the abduction debate summarized in this section, see particularly Bullard 1987, Hopkins 2000, and Klass 1989.

Strieber reported that in the last days of December 1985, he had plunged into a sudden depression shot through with terror and erratic behavior. Murky images in his memory finally coalesced into a clear recollection of being abducted from his bedroom and subjected to a series of brutal medical procedures by short, spindly, gray-skinned aliens with huge almond-shaped eyes. He contacted Hopkins, who found him a therapist to help him deal with his panic and depression, then had him hypnotized in the hope of getting more details. These duly followed, and within a few months Strieber began writing a book about his abduction. Its original working title was *Body Terror*, but Strieber later changed this to *Communion*.

Before the book was published, Hopkins and Strieber parted company explosively in a flurry of mutual accusations, largely driven by their different interpretations of the phenomenon. Hopkins insisted that myth, folklore, and popular culture had nothing to say to UFO abductions, and saw abduction as an essentially negative experience; Strieber flirted with elements of the ultraterrestrial theory made popular a decade before by Vallee and Keel, and argued that despite its frightening features, abduction was ultimately a positive experience, even a spiritual one. Few other UFO researchers agreed with this assessment. Meanwhile, critics pointed out close parallels between *Communion* and Strieber's earlier horror fiction and suggested that, as his fiction career faltered, Strieber had simply come up with a new way to market his latest novel.

None of this slowed *Communion*'s success. It became the first UFO book ever to climb to the number-one spot on the *New York Times* bestseller list, and it remained there for months. The enigmatic face of Strieber's alien captor gazed out from bookstore shelves around the world, and in the months and years that followed reports of alien abductions skyrocketed.

As abduction moved toward center stage in the imagination of the UFO phenomenon, a split paralleling the one between Hopkins and Strieber opened up in the abduction research community. A minority of researchers noted striking parallels between abduction accounts and material from folklore, spirituality, and near-death experiences, and argued that abduction might best be understood as an initiatory experience with a great deal of positive potential.[92] The majority rejected the idea that abduction had anything to do with any other dimension of human experience—especially rejecting those that strayed into the territory of the spiritual—and portrayed it in the same intensely negative terms as the monsters-from-space films of the 1950s.[93] As the twentieth century drew to its end, these two images of alien presence, the "good alien" and the "bad alien," struggled for primacy in the popular imagination.

Majestic-12

The year 1987 proved to be pivotal in the history of the UFO phenomenon for more reasons than this, however. That year, the small town of Gulf Breeze, Florida, got its fifteen minutes of fame in UFO circles, when local resident Ed Walters reported an encounter with an alien spacecraft that almost, but not quite, abducted him.[94] According to his account, he happened to have a Polaroid camera close by, and got a series of striking photographs of a luminous, top-shaped craft. Further encounters and photos followed, bringing Walters a blaze of publicity and a lucrative book contract.

Walters and the Gulf Breeze sightings were on their way to stardom in the UFO circuit, with the enthusiastic approval of several prominent researchers, when awkward facts began to surface. A model UFO made of disposable plates and scrap paper with Walters' writing on it turned up in the attic of his former house; an acquaintance of Walters explained how the photos were faked; additional evidence of Walters' skills at trick photography with his Polaroid surfaced as well. By the time Walters' book *The Gulf Breeze Sightings* saw print in 1990 the entire affair had turned into a civil war among UFO researchers, some of whom defended Walters' credibility while others dismissed him as a fraud.

---

92. See, for example, Mack 1999 and Ring 1992.

93. See, for example, Hopkins 1987 and Jacobs 1998.

94. For the events at Gulf Breeze, see Conroy 1990, Overall 1990, and Walters and Walters 1990.

The same fate on a larger scale awaited a more ambitious set of claims that also went public in 1987. These focused on a packet of papers labeled "Briefing Document: Operation Majestic 12," released to the UFO community that year by investigators William Moore, Jaime Shandera, and Stanton Friedman.[95] The documents, dated November 18, 1952, purported to be a preliminary briefing for President-elect Eisenhower on a secret project set in motion by President Truman in the aftermath of the crash of an alien spacecraft at Roswell.

According to the papers, a secret team of intelligence and military officials code-named Majestic 12—MJ-12 for short—was set up by Truman to coordinate research into two crashed saucers, one found at Roswell in 1947 and another recovered in 1950 on the Texas-Mexico border. The original members of the team were Admiral Roscoe Hillenkoetter, Dr. Vannevar Bush, Defense Secretary James Forrestal, General Nathan Twining, General Hoyt Vandenberg, Dr. Detlev Bronk, Dr. Jerome Huntsaker, Sidney Souers, Gordon Gray, General Robert Montague, Dr. Lloyd Berkner, and—in an ironic twist—Dr. Donald Menzel, the dean of American UFO debunkers. This group managed the U.S. response to the UFO phenomenon, which included extended contacts with aliens and a series of secret operations aimed at learning the secrets of alien technology and concealing the existence of the aliens from the public.

The prehistory of these papers goes back to the beginning of the 1980s, when UFO investigator William Moore was contacted by personnel from the Air Force Office of Special Investigations (AFOSI) and offered a tempting deal.[96] The AFOSI officers claimed to belong to a dissident group that no longer supported the Air Force's policy of UFO secrecy, and wanted to bring the Air Force's trove of evidence for extraterrestrial visits to Earth out into the open. They offered Moore access to secret material about UFOs. In exchange, they asked him to keep them informed on the activities of certain other UFO investigators,

---

95. For the MJ-12 papers, see Bishop 2005; Peebles 1994, 259–68; Sparks and Greenwood, 2007; and Thompson 1991, 173–79.

96. Bishop 2005 recounts the interactions between Moore and AFOSI in detail.

especially an electronics engineer in Albuquerque, New Mexico, named Paul Bennewitz.

Moore took the bait, and for most of the decade he gave regular reports on Bennewitz and other people in the UFO community to his AFOSI contacts. What he got in return was a glimpse at the Holy Grail of the extraterrestrial hypothesis: documents, apparently from the highest levels of the United States government, that claimed to prove ongoing contacts between U.S. authorities and alien beings from another world.

The first of these documents was passed to Moore by his main AFOSI contact, Staff Sergeant Richard Doty, in February 1981. This was a teletype message dated November 7, 1980, to the AFOSI office at Kirtland Air Force Base from higher-ups in Washington, D.C., about photos taken by Bennewitz. The message referred to a secret "Project Aquarius" and something called "MJ TWELVE." When Moore passed this document on to a TV station in 1982, and an employee of the station contacted the Air Force, AFOSI personnel investigated and stated that the entire document was a forgery, an assertion Moore rejected.

Further documents surfaced over the next few years, almost all of them through Doty. In 1983 Doty allowed Linda Moulton Howe, another UFO researcher who had entered the field by way of cattle mutilation research, to read a document claiming to be a presidential briefing paper expanding on the statements in the "Project Aquarius" teletype. The briefing paper claimed that one alien had survived the Roswell crash and been debriefed by Air Force personnel. It described several other contacts between the U.S. government and the aliens, gave information about the aliens' homeworld, and for good measure implied that Jesus of Nazareth had been created by extraterrestrials. A slightly different version of the same paper reached Moore in 1986 and soon found readers throughout the UFO community.

The crown jewel of the collection, though, was the MJ-12 document, which surfaced on a roll of undeveloped 35mm film mailed to Moore's ally Jaime Shandera in December 1984. By their own accounts, Moore and Shandera spent the next two years trying to authenticate the document's claims. In 1985, while searching the National Archives, they found a memo dated 1954 that referred to the "NSC/MJ-12 Special Studies Project." This and the briefing document finally convinced Moore and Shandera to go public with their find.

Like the Gulf Breeze sightings, or for that matter most of the other major events in the UFO field in the 1980s, the resulting controversy followed a familiar track. At first the MJ-12 papers were hailed by most UFO researchers as a breakthrough discovery that would finally blow the lid off the government coverup and force people to accept the reality of alien craft in Earth's skies. Later, problems with the "breakthrough" surfaced, and the initial enthusiasm dissolved into bickering between believers and disbelievers about the authenticity of the documents.

Defenders of the null hypothesis pointed out that the papers contained words and phrases more characteristic of 1984 than 1952, failed to match up to known facts about the alleged members of the MJ-12 group or the activities of other people involved, and lacked features standard on all authentic secret documents of the time.[97] As these challenges sank in, most UFO researchers distanced themselves from the claims surrounding the documents, while a minority continued to insist that MJ-12 was a reality.

What set MJ-12 apart from Gulf Breeze and other UFO hoaxes of the period was the extent to which it found eager listeners in another subculture of the time. In the aftermath of the cultural crises of the 1970s, a growing number of Americans began to suspect the worst of their government. In response, an underground network of speakers and self-published books took shape, arguing that American democracy was merely a facade behind which sinister forces plotted the enslavement of the planet. The UFO phenomenon, with its overtones of government conspiracy and unknown alien purpose, had many points of contact with this paranoid vision, and a fusion between the two came, once again, in 1987.

On December 27 of that year, John Lear—son of aviation pioneer William Lear of Lear Jet fame, and a former contract pilot for the CIA—issued a statement charging the United States government with

---

97. See, for example, Peebles 1994, 266–68.

selling out humanity to a race of evil aliens.[98] According to Lear, the MJ-12 group had succeeded in making contact with the aliens by the late 1960s, and established a treaty under which the U.S. government agreed to cover up the alien presence and their establishment of secret underground bases, along with their abductions and cattle mutilations, in exchange for extraterrestrial technology. The first alien base was established at the Groom Lake airbase in Nevada, with another built shortly thereafter beneath Dulce, New Mexico.

By the early 1980s, however, MJ-12 realized that their bargain with the aliens had been humanity's worst mistake. In 1979, sixty-seven Special Forces troops died in a failed attempt to rescue human captives from the Dulce base. Further hostilities followed, with the aliens winning every round. According to Lear, the aliens had all but completed their takeover of the world, and humanity could expect nothing more than a repeat of the Holocaust on a larger scale.

All this was grist for the extraterrestrial mill, and helped feed a growing climate of paranoia within the UFO community. As one wild claim built on another, few people noticed at first that much of Lear's rhetoric focused on a real location with its own aerial mysteries.

Dreamland

By the late 1980s the Groom Lake base in the Nevada desert, originally set up to handle test flights for the U-2 surveillance plane, had become the home of many of the most exotic aircraft in the U.S. military and intelligence arsenal.[99] The A-12/SR-71 Blackbird, still officially the fastest manned aircraft in history, first took to the air over Groom Lake; so did the first stealth aircraft testbed, an exotic diamond-shaped craft with the memorably weird code name HAVE BLUE; so did the F-117 Nighthawk, the first stealth fighter, and the B-2 Spirit, the first stealth bomber. Rumor mills in the aviation industry, then as now, buzzed with claims of more exotic craft flying out of Groom Lake, among them the TR-3 Black Manta, a variant of the F-117 stealth fighter rede-

---

98. For Lear's claims, see Lear 1989.

99. For Area 51 and the mythologies and subcultures that sprang up around it, including Lazar's claims, see Darlington 1997 and Patton 1998.

signed for tactical reconnaissance, and the SR-91 Aurora, a strategic reconnaissance plane with stealth technology built to replace the aging SR-71.

Surrounding the Groom Lake base was the Nellis Air Force test range, a sprawling region of sagebrush and sand the size of a small European country, where the Air Force kept its secret collection of captured Eastern Bloc aircraft and carried out a steady drumbeat of combat exercises. All through the second half of the twentieth century, if you wanted to find a place to observe flying objects that nobody in the United States government would willingly identify, Groom Lake was the place to do it.

Like most secret facilities, it had a plethora of names. Lockheed staff gave it the ironic label "Paradise Ranch," a handful of outdated maps assigned it the label of Area 51, military aircraft referred to the restricted space around it as "the Box," and its control tower used the code name "Dreamland." This latter name proved to be the most prophetic, for its emergence as a focus for UFO beliefs marked the point at which those beliefs finally left the evidence behind and plunged into a dream world full of sinister shadows.

Despite occasional references in the local media, Dreamland stayed off the radar screens of contemporary culture as effectively as though it had stealth technology of its own, until 1989. That was the year that a computer technician named Bob Lazar appeared on a TV show about UFOs, claiming that he had worked at Groom Lake as part of a U.S. military effort to reverse-engineer a crashed flying saucer.

Lazar, an associate of John Lear, claimed master's degrees from Cal Tech and MIT and a stint working at the Los Alamos National Laboratory. As a result of a chance meeting with famous physicist Edward Teller, Lazar claimed, he was hired in 1988 by a classified research program and began working at a facility near Area 51 code-named S-4, where several alien spacecraft were kept. His stint there was brief, due to his own unwillingness to follow security regulations, but he claimed that the U.S. government had retrieved living aliens as well as crashed saucers, and had worked out the basics of the gravity-field drive, powered by Element 115, that the alien craft supposedly used to travel through space.

Coming as it did in the wake of the MJ-12 controversy, these claims attracted an immediate audience, and helped power the growth of the new, conspiracy-oriented UFO belief system. The enthusiasm for Lazar's claims was such that very few people took the time to find out that neither Cal Tech nor MIT had any record of his attendance there. Nor did many of Lazar's fans ask why, if he was telling the truth, his public statements did not land him in prison for violating the stringent federal laws prohibiting disclosure of classified information.

In the wake of the media circus that sprang up around Lazar and his claims, the attention of the UFO community focused on Area 51 and its mysteries. One result was the birth of an informal network of amateur investigators, "the Interceptors," who prowled the Nevada desert just outside the boundaries of the Nellis test range. The tiny desert hamlet of Rachel, Nevada, the closest town to Area 51, became the Interceptors' headquarters. Rachel contained a grand total of two businesses—a bar and grill and a gas station—and a cluster of mobile homes housing the town's hundred or so residents. In the aftermath of Lazar's first public appearances, the bar and grill's owners added a few motel rooms and RV hookups and, with an eye to the UFO trade, renamed their business the Little A-Le-Inn.

Some of the Interceptors came to the deserts around Rachel to watch for flying saucers; others were more interested in the spyplanes that had been flying out of Groom Lake since 1955; still others simply wanted to challenge the U.S. government's secrecy policies, whatever might lie behind them. For a half dozen years in the early-to-middle 1990s, they formed one of those outlaw subcultures that periodically seize some corner of the American imagination. Dodging the "camo dudes"—private security guards hired by the Air Force to patrol the approaches to the Groom Lake base—to find viewpoints that gave them glimpses of the distant runways and hangars of Dreamland, the Interceptors gave the UFO field a quality of romantic adventure that it had been lacking since the heyday of the ultraterrestrial hypothesis in the 1970s.

By the middle of the decade, Area 51 had become as central to contemporary UFO legend as Roswell and the skies above Mount Rainier. Bob Lazar had been joined by several other people claiming inside knowledge of classified programs to reverse-engineer crashed saucers. The most outspoken of these was William Uhouse, who sold posters and playing cards at UFO conventions but claimed to have a mechanical engineering degree from Cornell—a qualification that proved just as elusive as Lazar's college degrees. Uhouse's story meshed with Lazar's in many details, and also had points in common with the MJ-12 mythology and several other central motifs in late twentieth-century UFO lore. Despite the usual lack of supporting evidence, Uhouse's claims met as enthusiastic a reception as Lazar's had.

Popular culture, always the final arbiter of UFO-related beliefs, had the last word in 1996 when the blockbuster movie *Independence Day* featured an Area 51 taken straight out of Lazar's and Uhouse's stories, complete with crashed saucers and aliens on ice. With an eye toward tourist dollars, the Nevada state government celebrated the release of the film by formally renaming Route 375, the highway that ran past Rachel, the Extraterrestrial Highway. A bill to make the name change had been introduced in the state assembly the previous year; the solemnity of the occasion may have been dented a bit by the fact that one of the bill's sponsors, Assemblyman Bob Price (D-North Las Vegas), attended the session in a Darth Vader mask.

Independence Day itself combined cutting-edge special effects with a plot that brought nostalgic feelings to many longtime watchers of UFO culture, drawing on motifs first marketed by such saucer-themed television shows of the 1960s and 1970s as *The Invaders* and *UFO*. Like these predecessors, the aliens in *Independence Day* came from a dying world to take over Earth as a new home for their species, and had to be thwarted by the usual flurry of improbable earthling heroics. The huge financial success of this hackneyed but reliable formula finished the process of expelling from popular culture the "good aliens" of the 1970s and 1980s. The monsters from space of the 1950s were back, with a vengeance.

The Reptilian Agenda

The 1990s saw these ideas percolate through the UFO community and popular culture alike, feeding a paranoid version of the extraterrestrial hypothesis in which the aliens and everything connected with them became a focus for primal fears. Two new writers—Milton William Cooper and David Icke—took center stage in this process.

Cooper, another protégé of Lear's, insisted that he had learned the horrible truth behind the UFO phenomenon while serving in a minor position in U.S. Navy Intelligence from 1970 to 1973. Cooper's version of the extraterrestrial hypothesis, published in his underground classic *Behold a Pale Horse* (1991) and a flurry of essays and manifestoes circulated over the Internet, took the stories circulated by Bennewitz, Lear, and Lazar to their furthest extreme.[100]

According to Cooper, no fewer than sixteen UFO crashes between 1947 and 1953 netted the U.S. government a good-sized truckload of dead aliens and saucer debris, along with one living extraterrestrial and a collection of human body parts gathered by the aliens. The world's ruling elites reacted by creating MJ-12, a secret world government focused on dealing with the alien threat. By 1954, MJ-12 had made contact with no fewer than four different extraterrestrial races—Cooper called these Grays, Large-nosed Grays, Nordics, and Orange—and established a treaty with the Large-nosed Grays, allowing the aliens to build more than a dozen underground bases and carry out abductions and cattle mutilations in exchange for advanced technologies, including flying saucers.

As suspicions grew that the aliens were cheating on their end of the bargain, MJ-12 tightened its grip on the world as it sought secret weapons against the Large-nosed Grays. In the meantime, Cooper claimed, human scientists had discovered that overpopulation and pollution would make Earth uninhabitable by the year 2000, and so alien-derived technology was used to build a new set of underground bases for the earth's ruling elites, and to build colonies on the moon

---

100. See Cooper 1991.

and Mars, while creating lethal plagues and other instruments of genocide to counter the population explosion.

In their quest to maintain control, MJ-12 assassinated John F. Kennedy, forced Richard Nixon out of office, managed the world drug trade, and was building secret concentration camps on United States territory into which dissidents would be interned once the Constitution was overthrown, martial law declared, and the New World Order imposed. To explain how the whole conspiracy worked, Cooper reprinted the full text of the *Protocols of the Elders of Zion*, a scurrilous anti-Semitic forgery concocted by the tsarist Russian secret police in the first decade of the twentieth century and adopted by Nazi Germany as a justification for the Holocaust.[101] A scattering of letters from unidentified sources, none of them particularly convincing, and a collection of public documents vaguely relevant to his accusations completed the panoply, providing the only excuse for evidence Cooper offered for his claims.

Most of the UFO community, to give it credit, rejected Cooper's claims with a great deal of heat. James Moseley, whose eccentric newsletter *Saucer Smear* rose in popularity through the 1980s and 1990s to become the most influential UFO periodical since the death of Raymond Palmer, dismissed Cooper's theories as "wild ravings," while Jacques Vallee, in his 1991 book *Revelations*, pointed out the gaping logical absurdities that ran through the entire Lear-Lazar-Cooper mythology.[102] Still, Cooper found his own following in circles in which belief in UFOs overlapped with angry political rhetoric that borrowed equally from the far left and the far right.

Cooper himself moved further into the fringes, and finally withdrew to his isolated Arizona home with a stockpile of guns and ammo, convinced that government agents would soon come pounding at his door. His refusal to pay taxes made this a self-fulfilling prophecy, and when he opened fire on the sheriff's deputies who came to serve him with court papers, he completed the process of making his fantasies

---

101.   Cohn 1967 remains the classic study of this document.

102.   See Peebles 1994, 278, and Vallee 1991, 52–58.

real. Well before his death in a hail of bullets on November 5, 2001, however, his place in the limelight had been taken by another theorist of cosmic paranoia who offered a story even more colorful and extreme than Cooper did.

This was David Icke, an erstwhile soccer player, sports announcer, and Green Party candidate from England who burst on the scene in 1995 with the first of a series of books announcing the conspiracy theory to end all conspiracy theories.[103] According to Icke, the ruling classes of the world can hardly be accused of selling humanity out to an alien species, because they themselves are aliens—specifically, blood-drinking, shapeshifting half-extraterrestrial hybrids descended from evil space reptiles from the constellation Draco, who rule the world by way of a network of secret societies wielding mind-control technologies. The reptile bloodlines include all past and present royal families of Britain, all of the other royal houses of Europe, and every one of the presidents of the United States, among many others.

Icke's theories fused the cosmic paranoia of the earlier UFO/conspiracy narrative with a skillful response to the New Age beliefs of the 1970s and 1980s. The "Aquarian revolution," the great change of consciousness imminently expected during the peak years of the New Age, never did happen to the satisfaction of its believers, and Icke offered a reason for the failure—the evil activities and mind-control technologies of the reptilians. They and they alone, he insisted, are responsible for making people believe in the supposed illusion of a world with limited resources and possibilities, where human beings can't automatically have whatever they want.

As a mythology of class warfare, which is essentially what Icke's theory offers, this goes far beyond anything else on record. Not even the most vitriolic Marxist ever accused the ruling classes of being evil space lizards who thirst for human blood and are personally responsible for everything bad that has ever happened to anyone. This invites parody, but at the same time there is a deeper and more troubling dimension to Icke's claims. Less than a century ago, another paranoid ideology

---

103. I have drawn the following summary from Icke 1995, Icke 1999, and Icke 2001.

claiming that all the world's problems were due to a wealthy minority that was allegedly not quite human boiled up out of the gutters of central Europe to launch the most destructive war in human history and send millions of victims to gas chambers. It is not exactly comforting that Icke, like Cooper, reprinted the *Protocols of the Elders of Zion*—the very document used to justify those atrocities—in one of his books.

If Icke's ideology has uncomfortable parallels to that earlier horror, it also represents the final triumph of popular culture in the UFO field. Nearly every element of Icke's theory can be found in the early 1980s TV series *V*, which featured shapeshifting extraterrestrial reptiles who disguised themselves as human beings and rule the world through mind-control technology. In the same way, the "bad alien" narrative elaborated by John Lear, Robert Lazar, and Milton William Cooper drew every one of its core elements from the science fiction of the previous two decades, with the flesh-hunting aliens and underground bases of the popular early 1970s British TV show *UFO* among the most obvious sources.

Less obvious but more pervasive was the influence of the pulp subculture that had imagined flying saucers into being in the first place. Students of the phenomenon as different as ultraterrestrial theorist John Keel and debunker Curtis Peebles noted how Raymond Palmer's ideas still permeated the popular imagination of the phenomenon, leading people on all sides of the UFO controversy to seek out equivalents of deros in the underworld and Green Men in the skies.[104] As Icke's ideas spread through the radical underground at the end of the century and beyond, the world imagined by the pulp science fiction writers had finally become real—at least in the imaginations of a growing number of true believers.

Twilight of the Saucers
More generally, conspiracy theories and hidden agendas had a tight hold on the collective imagination during these same years. As usual, popular culture was both a barometer and a feedback loop, amplifying

---

104. See Keel 1989 and Peebles 1994, 281.

the phenomenon it revealed. Fox TV's cult television show *The X-Files*, which ran from 1993 to 2002, portrayed a pair of FBI agents—one a believer in the paranormal, the other a skeptic—investigating mysteries in which UFOs and alien entities played a dominant role. The series slogan, "The Truth Is Out There," became something of a watchword in the UFO movement during those years, even as the prospect of finding anything like the truth about UFOs receded into something close to interstellar distance.

By the beginning of the twenty-first century, the UFO scene was spinning its wheels in ruts laid down decades earlier. Investigators continued to chase data about UFO sightings, though more and more often the deepening shortage of recent sightings forced them to revisit older investigations and try to tease more details out of cases that had been cold for decades. Abduction researchers continued to hypnotize people who thought they might have been abducted by a flying saucer, and argued endlessly about the nature and purpose of alien visitations they had never managed to prove in the first place. Controversies about the MJ-12 documents and other evidence for an Air Force coverup still sputtered; the paranoid wing of the UFO movement proclaimed the imminent alien takeover of the planet under the banner of the New World Order; believers kept on believing, debunkers kept on debunking, and the same arguments repeated themselves month after month and year after year.

There were many causes for this lack of progress, but among the most striking was the continuing decline in UFO sightings—especially in North America, once the homeland of the phenomenon. Though bursts of reports still came in now and then, the mass sightings of silvery disks or dancing lights so common in the 1950s and the 1960s never returned, and the black triangles that haunted the Hudson River valley and other locations in the 1980s sank into memory. The phenomenon was fading out, and in response, public interest faded out as well.

This twilight of the saucers found a grisly reflection on the morning of March 26, 1997, when police officers discovered the bodies of thirty-nine men and women in a mansion in a San Diego suburb, dead of self-administered poison.[105] Notes left behind by the group, Heaven's Gate, announced that its members believed they were leaving behind their "physical containers" in order to board a giant UFO cruising in the wake of the recently discovered Comet Hale-Bopp, which they expected to crash into the earth soon thereafter.

Behind this tragedy lay a long and troubling history woven from the raw materials of the UFO phenomenon. The leader of the group, Marshall Herff Applewhite, and his partner, Bonnie Lu Nettles, met in 1972 and began to preach a religion of their own creation three years later. Drawing from contactee beliefs as well as fringe Christianity, the Two (as their followers came to call them) claimed that those who made the transition to the "Evolutionary Stage Above Human" by following them, abandoning property and sexual desires, would be raptured onto flying saucers and saved from the imminent end of the world.

In the cultural crisis of the 1970s, their teachings found a following, and remained an active presence on the far end of the UFO community through the decades that followed. Jacques Vallee discussed them in his incisive 1979 book *Messengers of Deception*, as an example of the way UFO beliefs were changing into religious ideologies with ominous possibilities as tools of manipulation and control. Nettles died of cancer in 1985, but the members of Heaven's Gate, like the contactees chronicled decades earlier in *When Prophecy Fails*, focused their lives ever more fixedly on the prospect of imminent rescue by aliens. Unlike the Chicago group headed by Dorothy Martin, though, the misplaced faith of Applewhite and his followers backed them into a corner from which mass death was the only way out.

Surprisingly, the tragedy of Heaven's Gate did nothing to keep other believers in the contactee faith from making similar claims. The next year, in fact, a Taiwanese contactee group named Chen Tao garnered media attention around the world by proclaiming that God would appear on world television on March 25, 1998, and land in a flying saucer six days later. As the end of the millennium closed in, such claims became common. The announcement that some older

---

105. See Lewis 2001, 14–18 and 367–70.

computers might fail to function on January 1, 2000, because their software had not been designed to handle the rollover, sparked wild rumors of an imminent collapse of civilization.

Among contactees, the belief that the saucers would finally land once and for all spread like wildfire at the same time. One set of claims centered on the Great Pyramid in Egypt, where the Nine—the extraterrestrial gods introduced to the contactee movement by Andrija Puharich back in the 1950s, and channeled by dozens of mediums since his time—were expected to make an appearance at midnight on December 31, 1999. Rumors flew about the imminent discovery of a hidden chamber full of ancient Egyptian wisdom buried far below the Sphinx, and the old promises of a just and peaceful world arriving via flying saucer found new listeners all through the New Age community. Ironically, these claims sparked a corresponding panic among the more conspiracy-minded denizens of the world of alternative culture, who reinterpreted the arrival of the Nine as the imminent manufacture of a religious event and the imposition of a contactee theocracy by sinister cabals backed by military intelligence.[106]

The morning of January 1, 2000, nonetheless found the world in much the same state it had been in the night before. The fears of cybernetic apocalypse and the hope of a mass arrival by the Space Brothers proved, once again, to have no better basis than all the similar claims circulated in the contactee community over the half century since Kenneth Arnold's original sighting over the Cascade Mountains. Nor has anything dramatically changed the UFO scene in the years since the dawn of the millennium; the same debates have sputtered unproductively on as sightings remain few and far between, and the phenomenon moves further into the fringes of modern culture. Still, the evidence of history may just allow a different perspective to shed new light on the controversy—and on ourselves as well.

---

106. Picknett and Prince 1999.

Part Two
Exploring the Possibilities

We shall pick up an existence by its frogs.

Wise men have tried other ways. They have tried to understand our state of being, by grasping at its stars, or its arts, or its economics. But, if there is an underlying oneness of all things, it does not matter where we begin, whether with stars, or laws of supply and demand, or frogs, or Napoleon Bonaparte. One measures a circle, beginning anywhere.

—Charles Fort, *Lo!*

It can be clearly shown that the explanation offered does not account for the facts. Nevertheless, the facts are not disposed of by showing the explanation to be fallacious.

—Dion Fortune, *Applied Magic*

five

The Barriers to Understanding

M ore than sixty years into the history of the UFO phenomenon, a definite solution to the riddle of unidentified flying objects seems as far off as ever. Hundreds of thousands, perhaps millions, of people all around the world have seen strange things in the sky—silvery disks, black triangles, luminous blobs, points of colored light, and a panoply of other forms too diverse to catalogue. A much smaller number of people have encountered an equally diverse array of creatures associated with strange aerial objects. Several thousand people have reported that they were abducted by aliens, and an approximately equal number have claimed the role of contactees. Almost without exception, all these accounts show detailed and extensive similarities to ideas about aliens and extraterrestrial contact that appeared in popular culture decades before the UFO phenomenon went public in 1947. At the same time, in at least some cases, the witnesses do appear to have seen something genuinely strange.

Move out of the realm of testimony and look for physical evidence, and the trail becomes much thinner. A few marks on the ground that might have been produced by UFO landing gear have been found and photographed. A few scraps of metal and other substances that might have come from flying saucers have been obtained and tested, though none has shown any particular trace of an unusual origin. A modest collection of photographs has been amassed, though most of them have failed tests of authenticity and the remainder yield little information. An equally modest collection of supposed government documents have surfaced, none of them particularly convincing and most of them self-evident hoaxes.

It's useful to consider, as well, what has *not* happened over the last six decades. While human astronauts during the same period left a fair amount of hardware behind them, from dropped wrenches and spare parts to large chunks of spacecraft, not one scrap of unquestionably extraterrestrial technology has been left behind by a flying saucer's crew. Of the thousands of people who claim to have talked with aliens, not one of them has brought back a genuinely new piece of scientific knowledge or, for that matter, any other statement of verifiable fact previously unknown to human beings; even the spiritual teachings and moral philosophy passed on to contactees by the Space Brothers resemble nothing so much as the popular alternative spirituality of our own culture.

At least one other thing has not happened over the history of the UFO phenomenon. The contending sides in the dispute have failed to find any common ground from which an impartial investigation of the subject might be launched. For decades now, believers in the two main hypotheses have spun their wheels repeating past investigations and reiterating old claims, and a clear solution to the mystery remains nowhere to be seen. This deserves more attention than it has received so far.

Believers in the extraterrestrial hypothesis have argued at length that their solution has not been accepted because the Air Force or some other government body is suppressing the data that would allow them to prove their case. Believers in the null hypothesis, for their part, have argued at equal length that their solution has not been accepted because human beings, and more particularly Americans with poor scientific education, are ignorant and gullible. Both arguments attempt to explain the lack of agreement away, rather than actually explaining it, and neither one seems very convincing to those who are not already committed to one of the beliefs in question. A more careful look at the roots of the failure to solve the UFO puzzle is thus in order.

Problematic Paradigms

It's a common but quite mistaken belief that human knowledge builds on itself in a step-by-step fashion, with the discoveries of the present simply being added onto the discoveries of the past to make sense of the world. Instead, as Thomas Kuhn showed in his pathbreaking 1962 study *The Structure of Scientific Revolutions*, each generation's contributions to knowledge in a given field derive from a basic set of assumptions—a paradigm, in Kuhn's terminology—about the nature of the field and the way it should be approached. Each paradigm comes into being in response to the body of knowledge available at the time it was formulated.

As research continues, however, data that does not fit the paradigm begins to accumulate. Since scientists are human, and human nature is what it is, the challenging data is explained away, ignored, or dismissed as errors or forgeries. Still, as the body of knowledge in the field expands further and further, the anomalies pile up. Crisis arrives when the fit between the knowledge base and the paradigm becomes so bad that it is no longer possible for researchers using the paradigm to make any sense of the data at all. At this point a new paradigm emerges that makes sense of the most critical anomalies, the old paradigm goes onto the scrapheap of intellectual history, and the process begins all over again.

The classic example, cited by Kuhn and many others, is the Copernican revolution that replaced the old worldview of a solar system centered on the earth with the view we have now, with the sun at the center and the earth and other planets orbiting around it.[107] Putting the earth at the center was a matter of plain common sense in ancient times. Watch the skies from anywhere on Earth and it unquestionably

---

107. See Kuhn 1970, 68–69.

looks as though the ground beneath you is stationary and the sun, moon, planets, and stars move around it. The Greek astronomer and mathematician Claudius Ptolemy, who lived in the second century CE, worked out an elegant set of calculations based on an Earth-centered cosmos—one of the triumphs of ancient Greek science—that very nearly fit the observed movements of the planets in the sky.

"Very nearly," however, turned out to be more problematic than it looked. Over the centuries that followed, as astronomers and mathematicians grappled with the widening mismatch between the evidence and Ptolemy's calculations, difficulties piled up. So did attempts to tinker with Ptolemy's math and make it come out a little closer to accuracy. Long before Copernicus' time, most astronomers were convinced that something was drastically wrong with Ptolemy's system, though nobody could figure out what it was. The new Copernican system, though it was threatening to religious orthodoxies, was welcomed by many astronomers because it replaced Ptolemy's paradigm with one that allowed for a much better fit to the facts.

The classic sign of a paradigm in crisis is that it no longer provides clear solutions to the central problems in the field. The study of UFOs has been in this predicament since the phenomenon first took shape. This suggests that part of the difficulty in understanding the phenomenon is that the paradigm used to make sense of it is hopelessly inadequate to the task.

Numerous writers in the UFO field have proposed a shift in paradigms as a way to make better sense of the data. Some of these, to be sure, make proposals like the one offered by Don Donderi in his essay "Science, Law, and War: Alternative Frameworks for the UFO Evidence" (2000). Donderi essentially argues that since scientific reasoning will not support the claim that UFOs must be from outer space, proponents of the extraterrestrial hypothesis ought to switch to a kind of reasoning that does support that claim! By the same logic, defenders of Ptolemaic astronomy could have claimed that ordinary arithmetic should be scrapped in favor of some new system of mathematics that made their figures work.

More useful are proposals of the sort made by Jacques Vallee in several of his books, notably *Passport to Magonia*, arguing that the UFO phenomenon needs to be understood in the wider context of myth, folklore, and apparition, rather than being treated as a unique twentieth-century phenomenon. Yet the great difficulty in shifting paradigms usually lies in figuring out exactly what parts of the current view of the problem are getting in the way of a solution. As the example of the Copernican revolution showed, it's quite possible to waste centuries trying to fix the difficulties in a system because nobody realizes where the difficulties actually are. Before Copernicus' time, nobody apparently considered the possibility that the problem with Ptolemy was not in his calculations or his geometries, but in the apparently obvious, common-sense assumption he shared with almost everyone else—the assumption that the sun circles the earth.

With this in mind, let's look at the places where research into the UFO phenomenon has ground to a halt most dramatically, and see what that reveals about the problems in the field.

Unfalsifiable Hypotheses

One of the more telling things about the UFO controversy is the way that proponents of both leading hypotheses have tried to borrow the public reputation of science for their views. On the whole, supporters of the null hypothesis have been more successful in this endeavor, mostly because the contactee scene of the 1950s and 1960s tarred the extraterrestrial hypothesis with a whiff of occultism that has caused the hackles of scientific orthodoxy to rise ever since. Still, the claim that one or the other opinion about the origins and nature of UFOs is "scientific" or "unscientific" bespeaks a good deal of ignorance about what science actually is.

At its foundations, science is simply a method for testing claims about the nature of the material universe; it is a method, not a body of doctrines. Any proposition, about any field of human experience, can be explored in a scientific manner. It may be easier to get clear results in some areas of human experience than in others, but the only thing that determines whether a belief is scientific or not is whether it has been tested by the scientific method.

That method follows a simple but precise four-step process. The first step is identifying the problem—in the case of the Copernican revolution, this was the fact that Ptolemy's model of the cosmos just doesn't make accurate predictions no matter how much tinkering goes into it. The second step is choosing a hypothesis to explain what is going on—in the case of Copernicus, the revolutionary idea that the earth might circle the sun, and not vice versa.

The third step is the crucial one, and the one most often misunderstood in popular discussions of science. Having come up with a hypothesis, the scientist doesn't try to prove it. Instead, he or she sets out to *disprove* it, by putting the hypothesis to the test in an experiment designed so that things will turn out one way if the hypothesis is true, and a different way if the hypothesis is mistaken. In the case of Copernicus, the test was whether a cosmos with the sun at the center required less cumbersome mathematics and yielded better calculations of planetary motion than a cosmos with the earth at the center.

In scientists' jargon, a hypothesis that can be put to the test repeatedly in this way is a *falsifiable* hypothesis. To be of any use at all in science, a hypothesis has to be falsifiable—that is, its proponents have to be able to offer some conditions under which they will admit that the hypothesis isn't true. An *unfalsifiable* hypothesis is worthless in scientific terms. If it cannot be disproved, there is no way to know whether it's true or not.

The fourth step, finally, is publishing the results of the experiment in enough detail that anyone else interested can try the same experiment and check the results, putting the hypothesis to the test a second time. Once a hypothesis has been tested repeatedly in this way, it is accepted as a basis for further research—but it can always be disproved later on, if someone comes up with a different experiment that shows that it fails to fit the facts.

All this points up one of the core difficulties in making sense of the UFO phenomenon, because both of the two principal hypotheses in the controversy these days are unfalsifiable. There's no way either one can be disproved, to the satisfaction of its defenders, on the basis of the evidence available. In a 1997 study, Charles Ziegler pointed out that claims about the 1947 Roswell incident achieved this status in the UFO community a long time ago: "Can ufologists define the nature of the government evidence they would be willing to accept as conclusive proof that there was no cover-up, no alien visitation? The answer, I believe, is no, because any such evidence can be regarded as an element of a further cover-up."[108]

This same observation can be extended to the extraterrestrial hypothesis as a whole. Nothing in the entire observed range of UFO behavior offers any way of putting the extraterrestrial hypothesis to a definite test and showing whether or not UFOs are alien spacecraft. To a great extent, this is because the extraterrestrial hypothesis is what the logical theory of an earlier time called an argument from ignorance. Since we know precisely nothing about what the technological capacities of a spacefaring alien civilization might be—for that matter, despite the science fiction imagery that plays so great a role in the modern collective imagination, we don't even know if a spacefaring alien civilization is possible in the first place—any UFO behavior whatsoever can be compatible with the ETH. If UFOs behave like physical bodies, that supports the claim that they are spaceships; if they appear, disappear, and maneuver in ways that would be impossible for a solid body, that just shows how advanced alien technology is; if they appear on radar, that counts as evidence for their existence; if they do not, they must have some form of stealth technology far beyond our understanding, and so on. No matter what the evidence turns out to be, the ETH has an explanation for it.

This sort of nonlogic has been soundly criticized by supporters of the null hypothesis.[109] The irony here is that they have been just as guilty of propounding nonfalsifiable hypotheses as their opponents. The common NH argument that all UFO sightings should be assumed to be hoaxes, hallucinations, or misperceptions of ordinary objects

---

108. Saler, Ziegler, and Moore 1997, 70.

109. Sheaffer 1981 is as good an example as any.

unless proven otherwise is a case in point. Apply the same standard to nearly any phenomenon you care to name, and it will fail just as neatly. It is impossible to prove beyond a shadow of a doubt, for example, that the Apollo moon landings actually took place. A vast amount of evidence supports the claim, of course, but doubters can always argue that the whole thing was a gigantic hoax, supported by hallucinations and misperceptions. Try to prove them wrong!

In the same way, nothing in the observed range of UFO behavior offers any way of putting the null hypothesis to a definite test, because anything and everything can be compatible with the NH. If someone sees a light in the night sky, defenders of the NH can claim that it must have been a planet or star; if it didn't behave like a planet or star, the witness must have been delusional or drunk; if the witness says it landed in a nearby meadow, the witness must be lying; if investigation shows the marks of landing gear in the meadow, the marks must have been put there by hoaxers, and so on. No matter what the evidence turns out to be, the NH has an explanation for it.

Supporters of the null hypothesis have occasionally claimed that they would give up their opposition to the extraterrestrial hypothesis if a bona fide flying saucer landed on the White House lawn and turned out to be crewed by little green men from another world. This is a step in the right direction—the great majority of believers in the extraterrestrial hypothesis don't seem to be able to name any evidence at all that would disprove their faith—but in its own way it's just as unscientific. One thing that has been learned for certain about UFOs in the last sixty years is that they do not make overt public appearances of this sort, and insisting that the only acceptable evidence is something the phenomenon does not provide is ultimately just another evasion. To be scientific, a study of UFOs would have to make testable predictions about the observed behavior of the phenomenon, rather than demanding conditions contrary to observed fact and claiming victory when these are not met.

The decision of both of the major contending parties in the UFO controversy to embrace unfalsifiable hypotheses has thus done an immense amount to put a solution to the UFO problem out of reach.

Instead of approaching the UFO phenomenon as a mystery to be solved, both parties have assumed that their preferred solution was self-evidently correct, and focused their efforts on trying to prove it to the rest of the world. Behind this misdirection of effort lies another major source of confusion in the controversy—the tangled relation between knowledge and authority in an age of institutionalized science.

Struggles Over Legitimacy

That relationship shaped the two sides of the controversy in different ways. Beginning in the 1950s, as discussed in part 1 of this book, many believers in the extraterrestrial hypothesis focused their efforts on the quest to have UFOs recognized as a phenomenon worth serious scientific study.[110] The competing UFO organizations pursued this common goal in different ways. For NICAP, the way to legitimacy lay through congressional hearings that would blow the lid off the alleged Air Force coverup and reveal once and for all that the nation's military establishment knew that UFOs were extraterrestrial spacecraft. For APRO, the way to legitimacy lay through investigating and publicizing UFO sightings until the sheer volume of proof made the extraterrestrial origin of UFOs impossible to deny. Other groups and individual researchers pursued the grail of legitimacy in other ways.

A double helping of irony surrounded this search for legitimacy, however. First of all, it drove the UFO movement to distort its own data for the sake of acceptability. NICAP, on the cutting edge of the UFO movement here as elsewhere, for many years had a strict policy of refusing to accept any UFO report that included landings or occupants, no matter how reliable the witnesses might be. The reason for this policy was simply that such reports were more easily disbelieved by the general public, and thus undercut the goal of making the phenomenon respectable.[111] APRO had somewhat more lenient standards, a factor that helped feed quarrels within the movement. Still, the differences were merely a matter of degree; during the 1950s and 1960s,

---

110. See Jacobs 1983 for a summary of this quest.

111. Jacobs 1983, 221.

for example, NICAP, APRO, and every other UFO organization outside the contactee community itself heaped scorn on claims of contact with aliens in public, and worried in private that the contactees prejudiced the scientific community and the general public alike against UFOs. As a result, the picture of the phenomenon presented by the UFO organizations was shaped much more by what seemed plausible than by what people were actually experiencing in UFO sightings.

The second irony compounded the first, because the search for legitimacy was a fool's errand from the start. One of the most durable myths of contemporary Western culture holds that scientific knowledge stands outside the motives and pressures that shape every other human institution. This may be how scientists like to think of their profession, but it has nothing to do with the realities of research and publication in the highly competitive and politicized world of today's scientific community. As sociologists of science have been pointing out for decades, the forces that shape what is acceptable and what is not in morals, manners, and every other kind of public discourse act just as effectively in the sciences. These forces in turn play a massive role in the way that scientific practice defines our culture's mainstream model of reality.

James McClenon points out in his book *Deviant Science* that the scientific community—like every other community—defines itself largely by what it excludes.[112] A church, a club, a neighborhood, or a nation safeguards its own identity by distancing itself from people who don't fit its qualifications, and ideas that run counter to its opinions and values; so does the scientific community. People who lack a relevant doctorate and at least a few publications in peer-reviewed journals are roughly as welcome in scientific discussions as African Americans at a racially segregated country club, just as ideas from outsiders that challenge generally accepted theories about nature have approximately the same standing in scientific circles that devil-worship has in a conservative Christian church.

---

112. See McClenon 1984, especially 38–78, for the theory of social deviance that underlies this and the following paragraph.

The relationship between a community and the people it excludes has a fascinating twist. If membership in the community has value recognized by those outside it, outsiders often copy the community's customs and beliefs, hoping to be accepted by the community through adopting its standards. Since the community defines itself by what it excludes, though, these attempts trigger what sociologists call "status panic." As a result, the harder outsiders try to fit in, the faster they find themselves thrown out the door and the more rigid the boundaries become. Just as racism in the American South became progressively more extreme and violent as African Americans adopted white culture and values in the first half of the twentieth century, and declined again when African Americans affirmed their own identity as a distinct ethnic and cultural group in the aftermath of the Sixties, the scientific community has always reserved its harshest words for those excluded groups that try hardest to make their work fit scientific norms.[113]

This was the trap that closed around the UFO movement as it pursued its campaign to make the phenomenon a legitimate field of scientific research. Once UFOs had been stigmatized in scientific circles as a crackpot subject—a process that was well under way by 1950 and complete by the end of that decade—the movement's efforts to build a case that would satisfy the demands of the scientific community for hard evidence simply led the scientific community to set the bar higher and condemn the entire subject more fiercely.

Thus, while believers in the extraterrestrial hypothesis boxed themselves into a futile quest for respectability, the supporters of the null hypothesis labored to define their own stance in terms of one of the scientific community's own favorite narratives. In the late nineteenth and early twentieth centuries, influential writers such as Andrew Dickson White treated the nineteenth-century struggle between Darwinian evolutionary theory and conservative Christianity as the leitmotif of

---

113. Compare, for example, the relatively tame public reaction of the scientific community to Buddhism and Hermetic ceremonial magic—two active and popular movements in the contemporary Western world that promote radically nonscientific worldviews, but do not claim to be scientific—with the same community's reaction to parapsychology, creation science, and UFO studies, all of which claim to be scientific.

the entire history of science.[114] Their historical vision pitted visionary scientists as champions of reason and truth against the forces of ignorance and superstition—that is, in the terms of their narrative, the Christian church. While historians of science discarded this approach most of a century ago, it makes a compelling story, and since the middle of the twentieth century that story has been central to the scientific community's own self-image.

Supporters of the null hypothesis discovered the advantages of this narrative early on, and used them to the hilt, denouncing their opponents in the extraterrestrial hypothesis camp as the enemies of science and reason or ridiculing them as liars and fools.[115] This pervasive habit contributed mightily to the rise of a culture of mutual intolerance in the UFO controversy that helped drive members of both camps into increasingly extreme positions, and in the process obscured the phenomenon itself even further. At the same time, it led many supporters of both hypotheses to abandon a scientific approach to UFOs in favor of a rhetorical one.

The differences between the two are not small. Rhetoric starts with a hypothesis and then attempts to prove it, highlighting its strong points and bolstering or concealing its weak points through the skillful use of words. By contrast, as shown earlier in this chapter, science starts with a hypothesis and then attempts to disprove it, making predictions that can be put to the test and letting facts, not words, have the final say. Even as supporters of both major hypotheses tried to wrap themselves in the prestige of science, they adopted the methods of rhetoric, and the results were unscientific in every sense of the term. Once supporters of the extraterrestrial hypothesis came to identify their mission as proving the extraterrestrial origin of UFOs to an unbelieving world, and defenders of the null hypothesis came to see their task as defending science and rationality against a rising tide of popular delusion, the chances of a reasoned solution to the UFO mystery became slim at best.

---

114. White 1896.

115. See, for example, the last chapter of Sheaffer 1981 and all of Sagan 1995.

Confirmation Bias

The tactics of the two sides varied in large part because it takes different rhetorical methods to defend a theory than it does to assail one. Once the extraterrestrial hypothesis became the default interpretation for sightings of strange objects in the air—a process that, as we've seen, began long before the first modern UFO sightings in 1947 and was complete by the middle years of the 1950s—the debate over UFOs settled into the familiar mold of a "pro-UFO" party supporting the extraterrestrial origin of any oddity in the skies, and an "anti-UFO" party attacking that view in the hope of supplanting it with the null hypothesis. To a great extent, those roles determined the course of the arguments that followed.

Once the debate was phrased in those terms, the proponents of the extraterrestrial hypothesis had two massive rhetorical advantages. First of all, it's a commonplace of rhetoric that it's much easier to prove a positive case than a negative one. Believers in the extraterrestrial hypothesis simply had to make a strong case that at least *one* UFO came from another world, while believers in the null hypothesis had to prove that *every* UFO was something other than an alien spacecraft. This quickly turned the UFO controversy into a series of debates around a handful of high-profile cases that seemed most likely to support the ETH.

The problem with this refocusing of the debate is that it threw an already serious problem with confirmation bias into overdrive. *Confirmation bias* is what psychologists call the human habit of looking for evidence that supports one's beliefs, rather than evidence that challenges them. The scientific method is basically a method for short-circuiting confirmation bias by making researchers try to disprove their own theories.

When believers in the ETH set out to prove their case, rather than trying to test it, they opened the door to confirmation bias, but the pursuit of the perfect case—the sighting that would prove once and for all that Earth was being visited by beings from outer space—made confirmation bias almost impossible to avoid. Since candidates for the perfect case were by definition those that seemed to fit the ETH best, this directed the UFO debate toward those features of the phenomenon that supported the alien origin of UFOs, and away from those features that did not.

The second advantage held by partisans of the extraterrestrial hypothesis pushed the same effect even further. It's easier to build an argument on the basis of unquestioned assumptions shared by all parties in the debate than it is to question those assumptions. By 1955 or so, most Americans lost track of the fact that the catchy acronym *UFO* means "an object in the air that has not been identified"; it is not a synonym for "alien spacecraft." Devout believers in the null hypothesis fell into this dubious logic just as unquestioningly as their opposite numbers in the extraterrestrial camp; the partisans of the NH simply used the assumption to argue that since alien spacecraft did not exist, neither did UFOs.

This assumption, though, allowed supporters of the extraterrestrial hypothesis to use any scrap of evidence for the physical reality of UFOs or the reliability of witnesses as ammunition for their case. It also allowed them to pick holes in explanations offered by the other side; raise doubts that a given sighting could have been a hoax, hallucination, or misperception; and then claim that having excluded all other options, the only remaining possibility was an alien spacecraft. Now of course there were many other possibilities, but any exploration of these other options had to overcome the inertia of an assumption few people in the debate were willing to question. Once again, confirmation bias ran unchecked and distorted the evidence in favor of a preconceived conclusion.

The recent quarrels between proponents of "good alien" and "bad alien" versions of the abduction hypothesis cast a clear and unflattering light on the problems with this sort of thinking. Both sides have exactly the same evidence for their beliefs—the unsupported testimony, nearly all extracted under hypnosis, of people who claim to have been abducted by aliens. Both sides argue that their evidence is valid, while insisting that the other side's evidence is not, and that none of the other stories extracted using the same hypnotic procedure—say, the claims of Satanic ritual abuse believers—have any relevance to the matter. Both sides, in other words, are effectively insisting that what makes evidence count as reliable is the fact that it supports their point of view. This is confirmation bias with a vengeance, and comes close to justifying the harsh judgments aimed at such claims by believers in the null hypothesis.

The extreme form of confirmation bias is the belief that since a given claim is true, any evidence that supports it must be true as well. This far shore of illogic has been reached far too often by defenders of the extraterrestrial hypothesis in the course of the UFO controversy. In far too many cases, blatantly false information has been accepted by UFO researchers at face value, simply because it supports the point of view the researchers favor.

One example out of many is the alleged Aztec, New Mexico, UFO crash of 1949. First publicized in 1950 by Frank Scully in his book *Behind the Flying Saucers*, the Aztec claim was exposed in 1953 as a blatant fraud concocted by two professional confidence men and foisted on Scully for cash. The story dropped out of the UFO debate immediately thereafter, and nobody but debunkers mentioned it for some two decades after that.

In the late 1970s, however, ETH proponent Leonard Stringfield resurrected the Aztec hoax as one of a litany of supposedly crashed UFOs in the Air Force's possession, and the story has been repeated by a great many defenders of the ETH since then. At the same time, many of the details cited by Scully in his book about the Aztec crash reappeared, sometimes verbatim, in accounts of the Roswell incident published in the 1980s. In his study of the Roswell story as a modern myth, Charles Ziegler has argued that this shows the way that folktales normally grow, by picking up themes and details from other sources.[116] It's also arguable, though, that the details found their way from one story to another for no better reason than that they helped bolster the extraterrestrial case.

---

116. See Saler, Ziegler, and Moore 1997 for these points.

Logical Fallacies

The null hypothesis camp has made much of these failures of logic. Their critiques might have carried more force if their own side of the argument had been free from shoddy reasoning, but the reality has been uncomfortably far from this ideal. Just as backers of the extraterrestrial hypothesis fell victim to rampant confirmation bias in their efforts to prove what they believed was true, supporters of the null hypothesis let the search for effective rhetorical weapons against their opponents seduce them into reliance on logical fallacies.

A fallacy, in the language of logic, is a plausible argument that relies on false reasoning. Most of the fallacies known to modern logicians were analyzed centuries ago in the Middle Ages, and are still known by their medieval Latin names. The fallacies of the null hypothesis derive from these classic logical howlers, but combine them in highly imaginative ways to meet the needs of the debunking crusade. The resulting arguments are distinct enough that at least three of them deserve names of their own.

The first of these distinctive fallacies has been neatly defined in the words "Extraordinary claims demand extraordinary proof." There seems to be some question about who first formulated this adage, but it appears frequently in the writings of the late debunker and CSICOP member Carl Sagan, and so it seems only reasonable to name it "Sagan's fallacy."[117] Like most fallacies, it seems reasonable at first glance, but behind it lies a drastic distortion of logic. What this adage means is that evidence for one set of claims—"extraordinary claims"—ought to be judged by a different and more restrictive standard of evidence than other claims.

What makes a claim extraordinary, though? Jimmy Carter's 1969 UFO sighting offers a good example. What we know about the sighting is that a small group of businessmen watched an unusual light in the sky for a few minutes. Robert Sheaffer's claim that the witnesses saw the planet Venus, and somehow suffered a collective hallucination

---

117. The original authorship of this quote is debated, but its first documented appearance seems to be Sagan 1972, 62.

in which the planet seemed to turn red and approach within a few hundred yards of them, is surely just as extraordinary as the suggestion that the witnesses saw something strange in the sky, and reported it as they saw it. If the same group of men had sighted parhelia or ball lightning, say,[118] Sheaffer would likely have accepted their testimony as a matter of course. The only thing that makes Carter's sighting "extraordinary" is that believers in the null hypothesis want to argue that it did not happen.

This point can be made more generally. The evidence that has been offered to date for the real existence of UFOs—not, please note, of alien spaceships, but simply of things seen in the skies that have not yet been adequately identified by witnesses or investigators, which again is what the term actually means—would have been accepted by most scientists if it involved anything within the currently accepted range of natural phenomena. Sagan's fallacy attempts to justify this divergence, but in the process it violates several of the most basic rules of logic.

It's one of the classic fallacies—the Latin name for it is *petitio principii*—to insist that the evidence for one side of an argument ought to be judged by a different standard than the evidence for the other side of the same argument. It's another classic fallacy—*consensus gentium* is the Latin term for this one—to insist that because a given community of people believes that something is true, it is true. Sagan's fallacy combines these two in a triumph of circular reasoning. Once a claim has been labeled false by debunkers, the evidence that supports the claim is automatically considered less valid than the evidence that opposes it, because the standards of proof that apply to all other claims—and, in particular, to the claims of debunkers—no longer apply to it. Since UFOs don't exist, in other words, any evidence offered to prove their existence must be invalid, and the lack of valid evidence shows that UFOs don't exist.

The second core fallacy that undergirds the null hypothesis case also unfolds from *petitio principii*. It should probably be called Menzel's fallacy, after the late Donald Menzel, who used it relentlessly in his

---

118. See Greenler 1980 and Walker 1980.

writings on the UFO phenomenon. This fallacy relies on the unstated assumption that the burden of proof never falls on the null hypothesis. Any argument that opposes the null hypothesis, in other words, is presumed false unless the other side proves that it's true, but any argument that favors the null hypothesis is presumed true unless the other side proves that it's false—not to unbiased observers, mind you, but to the satisfaction of defenders of the NH. This doubtful logic has allowed debunkers to make lavish use of the fine art of the ad hoc hypothesis.

In the jargon of science, an ad hoc hypothesis is an explanation drawn up after the fact to make sense of the results of an experiment. In science, an untested ad hoc hypothesis has only slightly more standing than an unfalsifiable hypothesis, because it's possible to explain anything using either one. What makes an ad hoc hypothesis potentially more useful is that it can be tested in further experiments, and proved or disproved by the results.

This is exactly what defenders of the null hypothesis fail to do, however. Instead, they treat any ad hoc hypothesis that supports their case as a "solution," even when it has not been subjected to any experimental test. When Robert Sheaffer announced that debunkers had solved all the unexplained cases in the Condon Committee report,[119] for example, what he meant is simply that they had proposed ad hoc hypotheses to explain each of the sightings to their own satisfaction. This differs not a whit from what believers in the extraterrestrial hypothesis did with the same sightings; the choice of explanations was the only noticeable difference.

One of the classic examples of this fallacy is Menzel's own response to the Nash-Fortenberry sighting of 1952.[120] In this sighting, described in chapter 2, the pilot and copilot of a commercial flight reported seeing a series of glowing red disks moving through the air at high speeds. Menzel went to the media at once to announce that the disks had been city lights reflecting off haze, clouds, or humidity.

---

119.   Sheaffer 1981, 15.

120.   See Nash and Fortenberry 1952 and Tulien 2002.

When research showed that the sky was completely clear and humidity was low, Menzel announced that the sighting had been caused by fireflies that had somehow become trapped between the inner and outer glass of one of the cockpit windows. When ETH proponent James McDonald pointed out that no trace of the supposed fireflies had been found, Menzel announced a third solution—that Nash and Fortenberry had sighted a planet. At no point did Menzel offer any evidence for any of his claims, much less propose them as falsifiable hypotheses subject to proof or disproof by the scientific method; they were simply ad hoc hypotheses meant to explain away a troublesome sighting.

Sheaffer himself offered a fine example of Menzel's fallacy in his attempt to dismiss the Barney and Betty Hill case as a sighting of the planet Jupiter. He claimed:

> *To some it will seem incredible that any sane person could misperceive a distant (if brilliant) planet as a close-in structured craft, complete with portholes and alien faces peering out. But the examples of numerous other UFO cases prove conclusively that this does indeed happen.*[121]

Of course this proves nothing of the kind, because Sheaffer's claim amounts to nothing more than the fact that the same untested ad hoc hypothesis has been applied to other UFO cases by debunkers. Since it's precisely the validity of the hypothesis that is in question, this isn't exactly reassuring. If Sheaffer had presented evidence that such sweeping shifts in the evidence of the senses occur in cases unrelated to the UFO controversy, that might have been a different matter since, as we'll see, phenomena capable of causing the sort of experience reported by Barney and Betty Hill do in fact exist. Still, insisting that UFO witnesses must be seeing planets, and any details this hypothesis doesn't explain are caused by some factor that makes them see such things while looking at planets, is circular logic of the worst kind.

The third fallacy central to the null hypothesis case comes out of a different department of bad reasoning, and is common enough in

---

121. Sheaffer 1981, 35.

debunking efforts of all kinds that it should probably simply be called the Debunker's Fallacy. This is the insistence that if nobody knows the cause of some unusual event, or if the proposed cause doesn't fit current scientific theories, the event itself never happened.

In logician's jargon, the Debunker's Fallacy is a *fallacy of composition*, in which two issues are lumped together so that a response to one looks like a response to both. Logically speaking, "Did X happen?" is not the same question as "What caused X?" Furthermore, somebody may have a wrong answer, or no answer at all, to the latter question but still be able to give a truthful answer to the former one.

This habit has been a consistent problem in scientific research over the last hundred years or so, in contexts completely unrelated to the UFO controversy. One of the more embarrassing missteps in the twentieth-century earth sciences, in fact—the rejection of continental drift between 1923 and 1969—had its origins in exactly this fallacy.[122]

In 1923, the German geologist and explorer Alfred Wegener proposed that Earth's continents were once joined into a single land mass, and gradually moved apart to their current positions around the globe. He had a great deal of data backing up the claim—coastlines that fit together like pieces of a jigsaw puzzle, rock formations in eastern South America that continued without a break in the corresponding areas of western Africa, fossil life forms found only in sections of land that had once been joined, and much more of the same sort.

Despite all this evidence, two difficulties prevented Wegener's theory from being accepted, or even seriously considered, by the geologists of the day. First, it contradicted the prevailing geological theories of the time, which held that the continents had formed in place as the newborn earth cooled and contracted from its original molten state. The second difficulty was that Wegener did not have a good explanation for the force that caused the continents to move. He speculated that the continental masses, being made of lighter, granitic rocks, "floated" on the denser basaltic rocks of the ocean beds, but neither

---

122. See Oreskes 1999 for a good historical study of the rejection of continental drift.

he nor any of his handful of followers could suggest a driving force that could make the continents drift in this way.

The resulting controversy in 1920s geology has uncomfortably close parallels with the UFO debate of the last six decades. Mainstream geologists pointed out that Wegener's claims about the cause of continental drift didn't work, and argued on this basis that continental drift didn't exist. All the evidence pointing toward continental drift was explained away by ad hoc hypotheses that, in retrospect, had a noticeable resemblance to Menzel's imaginary fireflies.

This continued for almost half a century until the geological equivalent of a flying saucer parked on the White House lawn—magnetic surveys of the Mid-Atlantic Ridge that showed unshakable evidence of sea-floor spreading, and provided a driving force for continental drift at the same moment that it proved its existence—transformed Wegener's theory from crackpot pseudoscience to one of the foundations of modern geology. In the meantime, though, several branches of geology wasted half a century trying to understand the formation of continents and oceans on the basis of an inaccurate theory.

This process is hardly restricted to the history of continental drift, or for that matter the history of the UFO controversy. The study of ball lightning—an unusual form of electrical discharge that happens now and then during thunderstorms—has been bedeviled by the same difficulty. Nobody has yet proposed a workable theory that explains the reported behavior of ball lightning, and a significant faction among meteorologists have responded by insisting that ball lightning does not exist.[123]

Still, the UFO mystery may be the extreme example of this fallacy at work in twentieth-century science. Over the last six decades, thousands of people all around the world have experienced unusual lights moving through the skies. Many of them have not been able to explain what they saw, and many more have turned to explanations—the extraterrestrial hypothesis, in particular—that cannot be justified by the evidence, any more than Wegener's granite continents floating on basalt sea beds

---

123. Stenhoff 1999 provides a good account of the science of ball lightning.

could be supported by the evidence known to 1920s geology. The fact remains that many of these people have had the experiences they claim, and by fixating on the unacceptable explanation instead of the unexplained experience, modern science has fallen down on the job.

The Power of Narrative

While it's true enough to say that many UFO witnesses have seen something, this begs a much larger question, however, because what they have seen and reported varies so drastically from sighting to sighting and from close encounter to close encounter. One of the most perplexing things about the UFO mystery is that the phenomenon displays so few internal regularities. This raises a possibility too rarely considered: a phenomenon that behaves so inconsistently may not, in fact, be a single phenomenon at all.

Leave aside the obvious sources of confusion—the planets, stars, airplanes, meteors, and the like that so often cause people to think they have seen something unusual in the sky. What is left? If the extraterrestrial hypothesis were correct, the remaining unexplained sightings would fall into distinctive, repeating patterns that would tell us something about the alien spacecraft visiting Earth's skies. If the null hypothesis were correct, the remaining sightings would be unexplained only because of insufficient information or witness error, and they would tend to fall into patterns closely mirroring those of the ordinary objects that caused them.

This is not what the UFO evidence shows, however. Behind the currently accepted UFO narrative of silvery disks piloted by big-eyed Grays lies a phenomenon impossible to wrap up so neatly—a phantasmagoria that seems to follow the logic of dream and myth rather than the mechanics of interstellar travel or, for that matter, those of popular folly. Reflections such as these led UFO researchers as different as Carl Jung and John Keel to explore the possibility that the phenomenon might better be explored with the tools of the mythologist than those of the scientist, and much of value has come out of such explorations. Still, there may be more going on here than meets even the mythically literate eye.

In their very different surveys of UFOs as a modern myth, Keith Thompson and Curtis Peebles both identified the flurry of sightings and media reports that followed Kenneth Arnold's sighting as the myth's foundation, the "First Time" in which the narratives that would govern the entire phenomenon took shape. Look at the UFO mystery as a drama, and by 1947 it already had its definitive cast of characters—baffled witnesses of varying reliability, investigators pursuing their own ideas of the truth with more enthusiasm than common sense, reporters and media more interested in a good story than the facts, and the Army Air Corps, shortly to become the United States Air Force, announcing explanations for the sightings that made no sense to anyone else.

Of course the drama contained another role as well—that of the mysterious objects that would later be called UFOs. That role had been sketched out centuries in advance by the first authors to speculate about beings living on other worlds, and the sketch was filled in by many hands in the late nineteenth and early twentieth centuries. By the time Kenneth Arnold spotted nine strange objects over the Cascade Mountains, everyone in America knew somewhere in the back of their minds what spacecraft from another world ought to look like. After Arnold's epochal sighting, many of them saw those ideas take concrete shape in the skies as silvery flying disks.

That was not what Kenneth Arnold saw, though. This point has been missed so often in accounts of the UFO controversy that it deserves repeated emphasis here. The distinctive crescent shapes that Arnold saw near Mount Rainier were never seen again. What people saw when they watched the skies in the summer of 1947 were small silvery dots or disks, alone or in loose formation, high in the air. What they thought they saw, on the other hand, was the product of centuries of popular culture, focused through lenses as diverse as John Ballou Newbrough's Etherean gospel, Raymond Palmer's lurid magazine covers, and Meade Layne's network of occultists watching the skies for the coming of the ether ships.

As the UFO phenomenon unfolded in the wake of 1947, in turn, the same difference between what people saw and how they interpreted what they saw only grew wider. Blobs of colored light moved through the lower atmosphere, high bright lights soared high above, and a steady stream of exotic encounters brought the ambience of fairyland into the phenomenon. The passing decades scattered dead livestock in western meadows, moved huge black triangles across the night sky, put watchers onto ridges in the Nevada desert, and sent hundreds of people into the offices of amateur hypnotists, from which they emerged believing that they had been abducted by the Grays.

All these things, in turn, fed a thriving cultural narrative about visitors from other planets hovering in Earth's skies. So did many other things, of course. In the excitement of the moment and the emotional power of the narrative, however, one important detail got misplaced: the only thread connecting these wildly diverse experiences to one another was the narrative itself. Take away the expectation that everything unusual seen in the sky must be part of the narrative about alien visitation, and what remains is a set of phenomena that have no particular relationship to one another, except that all of them were pressed into service to carry out roles in the UFO drama—a drama that was originally scripted in the pages of science fiction pulp magazines, and has a great deal more to do with the fears, fantasies, and imagined future of modern industrial society than with any other factor.

Of all the sources of misunderstanding shaping the UFO phenomenon, the mistake of treating it as a single phenomenon has arguably been the richest. Once that mistake is recognized and removed, the entire mystery takes a radically different shape. The best way to make sense of that shape is to start with a closer look at the other options—the hypotheses about the origins and nature of UFOs that are not embraced either by the extraterrestrial hypothesis or the null hypothesis.

six

The Unexamined Hypotheses

A good grasp of the barriers to understanding just explored is crucial to making sense of the UFO mystery, because the circular reasoning and shoddy logic brought to bear on the subject are most of
what makes it a mystery. At the core of most arguments for the extraterrestrial hypothesis, as we've seen, is a bit of dubious logic claiming that if an unknown object seen in the air isn't a hallucination, a
hoax, or a misidentification of something more ordinary, it must by
definition be a spacecraft piloted by aliens.[124] The defenders of the null
hypothesis, far from challenging this questionable logic, have simply
taken it and stood it on its head, arguing that since an unknown object
in the air can't be a spacecraft piloted by aliens, it must by definition
be a hallucination, a hoax, or a misidentification of something ordinary. Neither version of the argument makes anything approaching
logical sense—a detail that has done nothing to weaken its hold on the
collective imagination of the modern world.

---

124. See, for one example out of hundreds, Hynek, Imbrogno, and Pratt 1998, 244–52, which
makes precisely this argument.

That hold has been so complete that the crucial problems with both popular hypotheses have rarely been noticed, much less given the attention they deserve. There are many good reasons for thinking that UFOs are not spacecraft from another planet;[125] still, the most important place the extraterrestrial hypothesis falls down, as already observed, is simply that its "aliens" aren't alien enough—or, for that matter, alien at all. As shown in the first four chapters of this book, the supposed aliens associated with the UFO narrative faithfully copy popular earthly ideas about extraterrestrial life, invented by science fiction writers and artists in the first half of the twentieth century and elaborated in various ways since then, in the service of a belief in progress that fills important emotional needs in today's society but need not have anything to do with the wider reality of life in the cosmos.

Real aliens, by contrast, would be *alien*. Intelligent creatures from a distant star system, shaped by an utterly different biology and the evolutionary pressures of another world, would not look or behave the way our expectations lead us to imagine them, much less copy the popular fiction and media of an earlier generation down to a fine level of detail. Instead, they would differ from our expectations in ways we could never anticipate. Thus when a defender of the extraterrestrial hypothesis insists that a "large and consistent body of UFO evidence . . . almost shouts 'extraterrestrial technology,'"[126] this claim—which amounts to saying that the UFO evidence closely matches our earthling fantasies about what extraterrestrial technology would look like— is in fact setting out the most conclusive evidence *against* the ETH.

The central problem with the null hypothesis is somewhat different. Despite all the rhetorical skills and logical fallacies expended to cloud the issue, it's impossible to dismiss the fact that some people do actually see some very unusual things in the sky. No matter how enthusiastically debunkers try to explain it away, for example, it remains the most likely hypothesis that Jimmy Carter and his fel-

---

125.   Vallee 1990 gives a good summary of these.

126.   Donderi 2000, 56.

low Lions Club members saw something out of the ordinary in the Georgia sky on the night of January 6, 1969. In the same way, and to an even greater degree, such classic multiple-witness sightings as the Westchester boomerang of 1983 and 1984, or for that matter the original wave of silvery disks in the summer of 1947, cannot be made to disappear by any amount of rhetorical handwaving. The witnesses to those sightings saw *something* unusual and, to them, unknown; the fact that they did not see spacecraft from another world does not prove that they saw nothing at all.

Other options thus need to be taken into account. On the outer edges of the UFO controversy, a wide range of alternative hypotheses have been proposed. Most books on the UFO controversy ignore them completely, but they deserve attention, not least because some of them explain the facts of the phenomenon at least as well as the more popular alternatives. We'll go through them one at a time.

The Anthropogenic Hypothesis

This alternative is the belief that UFOs are made and piloted by human beings here on Earth. Historically speaking, the anthropogenic hypothesis was the first widely accepted explanation for the UFO phenomenon. Kenneth Arnold himself, along with many of those who listened to his story or spotted "flying saucers" in the 1947 flap, believed at first that what they had seen were secret experimental aircraft belonging to the United States or the Soviet Union.

It was by no means an unreasonable guess. The United States had just demonstrated by way of the Manhattan Project that it was perfectly capable of developing and deploying advanced weapons systems in total secrecy, and no one doubted the Soviet Union's ability to do the same thing. Steadfast denials by the Air Force that UFOs were either American aircraft or threats to national security had little effect at first, since such denials had shrouded plenty of real phenomena in the war years.

By the 1950s, however, this first version of the theory became increasingly hard to support, as both sides of the Cold War pursued an expensive arms race involving weapons systems that would have been completely superfluous if either side had aircraft that could perform the way UFOs were believed to do. At this point, the anthropogenic hypothesis was rescued and reshaped from an unlikely quarter.

The final collapse of the Third Reich in 1945 broke the political power of Adolf Hitler's repellent ideology, but it left behind many true believers in that ideology, who cherished hopes that their Führer would reappear someday and resume the war against the "Jewish world conspiracy" fantasized by Nazi propaganda.[127] One group that embraced these ideas gathered in Vienna in the years immediately after the war around the seminal neo-Nazi thinker Wilhelm Landig. Like the founders of the Nazi party itself, the Landig circle drew heavily on Ariosophy, an occult system that mingled Aryan racial fantasies with older occult teachings.[128]

Like many people in America, Landig interpreted the first wave of UFO sightings in 1947 in occult terms, but Landig's occultism included sizeable helpings of Nazi ideology and the hope of a reborn Fourth Reich. All this inevitably fed into his version of the flying saucer myth. By the early 1950s Landig and his followers were claiming that the flying saucers were German secret weapons flying out of a secret base in the Arctic, the Blue Island, where an inner core of SS officers had retreated to prepare a counterstrike against the victorious Allies. Later on, details were borrowed from a minor prewar German expedition to Antarctica, and the "Last Battalion" of saucer-riding SS troops were relocated to an underground base somewhere beneath the Antarctic glaciers. By the 1960s this belief became part of an ideology of esoteric Nazism adopted by racist and neo-Nazi groups around the world.

Accounts of Nazi flying saucer tests during the war years were not long in coming. The earliest of these accounts included precise if fraudulent details about the names and designs of the supposed saucers, and a few of them seem to have been based on wildly distorted accounts of tests of documented experimental jet aircraft and heli-

---

127. See Goodrick-Clarke 2002 for a useful discussion of Landig's circle and its influence, and for much of the material described in this section.

128. Ariosophy is covered in detail in Goodrick-Clarke 1992.

copters in the last years of the war. As time passed and these stories mingled with the wider fund of rejected knowledge in modern industrial society, however, these pedestrian details gave way to more colorful accounts of secret societies and extraterrestrial contacts.

By the late twentieth century some neo-Nazi groups were claiming that the saucers had been built using instructions encoded in medieval documents by the Knights Templar, who were in contact with alien intelligences from Aldebaran; these blond, blue-eyed Aryan aliens had been contacted in the last days of the Third Reich, and had launched a vast invasion fleet that was scheduled to arrive in Earth's skies in 1998. Fortunately, like so many other predictions of imminent alien landings, this one failed to happen.

Well before the mythology reached this extreme, the claim that UFOs were German secret weapons flying out of an underground base came to the attention of science fiction author W. A. Harbinson. The first volume of Harbinson's *Projekt Saucer* series, titled *Genesis*, saw print in 1980. In this and the novels that followed it, a psychopathic American genius—think of a cross between Thomas Edison and Charles Manson—defected to the Nazi regime before the Second World War and became the head of a project to build advanced, saucer-shaped aircraft. As the Third Reich collapsed around him, he and his project team escaped to an Antarctic base and began laying the groundwork for a horrific plot of world conquest using flying saucers and mind-control technology. While they never made the mistake of letting historical fact get in the way of a rousing story, Harbinson's novels echoed (and may have shaped) the increasingly paranoid flavor of the UFO narratives of the 1980s, and his ideas have predictably been borrowed and recycled as fact by some of the more extreme ends of the contemporary UFO scene.

The rise of the Nazi-UFO mythology may well have helped the anthropogenic hypothesis find its way back into the wider UFO research community in the 1990s, when increased attention to the unusual aircraft flying out of the Groom Lake base in Nevada offered a reminder that other planets are not the only possible source of mysterious flying craft. What has occasionally been called the "federal hypothesis"—the hypothesis that UFO sightings are caused by experimental aircraft operated by some branch of the United States government—has surfaced now and again in Internet UFO discussions over the last two decades or so. While some tidbits of information that surfaced in the late 1990s lent unexpected support to this hypothesis, as we'll see in chapter 8, the federal hypothesis has received much less attention than it deserves.

A final version of the anthropogenic hypothesis without the horror fiction element has circulated in European and Latin American alternative circles for some decades now. According to this account, the brilliant Italian inventor Guglielmo Marconi faked his death in 1937 and retreated, along with a select corps of fellow scientists and technicians, to a hidden base in the eastern slopes of the Andes Mountains of South America. There he and his successors designed and built the first flying saucers, based on scientific principles far in advance of anything the world's governments have at their disposal. Eventually, the claim goes, this secret scientific elite will sally forth from their hidden base in their flying saucers, neutralize the world's armies with high-tech weaponry, and usher in a new age of peace and prosperity for the whole world. Despite the minor hindrance of a complete lack of evidence, this theory still has many supporters, especially in the Latin American UFO community.

The Intraterrestrial Hypothesis

The anthropogenic hypothesis, with and without its neo-Nazi coloring, has overlapped more than once with a much weirder set of UFO theories that trace the origins of flying saucers to a hypothetical realm inside the earth. The story of the hollow earth theory has been told many times, notably by Walter Kafton-Minkel and Joscelyn Godwin,[129] and can be passed over here. Its central claim is that the earth is a hollow sphere with a second surface on the inside, facing an interior sun, and openings at the poles through which intrepid travelers might be able to find their way—or may have already done so.

---

129. See Kafton-Minkel 1989 and Godwin 1993.

By the early years of the twentieth century, belief in a hollow earth had become one of many options available to those with a taste for intellectual heresy. William Reed's 1906 book *The Phantom of the Poles* and Marshall B. Gardner's 1912 opus *A Journey to the Earth's Interior*, which presented the classic hollow-earth case with colorful diagrams, were standard reading in alternative circles throughout the English-speaking world in the decades before the UFO phenomenon appeared. Thus the concept inevitably came into the hands of Raymond Palmer, who printed several articles about the hollow earth theory in the days before the Shaver Mystery pushed most other forms of rejected knowledge off the pages of *Amazing Stories*.

In 1957, as UFOs soared high above American landscapes, a new Palmer magazine—*Flying Saucers from Other Worlds*—first appeared alongside his existing titles *FATE* and *Search*. The early issues hinted teasingly that Palmer had discovered some astonishing new secret about the saucers. Later the same year, he let his readers in on the secret: the flying saucers came from inside the hollow earth! (He dropped "from Other Worlds" from the magazine title with that issue.) Consistency never troubled Palmer in the least, and he printed plenty of UFO stories focusing on the extraterrestrial hypothesis after revealing the saucers' inner-earth origins, but his proclamation made sure that the notion of a hollow earth would find its way to interested readers in the postwar world.

Still, the hollow earth theory resides on the outermost edge of fringe beliefs, and even among the true believers of rejected knowledge it finds very few supporters. The evolution of a fully developed intraterrestrial theory of UFOs was left to the same neo-Nazi theorists who filled out the anthropogenic theory with Knights Templar and Aryans from Aldebaran.

In the writings of such figures as Miguel Serrano, the Chilean diplomat, neo-Nazi occultist, and theorist of "Esoteric Hitlerism," the hollow earth became the ultimate refuge of the people of Hyperborea, the homeland of the prehistoric Aryans. Serrano claims that Hitler flew there in a Nazi saucer in the last days of the Third Reich and remained inside the hollow earth, directing a hidden war against the Allies, before finally returning to the homeworld of the Aryans in a distant galaxy.[130] It's easy to imagine Raymond Palmer printing stories of this sort in the pages of *Amazing Stories*; it's a good deal harder to imagine anyone taking them seriously, but Serrano and other members of today's neo-Nazi underground apparently do so.

The Cryptoterrestrial Hypothesis

It was probably inevitable, in the wake of the extraterrestrial and intraterrestrial hypotheses, that someone would split the difference and suggest that UFOs were the product of intelligent nonhuman entities living unseen somewhere on the surface of the earth. This proposal apparently first surfaced in the writings of biologist and Fortean researcher Ivan Sanderson, who argued in his 1970 book *Invisible Residents* that UFOs came from an underwater civilization far more advanced than present-day humanity—perhaps native to this planet, perhaps from somewhere else.

As evidence, he pointed to a collection of unusual phenomena associated with the world's oceans, and the fact that some UFO witnesses had seen flying saucers rising out of the ocean or descending into it. This wasn't much, especially since the Bermuda Triangle, one of the linchpins of his argument, was manufactured out of whole cloth and wild distortions of evidence by Vincent Gaddis and Charles Berlitz in two dubiously researched books in the 1960s. Still, the material supporting his case was no worse than the evidence used to back up the extraterrestrial hypothesis, and the fact that the world's oceans are a good deal closer to us than the nearest stars lent his argument a certain additional plausibility; unlike proponents of the extraterrestrial hypothesis, he didn't have to beg the question of whether interstellar travel is even possible.

For all that, Sanderson's theory read like science fiction, and not surprisingly it had been anticipated by at least one work in that genre—Edgar Pangborn's wry *A Mirror for Observers* (1954), which features Martian refugees hiding from human sight while trying to

---

130. Godwin 1993, 70–73 and 126–29.

guide human evolution. It helped inspire several other novels and at least one film, James Cameron's mostly forgettable 1989 movie *The Abyss*. Like so many of the imaginative attempts to revision the UFO phenomenon in the late 1960s and early 1970s, though, it failed to overcome the tight grip of the extraterrestrial hypothesis on the popular imagination, and vanished from sight when abduction accounts took center stage in the UFO controversy at the end of the 1970s.

The cryptoterrestrial hypothesis has recently been revived by UFO writer and Internet columnist Mac Tonnies, whose book on the subject—not yet in print as of this writing—will doubtless be worth a look. Still, unless some evidence turns up bolstering the claim that a technologically advanced nonhuman species inhabits the world alongside humanity, it should probably be left to science fiction.

The Time-Travel Hypothesis

The possibility that UFOs and their occupants might be travelers in time rather than space first surfaced in science fiction decades before it was proposed as a serious theory among UFO researchers; H. Beam Piper's classic *Lord Kalvan of Otherwhen* (1965) is one of many examples. Bruce Goldberg's 1998 book *Time Travelers from Our Future* seems to have been the first widely circulated work arguing that UFOs are time machines from a future Earth. Like most rivals to the extraterrestrial hypothesis, it has received little attention among UFO researchers and even less among debunkers.

Like the extraterrestrial hypothesis, the time-travel hypothesis starts out from the assumption that technological progress has no upper limit, and beings with a sufficiently advanced technology can overcome any limitation you care to name. If this turns out to be true, time travel would conceivably be within reach of a sufficiently advanced technology, and the outlandish behavior of flying saucers and their crews could be explained just as well if they came from thousands of years in the future rather than trillions of miles across space.

The downside to this point is that, like the extraterrestrial hypothesis itself, the time-travel hypothesis is an argument from ignorance. By definition, we have no way of knowing the possibilities and limits of a technology more advanced than ours, and so it's possible to argue that anything at all could be the product of some futuristic technology. Nor, it has to be said, is there any actual evidence for time travel. Goldberg's work relies on hypnotic regression of people who believe they were abducted by flying saucers in previous incarnations—a less than ironclad source of information by most standards—and nothing more solid supports it. Like the cryptoterrestrial hypothesis, or for that matter the extraterrestrial hypothesis, it's a great theory—and potentially a great theme for science fiction—but a great theory means nothing when the evidence to back it up simply isn't there.

The Zoological Hypothesis

The hypotheses we've examined so far all assume that UFOs must be machines of some kind, similar in concept to our own airplanes and spacecraft if more technologically advanced. One of the early theories circulated about the UFO phenomenon, though, suggests that they are not machines but living things, part of a previously unrecognized ecosystem existing either in the upper atmosphere or in outer space itself. This theory appears in the writings of Charles Fort, who used it in his wry way to account for the curious fact that people now and then report what look like flesh and blood falling out of the sky. It found expression in a number of UFO books in the 1950s and 1960s, of which Trevor James' *They Live In The Sky!* (1958) was certainly the most colorful and probably the most widely read.

The zoological hypothesis was certainly worth proposing at a time when human beings had never reached the upper atmosphere, much less ventured into space, and almost anything might have been found by early high-altitude aircraft or Skyhook balloons. Half a century later, this is no longer true, and no trace of the hypothetical sky animals has yet turned up. The zoological hypothesis thus filled its role in the scientific process; as a falsifiable hypothesis, it was put to the test and turned out not to be true. As far as I know, it has been completely forgotten in recent years, except by a handful of Fort scholars and UFO enthusiasts with a passion for intellectual heresy.

The Geophysical Hypothesis

The zoological hypothesis, whatever its problems, raises the point that UFOs might be natural rather than mechanical, and the possibility that some inanimate natural process creates them also needs to be considered. Such claims have been made since long before the dawn of the UFO age, of course. Before the UFO phenomenon emerged from obscurity in 1947, unusual lights in the sky were often identified as meteors or comets, and the attempt to identify UFOs with swamp gas—though it landed J. Allen Hynek in a great deal of trouble in 1966—quite possibly pointed to a significant explanation for some sightings. Still, recent decades have focused attention on another set of natural phenomena: the possibility that strain along geological fault lines might generate light phenomena that could explain at least some UFOs.

For thousands of years, people have reported strange lights in the sky immediately before, during, and after large earthquakes. While these reports were long dismissed as rank superstition, using arguments uncomfortably like those deployed by debunkers against the UFO phenomenon, earthquake lights have been repeatedly photographed and observed by qualified geologists, and while their cause is still a matter for enthusiastic debate, the basic reality of the phenomenon is accepted by many geologists today.[131]

The existence of earthquake lights demonstrates that some still-unknown factor related to tectonic stress—the pressure between moving rocks on opposite sides of a fault that drives earthquakes—can apparently cause luminous phenomena. The geophysical hypothesis argues on this basis that some related process gives rise to the experience of glowing balls of light ("earth lights") in tectonically active areas. These glowing balls of light are then interpreted by witnesses in terms of their own culturally shaped expectations, whatever those happen to be—flying witches in traditional East African cultures, the Wild Hunt in early medieval Europe, or spaceships from distant planets in the industrial societies of the twentieth century.

---

131. See, for example, Derr 1973.

This analysis is a great deal more subtle than most of the other theories surrounding UFOs. It makes room for both sides of the enigma—the reality of unusual things seen in the sky, and the way that this reality has been overlaid with interpretations drawn from popular culture—to a degree few other hypotheses even attempt. Unlike most other hypotheses about UFOs, it has also been tested to some extent through a series of innovative research projects in areas where nocturnal lights are frequently seen. Leicestershire, England; Hessdalen, Norway; the Yakima Indian Reservation near Yakima, Washington; the Mitchell Flats near Marfa, Texas; and several other locations have been investigated by teams using video cameras, magnetometers, seismic monitors, and other geological tools alongside ordinary observation.[132]

The results of these research initiatives have been intriguing, if not conclusive. Dozens of nocturnal lights have been photographed, and correlations between light phenomena and local changes in the earth's magnetic field have been measured. Historical research has also shown some remarkable correlations between nocturnal light phenomena and earthquakes, offering added support to the geophysical hypothesis. Another line of argument supporting it comes from the neurological hypothesis, described later in this chapter, which suggests that some of the stranger elements of the UFO phenomenon—experiences such as close encounters and abductions—can be generated by the impact of the earth's magnetic field on the human mind.

All in all, the geophysical hypothesis is among the strongest of the current theories about the origins of the UFO phenomenon. Ironically, it is also among the least popular. Rejected with equal heat by defenders of the extraterrestrial hypothesis and the null hypothesis, and ignored by the media and the general public, it has been championed by a small number of researchers, most notably Britain's Paul Devereux and Canada's Michael Persinger. Their work suggests that some UFO phenomenon may well derive from tectonic stress; what

---

132. See the summary in Devereux and Brookesmith 1997, 138–59.

nobody has been able to determine is how wide a net this hypothesis is able to cast.

The Demonic Hypothesis

The vast majority of hypotheses about the UFO phenomenon, including all those surveyed so far in this chapter, assume that UFOs are physical objects of a sort familiar to modern scientific thinking—machines in the case of the first four hypotheses, and natural phenomena in the fifth and sixth. Not all hypotheses accept this claim, however; some argue instead that UFO phenomena are spiritual rather than physical.

One traditional resource Western culture offers for talking about spiritual entities is demonology, the branch of Christian and Jewish theology that deals with the nature and activities of evil spirits, and one group of UFO researchers have used this resource to identify UFOs as demons. The demonic hypothesis was first proposed by a handful of Christian writers in the early 1950s and has remained a significant theme in conservative Christian circles ever since. Toward the end of the 1960s, it was embraced by Gordon Creighton, editor of the British UFO magazine *Flying Saucer Review* (*FSR*), and several other prominent British UFO researchers.

In its classic form, the demonic hypothesis argues that UFOs display all the hallmarks of demonic activity defined in biblical texts and Christian theology. The apparent ability of UFOs to violate the laws of physics, in this interpretation, can best be explained by the hypothesis that they are supernatural entities and thus not bound by material laws. Christian theology holds that all spiritual creatures are either servants of God (that is, angels) or opposed to him (that is, demons)—there is no middle ground—and the status of any particular spiritual creature can be identified by three principal tests. The first is that angels always speak the truth, while demons can tell the truth if it suits their purpose but prefer to lie; the second is that angels perform only good works, while demons can perform either good or evil works; the third is that angels teach and uphold Christian teachings such as the divinity of Christ, while demons oppose them.

By these three tests, supporters of the demonic hypothesis argue, UFOs are clearly demonic in nature. First, the occupants of UFOs repeatedly lie; for example, they often predict public UFO landings and global catastrophes that never take place. Second, the UFO literature is full of accounts of UFOs and their occupants performing evil works such as mutilating cattle and abducting and sexually abusing human beings. Third, contactees and abductees alike report that they are encouraged to adopt a set of beliefs that UFO demonologist David Ritchie characterizes as "collectivism; the unification of human society into some kind of global regime; veneration, bordering on worship, of nature and natural objects; faith in occult principles and practices, such as mediumism or 'channeling'; discouragement of traditional Judeo-Christian religious beliefs, such as the doctrine of the divinity, crucifixion, and resurrection of Christ, and a syncretic set of religious beliefs with identifiable parallels in Buddhism, Hinduism, and shamanism."[133] Since all these are incompatible with traditional Christian teaching, the spiritual entities behind the UFO phenomenon must be demonic rather than angelic.

These arguments borrow their force from the theological viewpoint that lies behind them, and will be convincing only to those who believe in the essential truth of the Christian faith. It also requires the acceptance of a dimension of reality—the spiritual—whose existence is flatly rejected by many people nowadays, and reduced to psychological or neurological terms by many others. Still, the demonic hypothesis points up details of the UFO phenomenon that other hypotheses miss, notably the physically improbable behavior attributed by UFOs and their curious association with a distinctive set of religious beliefs opposed to those of traditional Christianity. Whether or not the specifically Christian interpretation of these factors is valid, they deserve to be included in any complete view of the phenomenon.

---

133. Cited in Lewis 2000, 105.

The Ascended Masters Hypothesis

The same perspectives that lead some traditional Christians to identify UFOs as demonic entities have encouraged a good many people
in alternative religious movements to propose what is essentially the
opposite interpretation, and identify UFOs as positive spiritual entities. The more diverse belief systems of the alternative spirituality
scene have fostered a very wide range of identifications of this sort.
Some writers whose beliefs draw on Christian imagery have suggested
that UFO occupants are angels; others have borrowed concepts from
other cultures and spiritual traditions to identify UFO occupants with
shamanic guardian spirits, ancient Egyptian gods, and the like; but
the most popular claim, backed by the contactees of the 1950s and
widely held in today's New Age scene, considers UFO occupants to be
ascended masters.

The concept of the ascended masters derives from Theosophy, the
most influential of the nineteenth-century occult movements in the
Western world, by way of popular early-twentieth-century alternative
religious groups such as the I AM Activity and Soulcraft. According
to these teachings, every soul in the entire cosmos undergoes a slow
process of spiritual evolution, and ascended masters are those souls
who have risen to levels far above the human through the process of
ascension, a spiritual transformation that frees the soul from ordinary
birth and death. To many believers in this teaching, Jesus of Nazareth
is one of the ascended masters, alongside the Buddha, the Comte de
St.-Germain, and many more.

The ascended masters, in this belief system, are the spiritual
guardians of the cosmos, and those assigned to Earth are responsible for fostering the spiritual advancement and eventual ascension of
every being on our planet. The development of nuclear weapons in the
1940s marked the coming of a time of crisis for the earth that could
end in a Utopian planetary transformation or the total destruction of
humanity and the planet itself. The arrival of the first UFOs in 1947,
according to this view, was the response of the ascended masters to
this crisis—a demonstration to the materialistic majority that beings
with an incalculably more advanced technology also existed in the

cosmos, and a way of passing on important metaphysical teachings to the spiritually advanced minority.

All of the points raised by traditional Christians in favor of the demonic hypothesis have their opposite numbers in the ascended masters hypothesis. Like proponents of the demonic hypothesis, believers in the ascended masters hypothesis point to the apparent ability of UFOs to violate the laws of physics at will as evidence that they use spiritual powers rather than material technology. The claims that UFO communications include lies, and UFO actions include evil deeds, are countered in a variety of ways; some versions of the ascended masters hypothesis, for example, suggest that there may also be negative spiritual powers involved who try to discredit the ascended masters by passing on false claims and carrying out evil actions in their names. Finally, believers in the ascended masters agree that UFOs pass on a distinctive set of spiritual teachings, but since those teachings are essentially those of the contactee and New Age community, this is a positive point rather than a negative one.

Like the demonic hypothesis, the ascended masters hypothesis makes sense only in terms of the traditions and teachings that undergird it, and those who approach it as outsiders are unlikely to find much value in it. This limitation has helped foster another hypothesis about UFOs, which approaches the phenomenon along the same lines as the demonic and ascended master hypotheses, but avoids embracing any set of assumptions about it other than those derived from the evidence itself.

The Ultraterrestrial Hypothesis

This approach, the ultraterrestrial hypothesis, is the one theory about the origin of UFOs that seriously challenged the dominance of the extraterrestrial and null hypotheses in the UFO controversy. Present in embryonic form in the writings of Charles Fort, it became widely popular after UFO researchers John Keel and Jacques Vallee presented it in a series of influential books and articles between 1969 and 1979.

The starting point of the ultraterrestrial theory is the argument that UFOs and their occupants do not behave like physical nuts-and-bolts spacecraft at all. They appear and disappear like ghosts, and sometimes can be seen by some witnesses and not by others in a situation in which a physical object would be visible to all. They show close similarities to themes from contemporary popular culture, but they also closely resemble legendary beings recorded in the folklore of cultures around the world. Thus, according to this way of thinking, the answer to the UFO phenomenon is to be found somewhere in the complex realm of human experience that reaches from the mind through the debatable ground of psychic phenomena into the world of myth, magic, and spirituality.

This suggestion understandably came in for heavy fire from both of the established positions in the UFO controversy. Defenders of the extraterrestrial origins of UFOs have generally dismissed it out of hand. The other end of the controversy responded with even less patience; Robert Sheaffer, whose book *The UFO Verdict* saw print when the ultraterrestrial hypothesis was at the peak of its influence, offered a typical response; he dismissed Vallee and Keel as "off the deep end" and insisted that their reasoning can be used to justify belief in the Easter Bunny.[134]

If nothing else, this shows how little attention Sheaffer paid to the history of his subject. Charles Fort faced and flattened the same argument half a century before, pointing out the difference between the phenomena he tracked and Santa Claus: ". . . I am particular in the matter of data, or alleged data. And I have come upon no record, or alleged record, of mysterious footprints in snow, on roofs of houses, leading to chimneys, Christmas eves."[135] Predictably, though—despite the notable absence of several hundred thousand reports by reputable witnesses of "unidentified furry objects" leaving colored eggs on lawns on Easter mornings—Sheaffer's gibe has been much repeated among his fellow debunkers.

For all that, the ultraterrestrial theory is not without serious problems. In some sense, it is an argument from ignorance far more

---

134.   Sheaffer 1981, 172–73.

135.   Fort 1974, 643.

impenetrable than the one surrounding the extraterrestrial hypothesis, since—at least in theory—we know a little bit about what other planets and their inhabitants might be like, but we know precisely nothing about Keel's "superspectrum" except the limited conclusions that can be drawn from the actions of the ultraterrestrials themselves.

Balanced against this difficulty are the two great advantages of the ultraterrestrial hypothesis—first, the way that it allows the UFO phenomenon to be considered as a whole, with all its bizarre details intact, instead of being edited down to fit the limits of some more restrictive hypothesis; and second, its attention to the possibility that UFOs might represent a range of human experience not well addressed from within the worldview of modern industrial cultures. Whether Keel's idea of a superspectrum is more useful as an explanation than the Christian doctrine of hell or contactee teachings about other planes of being is another matter, difficult to decide on the basis of the very limited evidence at hand.

The Neurological Hypothesis

The hypotheses we've examined already start from the assumption that whatever UFOs are, they are actually present in the skies of our planet, and people who encounter them participate in the encounters only as passive witnesses. This apparently commonsense view has been forcefully challenged by the neurological hypothesis, a theory that UFO experiences are not produced by alien spacecraft in Earth's skies but by neurochemical events in human brains.

The main proponent of this thesis is Canadian neurologist Michael A. Persinger, who has defended it ably in numerous scholarly papers and a cowritten book. Persinger points out that most of the experiences associated with the UFO phenomenon can be found in the clinical and experimental literature on temporal-lobe epilepsy (TLE), a poorly understood syndrome that can be triggered by magnetic fields. In a series of elegantly designed experiments, Persinger exposed subjects to pulsing magnetic fields and produced hallucinations that showed strong similarities to UFO close encounters.[136] Since hundreds of modern technologies produce magnetic fields, and the earth's own magnetic field has its own ebbs and flows, Persinger makes a case that these might be causing UFO experiences in people who then honestly report what they perceived.

Another name that sometimes surfaces when the neurological dimensions of the UFO phenomenon comes up is Julian Jaynes. In his 1976 book *The Origin of Consciousness in the Breakdown of the Bicameral Mind*, Jaynes argued that modern human consciousness is a recent thing, born around 1250 BCE with the collapse of the "bicameral mind." In that older form of consciousness, the personality existed in one half of the brain, and the other half was perceived as a separate being, a god or guardian spirit, that communicated with the personality through auditory and visual hallucinations. Jaynes argued that today's mystics and visionaries were simply experiencing a throwback to this older way of brain functioning. People who experience UFOs and abductions could readily fit into the same category.

Unlike most UFO theories, the neurological hypothesis offers a reasonable explanation for the hallucinatory qualities of the UFO experience and the ways in which it shapes itself to fit popular culture and the expectations of witnesses, without rejecting the honest testimony of witnesses who have experienced very strange things. It also combines well with the geophysical hypothesis, as suggested earlier, to produce a general theory of the UFO phenomenon sharply different from most of its rivals.

The combined hypothesis starts from the fact that the sort of tectonic stress that seems to create earth lights can also affect the local terrestrial magnetic field. If these effects produce pulsing fields of the sort used in Persinger's experiments—and the studies mentioned above offer evidence that this does happen—hallucinations like the ones experienced by Persinger's experimental subjects would be a likely result. Combine objectively real moving lights in the sky with a tendency toward sensory hallucination among witnesses and you have

---

136. Persinger 2000.

the perfect formula for UFO experiences. Since hallucinations always draw on the content of the subject's mind, the potent role of media portrayals and popular culture on the UFO phenomenon could be explained by this theory.

Like the ultraterrestrial theory, this expanded version of the neurological theory thus manages to embrace the entire spectrum of UFO experiences, or at least a much larger part of that spectrum than most of its rivals. Unlike the ultraterrestrial theory, it also makes a good assortment of falsifiable claims about the UFO phenomenon, some of which have been tested already and passed the test. Whether or not it gives the final explanation to the UFO mystery, it manages at least to open doors left closed by the dominance of the extraterrestrial and null hypotheses over the last sixty years.

Summing Up the Hypotheses

The sheer diversity of the explanations proposed for the UFO phenomenon over the last six decades offers a good measure of the complexity of the subject. There are few phenomena in existence that have attracted so varied a set of proposed explanations. Still, that diversity is in some ways more apparent than real.

Each of these varied positions in the controversy unfold from the implications of a fundamental disagreement about what UFO witnesses observe. Of the twelve hypotheses discussed in this chapter, seven—the extraterrestrial, anthropogenic, intraterrestrial, cryptoterrestrial, time travel, zoological, and geophysical hypotheses—identify UFOs as material objects, more or less accurately perceived by witnesses; without too much irreverence, these might be called the "hardware hypotheses." The five remaining hypotheses—the null, demonic, ascended masters, ultraterrestrial, and neurological hypotheses—reject this claim, and suggest instead that UFOs are apparitions.

This latter term bears careful attention. Suggesting that UFOs are apparitions is not the same thing as saying that they don't exist. It means that the experience of seeing a UFO does not directly reflect the cause of that experience, the way that the experience of seeing a coffee cup reflects the coffee cup. Persinger's geomagnetic theory provides a good example. If he is right, something real—a pulsing magnetic field within a certain range of frequencies—causes people to experience UFOs. At the same time, the witnesses don't experience the pulsing magnetic field; they experience the hallucination that the field causes when it hits their brains.

In the same way, if the null hypothesis is correct, witnesses don't directly experience the misjudgments and illusions that make them think they have seen something unknown in the sky. Interestingly enough, the same distinction even works with the three hypotheses that identify UFOs as the work of disembodied intelligences. Traditional Christian theology, for example, holds that what human beings experience when they encounter a demon is not the demon itself, but a form or image created by the demon for its own purposes.[137] Most modern alternative religious traditions share the same view of the relation between spiritual apparitions and the realities behind them, and of course Keel's discussions of the superspectrum embrace the same awareness of the gap between what witnesses see and what is actually going on.[138]

The currently recognized possibilities surrounding the UFO phenomenon thus arrange themselves around the basic distinction between physical objects and apparitions. If UFOs are physical objects, they might be artificial or natural; if artificial, they might be created by human beings or something else, and they might come from some location on Earth or from somewhere else. If natural, they might be living or nonliving. If they are apparitions, those apparitions might be objectively real entities—demons, ascended masters, or ultraterrestrials—or they might be purely subjective experiences; if the latter, they might be produced by the human nervous system, or by the perceptual and psychological patterns that shape our experience after the nervous system gets done with it. Lay those options out in order, as in table 2, and you have the hypotheses outlined in this chapter.

All this may seem abstract, but it has crucial implications for our investigation. In most cases, it's actually not that hard to tell the difference

---

137.   See, for example, the warning of the apostle Paul in 2 Corinthians 11:14 that the devil can appear in the form of an angel of light.

138.   See Keel 1991, 163–68.

between a material object and an apparition, even at second or third hand. If a material object shows up at some particular place and time, anybody with normal sensory apparatus will experience it in something close to the same way. The psychological effects that make witnesses to auto accidents recount different stories always have to be factored in, of course, but even so, witnesses to auto accidents generally agree on the basics—how many cars were involved, for example, not to mention that the objects that collided were cars rather than dragons, dirigibles, or spacecraft from Zeta Reticuli.

Thus an unusual material object in a public setting commonly attracts a sizeable number of sightings, most of which agree with one another about the general nature of the thing that was seen. If the object reappears at a different place and time, or if more than one exists, sightings can be compared to one another and detailed points of similarity will generally come up. Furthermore, observations of material objects will reliably follow the known laws of nature.

Apparitions are another matter. It's quite possible for two or more people to experience the same apparition—psychologists have long recognized a syndrome called *folie à deux*, in which two people enter into a common delusion that can include full-blown hallucinatory experiences—but this happens only when all the witnesses are affected by a common factor that upsets the normal function of their senses, nervous system, or mind. If an apparition is seen at a particular place and time, only those people affected by this common factor will experience it. Some indication of an altered state of consciousness will usually be reported by the witnesses, whether or not they themselves recognize this for what it is, and reports of witnesses to the same apparition may vary widely from one another, and most often have little in common with reports of those who have witnessed other apparitions elsewhere or at different times. Furthermore, apparitions do not obey the same natural laws as material objects, and very often behave in ways that material objects cannot.

Thus it's possible, and useful, to ask which of these corresponds most closely with the UFO phenomenon—or rather, as suggested in chapter 5, with the various phenomena that have been lumped under

---

TABLE 2

UFOs are either . . .

I. Material objects, and are either . . .

  A. Artificial, and are either . . .

    1. Made by human beings . . .

      a. On the earth . . .

        1. At the present time—*anthropogenic hypothesis*

        2. In the far future—*time-travel hypothesis*

      b. Or somewhere else—*intraterrestrial hypothesis*

    2. Or made by nonhuman beings . . .

      a. On the earth—*cryptoterrestrial hypothesis*

      b. Or somewhere else—*extraterrestrial hypothesis*

  B. Or natural, and are either . . .

    1. Living things—*zoological hypothesis*

    2. Nonliving natural phenomena—*geophysical hypothesis*

II. Or apparitions, and are either . . .

  A. Objectively real, and are either . . .

    1. Best understood via Christian theology—*demonic hypothesis*

    2. Or best understood via alternative faiths—*ascended masters hypothesis*

    3. Or best understood outside either option—*ultraterrestrial hypothesis*

  B. Or only subjectively real, and are either . . .

    1. Produced by the nervous system—*neurological hypothesis*

    2. Or produced by perceptual and psychological factors—*null hypothesis*

---

the heading of UFOs. The answer, of course, is that some UFOs fall into one category and some into the other. The UFO phenomena that behave like material objects include a small number of well-defined types routinely sighted by multiple witnesses: the silvery disks of the original 1947 wave and its sequels in the mid-1950s; brightly colored lights at high altitudes, which became common in the 1950s and have continued ever since; black triangles of the Westchester Boomerang type, which were mostly seen in the 1980s; and relatively small moving lights in areas under tectonic stress, which have been observed and photographed since time out of mind.

Most other UFO sightings, on the other hand, behave like apparitions. This includes nearly all the UFO experiences that have shaped and supported the extraterrestrial hypothesis and defined the UFO phenomenon for the last sixty years, including many close encounters and all abduction experiences. By sorting out the role of apparitions in shaping the UFO narrative of our time, we can begin to approach the hard core of fact underlying six decades of confusion and controversy.

Part Three

Solving the Mystery

It is out of blasphemy that new religions arise.
It is by thinking things that schoolboys know better
than to think that discoveries are made. It is because
our visions are not delirious enough, or degraded, or
nonsensical enough, that all of us are not prophets.
—Charles Fort, *Wild Talents*

It is an old maxim of mine that when you have
excluded the impossible, whatever remains, however
improbable, must be the truth.
—Arthur Conan Doyle,
"The Adventure of the Beryl Coronet"

seven

The Natural History of Apparitions

The suggestion that a very large number of UFO witnesses experience apparitions rather than seeing material objects will doubtless raise hackles among most members of the UFO research community. Those who have committed countless hours of hard work to the task of proving that UFOs are spacecraft from distant planets are unlikely to welcome the suggestion that they have been building their theories on a foundation of dreams, visions, and altered states of consciousness. Still, this proposal explains a great many things about UFOs for which the extraterrestrial hypothesis, and for that matter the other hardware hypotheses, provide no meaningful explanation at all.

The first point that has to be made here is one that has already been mentioned repeatedly in the course of this book—the extraordinary parallels between reports of UFO experiences and the portrayals of aliens and their spacecraft in science fiction literature and media, beginning long before the emergence of the phenomenon in 1947 and continuing right up to the present. These parallels cut to the heart of nearly any claim that UFOs are real material objects, and pose a particularly daunting challenge to the extraterrestrial hypothesis. It might make a clever science fiction story to claim that alien beings from a distant planet surreptitiously landed on Earth in the 1930s, spent hours reading through stacks of *Amazing Stories* back issues, modeled their spacecraft and their activities on the stories concocted by Raymond Palmer and his friends, and proceeded to update themselves and their technology to keep abreast of earthling science fiction movies and TV programs for decades thereafter. Still, as a serious proposal about the origin and nature of UFOs, this is the great-grandmother of all circular arguments—and yet some such assumption would be needed to explain what is, after all, one of the most significant facts about the entire UFO experience.

This same problem can be traced back to the first modern parallel to today's UFO phenomenon, the phantom airship sightings of 1896 and 1897. Perhaps the most crucial point about those sightings has also been the point most often missed: the airships observed in America's skies that year would not have been able to fly if somebody had actually built them. In place of effective propellers and gasoline motors—the technology that actually made working airships possible—the phantom airships were equipped with flapping wings and other technologies that were tried in the quest for viable air travel, and failed. On the other hand, the phantom airships were exact copies of what people at the time *thought* airships would look like.

A few historical studies from within the UFO community, notably Michael Busby's *Solving the 1897 Airship Mystery* (2004), have made heroic attempts to argue that the phantom airships were physically real craft produced by some secret airship program. Still, the evidence all points toward the opposite conclusion: that the airships of 1896 and 1897 were apparitions, reflecting the expectations and assumptions of witnesses, rather than actual dirigibles. This strongly suggests that the same conclusion applies to the alien spacecraft sighted from 1947 to the present, which have the same relationship to popular notions about extraterrestrial life in the twentieth century that the airships had to popular notions about air travel in the nineteenth.

The second point that finds a ready explanation if UFOs are apparitions, and faces much more difficult challenges if they are actual spacecraft, is the astonishing diversity of UFO experiences reported by credible witnesses. This has too rarely been taken into account in the UFO debate, but it's a factor of massive importance. Start with the most basic question: when people see an unidentified flying object, what does it look like? While the image of the metallic flying disk still monopolizes much of the discussion in UFO circles, disks of any sort account for a very modest percentage of all UFO sightings. Among UFOs that come close enough to observers to have their shapes clearly distinguished, spheres, ovoids, cylinders, triangles, rocket shapes, and football shapes are all at least as common as disks in the UFO sighting literature, and formless blobs of light are more common still.

Examine witnesses' accounts of UFO occupants and the same diversity appears again. An astonishing array of creatures have been reported in and around UFOs, ranging from ordinary humans through "Grays" to reptiles, robots, claw-handed giants, animated geometric shapes, and little green men, among many others. If UFOs are actually spacecraft from other worlds landing on Earth, their occupants include thousands of distinct species, flying just as many distinct kinds of spacecraft. It seems hard to credit the claim that our backwards planet, located in an out-of-the-way corner of a nondescript galaxy, would be of interest to so many alien civilizations, and harder still to ignore the close resemblance between so many of these sightings and the images of alien beings in twentieth-century science fiction literature and cinema. The vast majority of books written to defend the extraterrestrial finesse this problem by focusing on a handful of alien types—above all the "Grays"—and dismissing or ignoring the rest. Yet this won't do; if the phenomenon is real, all the evidence—not just the bits of it that support some preferred hypothesis—have to be taken into account.

The third point that supports the suggestion that UFOs are apparitions relates to the remarkable scarcity of any evidence for UFOs other than the testimony of human witnesses. In particular, technologies that ought to be providing clear evidence for the presence of alien spacecraft in Earth's skies, if that was actually the cause of the UFO phenomenon, do nothing of the kind. As I write these words, tens of thousands of webcams hooked up directly to the Internet provide views of scenes around the world, and millions of people carry cell phones equipped with digital cameras everywhere they go. If UFOs are material craft cruising through Earth's skies, a significant number of them should be showing up on webcams and having their pictures snapped by startled witnesses around the world. The fact that this is not happening poses a major challenge to the extraterrestrial hypothesis, and to all the other hardware hypotheses as well.

The lack of physical traces left behind by UFOs is another piece of evidence pointing in the same direction. Every kind of technology human beings have ever used, no matter how simple or complex, leaves traces of its presence behind. The more advanced a technology, in fact, the more likely it is to leave distinct traces, because the materials comprising an advanced technological device and the processes that make it work are both further from the ordinary workings of nature than those of simpler devices. If a jet airplane and a dugout canoe both crashed on the same desert island, for example, which one would leave more definite evidence of its presence? The same point would likely be even more true of extraterrestrial technologies far in advance of earthling science; we might well not be able to understand the traces, but solid physical evidence that something very strange had happened would not be hard to find.

Nor is anything so dramatic as a crash the only thing that would necessarily provide definite traces of an extraterrestrial presence on Earth. Look at the way physical traces of the human presence in outer space have proliferated each step of the way from Sputnik to the latest space shuttle launches. Astronauts drop spare parts on spacewalks, spacecraft spray out a dozen different kinds of rocket fuel into space, and pieces of hardware from stray screws to massive booster stages end up strewn throughout orbit. If the earth were being visited by extraterrestrials, they might well be less sloppy than our astronauts have been, but exploration is a notoriously messy process. Of the hundreds of UFO occupants seen repairing their craft on the ground over the years, for example, it's remarkable that not one has apparently ever dropped the alien equivalent of a screw or left a splash of saucer fuel on the ground.

Now of course it's quite possible to come up with any number of unfalsifiable ad hoc hypotheses to explain the lack of photographic, videographic, and physical evidence for the material reality of UFOs, and indeed this has been done. It has been claimed, for example, that the aliens have technology so advanced that they can interfere with our cameras at will and influence people's minds so that they don't think of taking pictures when a UFO is in sight. It has also been claimed that the U.S. government has managed to locate and hide away every scrap of evidence for an alien presence in Earth's skies. Arguments of this sort, however, rest on the same sort of circular logic diagrammed in chapter 5: they assume what they claim to prove, and explain away conflicting evidence instead of explaining it.

This last point has repeatedly been made by defenders of the null hypothesis, and for good reason. It's with the next step in their reasoning—the claim that since there is no serious physical evidence for the material reality of UFOs, no one is actually experiencing anything unusual at all—that they run off the rails. Proving that UFOs are apparitions is not the same thing as proving that they are the only kind of apparition for which the null hypothesis makes room, the kind caused by misinterpretation of ordinary objects.

Of course it's true that some reported UFO sightings are caused by ordinary objects such as airplanes and mirages, or are the product of hoaxes and rumor panics. Still, there are plenty of cases that cannot be shoehorned into this kind of explanation without doing violence to the facts. A very large number of UFO sightings involve experiences that clearly go beyond what can be explained by the ways the human mind and senses function under ordinary conditions. Once again, this does not mean those experiences were caused by spacecraft from other worlds; it does mean that some factor outside the null hypothesis has to be taken into account.

The Oz Factor

Consider the following case from Rochdale, England, collected and published by British UFO researcher Joseph Dormer.[139] The witness, an adult woman, and her elderly mother were at home near dusk on a November day. When the mother went to draw the curtains, she saw an unusual craft hovering in the sky nearby and called her daughter's

---

139. Barclay and Barclay 1993, 130–32.

attention to it. They both observed a big cylindrical craft, perhaps one hundred feet long, with portholes along its length. Figures in "silver space suits" moved about inside the craft. The witness and her mother both watched the craft for what seemed like some minutes, and both found themselves unable to speak or move during that time. Abruptly, the craft "vanished into thin air." The witness noted that an entire hour had gone by during the apparently short time she and her mother watched the craft. No other witnesses appear to have come forward to report sightings of the same craft.

Doubtless defenders of the extraterrestrial hypothesis might claim that a spaceship from a distant world visited Rochdale that evening, and used advanced technology to show itself only to two women. Equally, some defender of the null hypothesis might claim that the witness and her mother saw the planet Venus or some other conventional object, and somehow misinterpreted it as a hundred-foot-long cylindrical UFO. Still, at least three points about this sighting suggest that the witnesses observed an apparition rather than a material object.

First and most obviously, hundred-foot-long material objects made of metal and glass do not instantly vanish into thin air, while it's a commonplace of folklore and tradition that apparitions very often do. Second, nobody else in the town of Rochdale reported seeing the spacecraft that was apparently hovering above their roofs. When a hundred-foot-long blimp, for example, flies over a town during daylight hours, many people notice it. Why did only the two witnesses in question see such a remarkable object, if it was physically present? If it was an apparition, on the other hand, the entire account makes perfect sense.

The third point, however, is the crucial one. The witness and her mother were clearly in an altered state of consciousness during the experience, as shown by their inability to move or speak and the distortion of their time sense that made an hour pass by in what seemed like a few minutes. Evidence of changes in consciousness like this are extremely common in accounts of UFO close encounters, even in those collected by the most dogmatic believers in nuts-and-bolts spaceships from distant worlds.

UFO researcher Jenny Randles has coined the term "the Oz factor" for the very common report from UFO witnesses that they seemed to enter another reality just before sighting a mysterious object in the sky.[140] Many witnesses experience the same inability to speak or move as the two women in the Rochdale case, and subjective distortions of time are even more common in close encounters. Other signs of altered states of consciousness routinely reported by UFO witnesses include unexplained total silence, even in situations where sounds would otherwise be heard, and seeing other people who appear to be frozen in place or who pass by the scene of the encounter without apparently noticing anything.

These points have been cited by proponents of the neurological hypothesis, and it's entirely possible that in some cases—perhaps a significant number of cases—pulsing magnetic fields of the sort explored by Persinger's tests might have been involved in generating the altered states in question. Still, it's hardly necessary to bring in exotic physical factors when the human nervous system has been shown to enter altered states of consciousness quite readily all by itself.

In this light, for example, it's not exactly hard to account for the thousands of UFO sightings for whom the only witnesses are the passengers in a single car driving somewhere at night on a lonely road. "Highway hypnosis," induced in drivers by the monotony and sensory deprivation of road trips, is a common hazard faced by long-haul truckers and other people who drive long distances, especially at night. Many people have had the experience of suddenly realizing they are dozens of miles farther down the road than they thought they were, with no recollection of the road they have traveled; in some cases, dream imagery spills over into the process, leaving dim memories of improbable events to fill the gap. The relevance of this phenomenon to cases of the Barney and Betty Hill type should be obvious.

At least one other method for entering into altered states of consciousness has an even more precise relevance to the UFO phenomenon, though you have to know your way around occult literature to find it these days. Occultists spend a good deal of time learning to evoke apparitions at will, for a variety of reasons; crystal balls, magic mirrors, and

---

140. In Randles 1983.

similar tools have been mainstays of occultism for centuries because they foster the altered states of consciousness in which apparitions are most easily experienced. Still, there is another very widely practiced method for reaching the same state: *gazing up into the sky.*

The knowledge lectures of the Hermetic Order of the Golden Dawn, the most prestigious of the late-nineteenth-century occult orders, include detailed instructions in this practice. In order to gain "astral vision"—the Golden Dawn term for perceiving apparitions—the student gazed into the sky without blinking for extended periods, until he or she began to see apparitions.[141] The same technique was a matter of widespread public knowledge back in the Middle Ages and Renaissance, when occult traditions were more widely studied than they are today, and such literary classics as Richard Burton's *Anatomy of Melancholy* discuss it as a matter of course.[142] The popular slogan "Watch the skies!" takes on a notably different meaning in this context.

Many other factors can play a role in fostering altered states of consciousness in which apparitions are seen. The core point that has to be grasped, though, is that UFO apparitions can be produced by *any* method of entering into an altered state of consciousness. Because apparitions take much of their content from the mind of the person who perceives them, the presence of colorful and emotionally charged UFO-related imagery from popular culture in the minds of most people nowadays guarantees that whenever people slip into an altered state, one of the things that frequently results is a visionary or hallucinatory experience that draws on the rich fund of UFO imagery.

Still, the most significant factor at work in the modern UFO phenomenon that is known to make witnesses experience apparitions is one that many UFO researchers themselves apply to people who believe they have interacted with aliens from other worlds. This factor is, of course, hypnosis, and its role in creating the UFO abduction experience of the last three decades offers a good look at the mechanisms underlying the entire phenomenon.

---

141. Regardie 1971, vol. 4, 104.

142. Burton 2001, 183..

Hypnosis, Memory, and Fantasy

Although a small minority of people who report being abducted claim to remember their experiences without help, the great majority of cases rely on memories recovered under hypnosis. The theory is that abductees have their memories more or less completely blotted out by an alien technology, but that hypnosis allows those memories to be recovered completely and accurately. These claims echo themes that have been repeated endlessly in popular culture, but there are at least two glaring problems with them. On the one hand, they beg a flotilla of questions about the supposed alien technology that hypnotism is said to overcome; on the other, they are based on a completely false picture of what hypnosis is and what it can do.

According to the extraterrestrial interpretation of abduction accounts, to begin with, aliens from some distant planet are secretly abducting millions of human beings for purposes of their own, and then using technologies centuries or millennia in advance of ours to erase the memories of the abductions from the minds of their victims. This memory erasure, however, is so weak and impermanent that an amateur hypnotist with no professional training or relevant experience can punch through it in a matter of minutes and reveal all the details the aliens are apparently trying to conceal. While hypnosis has a mixed track record in every other legal and therapeutic context—like any other technique, it has its failures as well as its successes—it is apparently omnipotent in the face of an alien technology far beyond anything humans can even begin to duplicate. If the abduction literature is anything to go by, whenever somebody who has had a "missing time" experience undergoes hypnosis with an abduction researcher, a detailed account of alien abduction spills out within the first few sessions.

Once again, of course, it's possible to come up with an unfalsifiable ad hoc hypothesis to explain all this. It might be argued, for example, that the aliens know all about our methods of hypnosis, expected some of their abductees to go to hypnotherapists and spill the beans, and factored this into their plans in advance. As before, though, this is circular logic that assumes what it is trying to prove.

More generally, it's a misconception to think of hypnosis as a way to produce some sort of "instant replay" of suppressed memories. Even a brief survey of the professional literature on hypnosis reveals a very different picture. Hypnosis can be an effective way to reduce anxiety, and therapists have been using it successfully for more than a century to help patients deal with memories that are ordinarily too stressful to call back to mind. Memories recalled by patients in hypnotic regression, however, are consistently mixed with liberal helpings of distortion and fantasy.[143] This doesn't limit their clinical value—a fantasy can be a powerful vehicle for releasing pent-up emotions and catalyzing positive change—but it does limit their value as evidence for anything outside the therapeutic setting.

This difficulty isn't simply the product of incompetent hypnotherapy. It's built into the mechanism of hypnosis itself, because the same processes in the mind and brain that let hypnosis quell anxiety and enhance suggestibility also undercut the mind's ability to distinguish between memory and imagination. Worse, this confusion stays in place after hypnosis is over. The professional literature discusses this problem in great detail.

Surveying the uses and pitfalls of hypnotic memory retrieval in criminal cases, for example, Roy Udolf's classic *Handbook of Hypnosis for Professionals* warns, "The accuracy of information obtained in this manner [that is, by hypnotic regression] is, of course, open to serious question. It would be unsuitable for use as evidence, for it is likely to be a mixture of indeterminate proportions of fact and fantasy. The real value of the method is its ability to develop leads which may ultimately help uncover independent evidence."[144] Dr. Martin Orne, a professor of psychiatry and hypnotist who has worked on high-profile criminal cases such as the murder trial of "Hillside Strangler" Kenneth Bianchi, similarly cautions, "At the present stage of scientific knowledge, we cannot distinguish between veridical recall and pseudomemories elicited during hypnosis without prior knowledge or truly independent proof."[145]

---

143.   See, for example Udolf 1981, 131–33.

144.   Udolf 1981, 243.

145.   Orne, et al., 1988, 55.

The "Satanic ritual abuse" panic of the 1980s and 1990s shows how this phenomenon can feed on itself and snowball into an international phenomenon.[146] In the early 1980s, a handful of individuals went public claiming that they had been victimized by Satanic cults that bred babies for sacrifice. Most of these claims came straight out of popular culture—notably the 1968 hit movie *Rosemary's Baby*, which contained nearly every theme of the emerging panic—but they were taken seriously by networks of social workers and evangelical Christians, who had their own motives for believing such claims. Hypnotherapists played a central role in all this by recovering supposed memories of Satanic ritual abuse. The result was a classic rumor panic in which hundreds of families were torn apart and dozens of people spent time behind bars on charges supported only by the testimony of their alleged victims, extracted under hypnosis.

Abduction researchers have repeatedly denied that the phenomenon they study shares any significant common ground with the Satanic ritual abuse frenzy. Leading abduction proponent Budd Hopkins, for example, addressed similarities between UFO abductions and Satanic ritual abuse in a 2000 essay and dismissed the parallels as "specious."[147] From nearly any perspective other than Hopkins', though, the two phenomena are effectively identical.

Both raise the specter of a vast but unseen epidemic of physical and sexual violations carried out in secret, involving repeated abuse of selected individuals who suffer loss of memory as a result. In both cases, the phenomenon centers on reproduction—abductees who claim to have given birth to human-alien hybrids have their exact parallel in Satanic-abuse survivors who claim to have been used as "breeders" to produce babies for sacrifices to the devil. In both cases, the phenomenon copies every detail of fictional narratives exploited to the hilt by popular culture for many decades—compare the claims made in the Satanic abuse furor of the 1980s with the plot of *Rosemary's Baby*, for example, and you'll find an exact equivalent of the parallels between UFO abduction claims and the science fiction of previous decades. In both

---

146. See Victor 1993 and Ellis 2000 for good accounts of the Satanic ritual abuse furor.

147. Hopkins 2000, 236.

cases, the only unambiguous evidence for the phenomenon that has ever been presented consists of the testimony of alleged victims, most of whose memories have been extracted by hypnosis.

Abduction researchers have argued that unlike Satanic ritual abuse therapists, they do not use leading questions, though this has been challenged by outside witnesses. They also point out that abductees undergoing recall can't simply be made to remember whatever the therapist wants them to remember. Abduction therapists routinely use "false leads"—that is, leading questions that contradict some of the consistent patterns in the abduction experience—and report that authentic abductees reject the false leads. An example cited by Budd Hopkins is typical: the therapist asks the abductee who is reliving the abduction experience if he or she can see the legs of the examination table. In nearly all abduction reports, the examination table has no legs—it is either a pedestal table, a solid block, or a floating slab—and abductees consistently correct the inaccurate suggestion, rather than confabulating table legs.[148]

While the role of hypnotist expectations in shaping hypnotic experience can involve cues a good deal more subtle than this, Hopkins' point is a valid one. Thomas Bullard's two-volume survey of the abduction experience similarly argues that abduction accounts contain a wealth of consistent features that remain constant from investigator to investigator, again suggesting that whatever is going on isn't simply a function of investigators asking leading questions and getting the answers they expect.[149] Clearly, the experiences of abductees draw on something other than their own fantasies and the expectations of investigators. Proponents of the extraterrestrial hypothesis argue that this "something" must be the behavior of alien spacecraft and their crews, but there's another source much closer to hand—twentieth-century popular culture.

Abducted by Popular Culture?

Every detail of the entire abduction phenomenon, in fact, can be traced straight back to modern media portrayals of abduction by aliens. This shows up in hard numbers as well as more subtle measures. Abduction

---

148.   Hopkins 2000, 220.

149.   Bullard 1987.

reports were almost unheard of before John Fuller's *The Interrupted Journey* gave the phenomenon its core narrative. After 1966, when Fuller's book first saw print, a trickle of abduction reports reached investigators; Dr. Leo Sprinkle, one of the most active (and controversial) researchers in the UFO abduction field, encountered only six cases during the decade following Fuller's book. The 1975 TV movie *The UFO Incident*, a docudrama based on Fuller's book, brought a modest flurry of new reports, and Sprinkle found another six cases over the next two years. In 1977, the phenomenal success of *Close Encounters of the Third Kind* sent the entire process into overdrive; the two years following its premiere brought Sprinkle eighteen additional cases. Another study found a total of only fifty abduction cases cited in UFO literature from 1947 to 1976, while one hundred more were reported in 1977 and 1978 alone.[150]

The same media events had equally striking effects on the way aliens were experienced by abductees and others. *The UFO Incident* portrayed the aliens who kidnapped the Hills as very short, gray-skinned, and hairless, with huge slanted eyes. These weren't the aliens Betty Hill described—hers stood fully five feet tall, and had black hair and long noses "like Jimmy Durante's"—but after *Close Encounters of the Third Kind* borrowed the same image for its aliens, it became an American icon, and by the early 1980s the great majority of abduction reports featured small gray aliens with slanting dark eyes.

The possibility that popular culture could function as a source for abduction experiences has of course been challenged by abduction researchers. Thus in *The Threat* (1998), one of the most strident of the "bad alien" books published so far, historian and UFO researcher David Jacobs argued that his horror-movie scenario—an imminent alien takeover of the earth using abductees and their hybrid offspring as a fifth column—can't simply be pigeonholed as a reflection of popular culture. "My conclusion that alien integration will soon bring about dramatic social change bears no relationship to other more familiar apocalyptic visions," he insists. "I am aware of my conclusion's superficial similarities to science fiction or millennialism, but the evidence does not warrant this link."[151]

---

150.   Peebles 1994, 234–35.

151.   Jacobs 1998, 255.

The problem here is that the relationships Jacobs disclaims can be found all through the material he presents, and the similarities he dismisses out of hand are the opposite of superficial. Every detail of Jacobs' theory, in fact, surfaced in twentieth-century science fiction literature and cinema long before it began to be reported by abductees. To begin with, the idea that aliens can interbreed with human beings—while it's a tour de force of biological improbability[152]—has been a staple of science fiction since the beginning of the genre, featuring in everything from such serious SF stories as Roger Zelazny's 1963 classic "A Rose for Ecclesiastes" to classic kitsch B-movies such as *Devil Girl from Mars* (1954) and *Mars Needs Women* (1967). The idea that aliens could take over the world using implant-equipped human beings as their proxies has at least as long a track record in the genre—one popular young-adult work on that theme, John Christopher's *Tripods* trilogy, was among the books we were assigned to read in my junior high school English classes in the 1970s. The role of alien-human hybrids as a fifth column echoes John Wyndham's *The Midwich Cuckoos* along with scores of other works, and so on.

Nor are detailed accounts of classic alien abductions lacking in popular culture from the early twentieth century. To cite only one out of hundreds, a sequence from the comic strip *Buck Rogers in the 25th Century*, published in 1930, has a character abducted by a spherical spacecraft and kept in an "electro-hypnotic trance" on a classic UFO examination table without visible legs, while the alien crew probed her mind and memories.[153] (Look at examination tables in science fiction films and TV shows, in fact, and you'll see very few tables with legs.) Since the only evidence for Jacobs' theory consists of abductees whose memories fit his "bad alien" model—nearly all of them extracted under hypnosis, and all of them without exception subject to cultural influence—the evidence warrants exactly the link he rejects.

It's also not irrelevant that the split in the abductee research community between "good alien" and "bad alien" scenarios precisely dupli-

---

152. Alien life forms would inevitably have a biochemistry radically different from ours, and creating a human-alien hybrid would be more complex than trying to crossbreed a human being with a petunia. It would be much easier for a civilization with genetic technology advanced enough to do this to synthesize the genetic material it needed directly, without having to abduct sperm and egg donors from a (to them) totally alien species.

153. See the panels reprinted in Lewis 2000, 57.

cates the divide in contemporary apocalyptic thought discussed at length by scholars such as Philip Lamy.[154] Lamy points out that in modern times the classic Christian discourse of apocalypse has given way to "fractured" forms that stress either the hope of the New Jerusalem or the fear of the advent of Antichrist, but in either case replace the furniture of traditional religious myth with images out of various modern secular mythologies. The prophecies of imminent salvation or doom via UFO that have emerged from the abductee movement share another feature with other modern apocalyptic traditions: the "Great Change" they predict is as inevitable in theory as it is endlessly postponed in practice.

The role of popular culture as a source of hypnotically obtained UFO accounts was pointed up forcefully in a study carried out in 1977 by Alvin Lawson, a professor at California State University at Long Beach. Lawson used surveys to select a pool of student volunteers who had no interest in UFOs and whose only exposure to UFO lore came from the mass media. He hypnotized them, told them they were being abducted by a UFO, and had them recount their experiences during the imaginary abduction. The students produced a range of abduction narratives very similar to the ones reported by "real" abductees, and—though Lawson either did not notice or did not mention this—equally similar to the science fiction abductions already mentioned.[155]

Abduction researchers have insisted that important differences remain between their own results and those obtained by Lawson, but differences just as great exist between what today's researchers consider standard abduction accounts and older cases such as the Hill and Hickson-Parker cases.[156] It would be enlightening to see if the differences Lawson found would still exist if his study were repeated today, now that the standard abductee narrative has become a widespread theme in popular culture.

Nor do all abduction accounts make sense in terms of the extraterrestrial hypothesis. The close encounter of Constable Alan Godfrey is a

---

154.   Lamy 1998.

155.   Lawson 1980.

156.   In place of the ubiquitous "Grays" of current abduction narratives, to cite only one difference, Betty Hill described aliens with black hair and "noses like Jimmy Durante's," while Charles Hickson and Calvin Parker described wrinkled, neckless creatures with crab claws in place of hands, and ears and noses that extended straight out to points.

case in point.[157] In the early hours of November 29, 1980, Godfrey was on patrol in his car near the small town of Todmorden in England, looking for strayed cows, when he saw a luminous saucer in the air, and observed it long enough to make a sketch. Suddenly he realized he was some distance away, still in his police car, and the saucer was gone. Under hypnosis, he recalled a classic UFO abduction—except that the captain of the saucer was a Jewish man named Yoseph, dressed in the clothing of the ancient Israelites, and the saucer's crew consisted of a group of dwarfs and a large black dog. Anomalous in terms of the UFO myth, this last crew member is anything but out of place in the wider context of British folklore, in which spectral black dogs are among the most commonly reported apparitions in legend and contemporary experience alike.[158]

Another example from the records of UFO abductions makes the same point. On August 22, 1952, Cecil Michael of Bakersfield, California, had a close encounter with a flying saucer and was abducted by its strange-looking occupants.[159] This was early in the contactee movement, when guided tours of space were apparently a common experience among those picked up by flying saucers, but Michael was headed for a destination George Adamski never visited. The saucer deposited him in hell, where he had a conversation with Satan himself before being rescued and returned to his home by Jesus Christ. Here an older set of culturally powerful imagery—that of the Christian faith—filled the slot more often occupied by science fiction.

The annals of the UFO phenomenon contain thousands of such anomalous cases. From the point of view of most of the popular hypotheses about the phenomenon, they are a profound embarrassment, and have thus been tucked safely out of sight in most discussions of the subject. From any broader perspective, though, they offer a crucial key to understanding.

It takes circular logic to argue that one set of imagery—say, the set derived from twentieth-century science fiction, which defines abduction as the work of alien astronauts—should be accepted automati-

---

157.   Barclay and Barclay 1993, 155–56.

158.   See, for example, Bord 1980.

159.   Michael 1971.

cally as true, while all others ought to be dismissed as deception or delusion. Believers in the demonological hypothesis have argued on identical grounds that experiences such as Cecil Michael's represent the true shape of the UFO phenomenon, while other accounts simply reflect Satanic illusions, and their arguments stand the test of logic as well or, rather, as poorly as those of the extraterrestrial hypothesis.

Otherworld Journeys

All this has provided plenty of ammunition for proponents of the null hypothesis, who have argued along the lines just given that the entire abduction phenomenon is an artifact of the limitations of hypnotherapy and the influence of mass hysteria. The one problem with this dismissal is that the same phenomenon has parallels just as striking with another phenomenon with a worldwide distribution throughout recorded history.

Consider the following account of an abduction recorded in South Dakota early in the twentieth century. The abductee, a nine-year-old boy at the time of the abduction, came down with a sudden unexplained illness that left him too weak to walk. While lying in his bed one day, he saw two humanoid figures descending toward him from the sky, each of them carrying a rodlike object with electrical sparks coming from one end. The two beings called to the boy and told him to come with them, and he felt himself rising from the bed, feeling "very light." Something "looking like a small cloud" descended to pick up the three of them. Once on board, the boy described looking down at his home from above. The rest of the story is considerably less like today's abductions, because the boy grew up to be the Lakota holy man Black Elk, and the thunder beings who came for him took him on a medicine journey that became the source of his powers.[160]

Otherworld journeys of this sort can be found throughout the world's folklore, theology, and occult traditions. Certain themes that run through these journeys also play a prominent role in the abduction phenomenon. Countless shamans, saints, and visionaries, as well as abductees, all report that their experiences begin with the arrival of one or more entities, nonhuman but usually humanoid, who extract

---

160. For the complete account of Black Elk's "abduction," see Neihardt 1988, 20–47.

them from their ordinary circumstances and take them into a place where ordinary rules no longer seem to apply. The "Oz factor," with its pervasive sense of entering an alternate reality, also appears in otherworld journeys of every kind.

The relationship between apparitions and abductions is pointed up in even more detail by cases in which the "abduction" clearly took place in the realm of the mind. In one famous abduction case, the 1973 Maureen Puddy abduction,[161] the physical body of the abductee remained in ordinary reality under the observation of two UFO researchers while she experienced an abduction. This parallels one of the most common themes in shamanic and visionary experience, in which the body of the shaman lies inert while he or she undergoes strange experiences in a not-quite-physical place.

Body modification is another common feature. Siberian shamans in their initiatory trances experience having their organs removed and replaced with new, magical organs, just as abductees undergo baroque medical procedures and experience having implants placed in their bodies. Just as visionaries around the world have claimed that they receive spiritual gifts from their experiences, too, a sizeable number of abductees believe that they have gained psychic powers in the aftermath of their abductions.

Still, these cross-cultural features are only half the story. Themes and expectations drawn from the experiencer's own culture play at least as important a role in structuring otherworld journeys. In medieval Europe, visionaries described visits to heaven, purgatory, and hell and reported encounters with God, angels, and devils;[162] in traditional Japan, figures and locales from Buddhist and Shinto mythology filled the same role;[163] in Black Elk's vision, that role was filled by the thunder beings and sacred mountains of the Lakota; and in abductee accounts, it's filled by the spaceships and aliens of today's UFO faith.

In his study of flying saucers as a modern myth, Carl Jung drew attention to exactly these points in a discussion of Orfeo Angelucci,

---

161. Magee 1978.

162. Zaleski 1987 provides a useful summary.

163. See Blacker 1975.

one of the more popular contactees of the 1950s.[164] According to Angelucci, he first saw a UFO in 1946, almost a year before the phenomenon caught the public imagination. In the banner year of 1952 he encountered another UFO, a glowing red disk that nobody else could see, and he entered into a telepathic conversation with its occupants, a pair of supernaturally beautiful and wise human beings who instructed him about humanity's place in the cosmos.

Angelucci had two other contacts the same year, and received further mystical teachings that drew heavily on Theosophy and other forms of popular occultism.[165] In 1953 he spent a week in a somnambulistic trance, after which he reported traveling in the spirit to the planetoid home of his teachers Orion and Lyra. In the wake of these experiences he quit his job as a mechanic, became a teacher of popular occultism, published a book titled *The Secret of the Saucers* (1955), and remained one of the leading figures on the contactee circuit well into the 1960s.

Jung pointed out that every detail of Angelucci's narrative has exact parallels all through the literature of spiritual experience. From the first appearance of otherworldly powers in his life, through his initial contact, his period of instruction, and his trance journey to the Otherworld, Angelucci's story is a classic account of the process of shamanic initiation. The only detail that differentiates it from the nearly identical stories of Siberian and Native American shamans is that Angelucci's Otherworld is found in outer space.

It's traditional to call on the evidence of these visionary experiences to support claims of the reality of the cultural forms they echo—preachers in medieval Europe, for example, made much use of contemporary accounts of otherworld journeys to argue for the reality of heaven, hell, Satan, and the like—and UFO researchers who use abduction accounts to back up the extraterrestrial hypothesis are thus in good company. Still, many of the cultures that pay close attention to these visionary experiences draw more from them than confirmation of an existing worldview.

---

164. Jung 1978, 112–20. See also Reeve and Reeve 1957, 222–32.

165. It is interesting that Jung, who had a substantial knowledge of occult traditions, seems to have missed the popular occultism permeating Angelucci's narrative—for example, Angelucci's identification of Jesus as a "Lord of the Flame," a term straight out of Blavatsky's *The Secret Doctrine*.

Thus Black Elk's people, for example, embraced his vision and those of other visionaries of the same period in an effort to make sense of the catastrophic changes that followed the white invasion of the Great Plains.

They were by no means unwise to do so. Jung's essay on flying saucers points up the role that visionary experience can have in pointing up the unresolved issues and cultural struggles of an age. For that matter, it may not be accidental that during a period when the abortion issue has been a flashpoint throughout American culture, hundreds of people have experienced brutal reproductive surgery at the hands of beings who look remarkably like human fetuses.

Thus the epidemic of abduction experiences provides dubious support at best for the claim that flesh-and-blood aliens from a distant world are visiting Earth. Rather, it finds its meaning in the cultural crisis of the present time, a crisis that has seen the decline or outright collapse of most traditional forms of spirituality alongside the failure of rationalist materialism to make good its claim to take religion's place. In other times, the disintegration of familiar religious forms has sparked the rise of new spiritualities at the hands of individuals whose lives and experiences closely parallel those of shamans, prophets, and mystics around the world. The contactees, abductees, and witnesses of close encounters may well count in these same ranks.

The Shamanic Dimension

This suggestion gains powerful support from research conducted by Dr. Alex Keul and Ken Phillips into the background of UFO witnesses. The Anamnesis Protocol, a systematic questionnaire given to UFO witnesses, people who have experienced other strange occurrences, and control groups who have had no unusual experiences at all, has shown consistent, statistically significant psychological differences between people who experience strange things and people who do not.[166]

UFO witnesses are not, despite the claims of null hypothesis supporters, any more likely to believe that UFOs are from outer space, to be members of religious groups, or to be interested in the paranormal. Rather, compared to control groups, people who report a

---

166. See, for example, Barclay and Barclay 1993, 46–49.

close encounter with a UFO are significantly more likely to be dissatisfied with their lives, to have problems with nervousness, to recall their dreams, to have had flying dreams or dreams about UFOs, and to report experiences of ESP, especially after their UFO encounter. These may seem like a grab bag of unrelated psychological traits, but they are nothing of the kind. In cultures around the world, these are recognized as among the hallmarks of a potential shaman.

For most of the last two thousand years, people with the distinctive talent for this kind of experience have had very few options in the Western world. From the early Middle Ages up to the first stirrings of the modern world, those whose visions happened to match up well enough with the religious orthodoxies of their time ended up in monasteries and convents, where their experiences were treated as signs of sanctity, while others risked execution as heretics and witches. More recently, with the hardening of prejudices against all forms of altered states of consciousness, those who had such experiences learned to hide that fact from others, or landed in mental institutions where they could count on being drugged and electroshocked into a semblance of normality.

In societies less hostile to the human talent for visionary experience, by contrast, such people typically find a valued place as shamans, medicine persons, mystics, and the like. Most cultures outside the modern industrial West have a wealth of traditional lore and technique that can be used by visionaries to help direct their gifts into constructive channels. The apparitions that stalk through the dreams and nightmares of a society can serve as a kind of early warning system for social stresses. Just as psychotherapists elicit the dreams of their patients in order to open the door to insights not otherwise accessible to the conscious mind, the waking dreams of a society's visionaries can cast an unexpected light onto the popular imagination and collective consciousness of their time.

It's for this reason that in many other societies—ancient Rome and imperial China come to mind—reports of strange occurrences, apparitions, and visions were assiduously collected as a way to track subtle changes in public opinion and the relationship between the people and their government. No Roman augur or Chinese mandarin would have been deaf to the messages of sixty years of UFO-related apparitions as they mirrored back hopes of world peace, fears of nuclear holocaust, deep ambivalences toward technology and scientific progress and, most recently, a massive loss of faith in governmental institutions and a sense of widening schism separating politicians from their constituents. To the extent that the endless disputes between partisans of the extraterrestrial and null hypotheses have kept these messages from being heard, we are all arguably the poorer.

In the modern industrial world, the task of watching the ebb and flow of imagery in the collective imagination has been left by default in the hands of occult lodges and secret societies. Disciplines for experiencing apparitions, as mentioned earlier in this chapter, form one important branch of occultism.[167] Another, rarely discussed in modern occult literature but present in the writings of such classic occult authors as Giordano Bruno and Cornelius Agrippa, consists of using various subtle means to shape the visionary dimension of human experience. Historian Ioan Couliano has pointed out that modern advertising, seen through the lens of traditional occult philosophy, is a form of magic using emotionally charged imagery to shape people's thoughts and behavior[168]—and the history of the UFO phenomenon arguably shows definite signs of the same process at work.

Thus the fact that occultists such as Meade Layne and Harold Sherman appear to have predicted the beginning of the UFO phenomenon in advance, and played such a significant role in its early days, may be more important than it appears. On the one hand, they may have been responding to decades of science fiction imagery a little before their neighbors did; on the other hand, they may have been using that imagery to accomplish purposes of their own.

This latter possibility gains credence from the fact that at least one other organized group can be shown to have used the UFO phenomenon deliberately to shape public opinion. The existence of this group and its involvement in the UFO controversy are a matter of public record, and its deliberate use of UFO reports as a matter of deception has been made public more than once. The organization in question is the United States military.

---

167. See Greer 2007, 215–35, for examples.

168. Couliano 1984.

eight

The Last Secret of the Cold War

As Jung pointed out presciently in 1958, there is a world of difference between the physical basis for UFO sightings and the extraordinary wealth of mythic imagery and speculation that has been loaded onto a collection of moving lights in the sky.[169] This distinction has rarely been grasped, not least because both the extraterrestrial hypothesis and the null hypothesis lump all UFO experiences together as a single thing with a single cause, but it's crucial to any real understanding of the UFO phenomenon.

A large percentage of all UFO sightings, as shown in chapter 7, have the distinctive characteristics of apparitions. They appear to individuals or very small groups of people in altered states of consciousness, violate the laws of nature that normally govern material objects, vanish without leaving material traces, and closely reflect psychologically potent imagery in the popular culture of their time. They form a feedback loop that turns the images of popular culture into the raw material of experience, reflecting the imaginary aliens of science fiction back into the collective

---

169. Jung 1978, 107–9.

imagination and allowing three generations of UFO researchers to convince themselves that UFOs must be alien spacecraft from other worlds, because their appearance and actions mirror back to us the way we expect alien spacecraft to look and behave.

Yet it's important to remember that not all UFOs fit these parameters. Some UFOs are seen at the same time by large numbers of people, who show no signs of participating in an altered state of consciousness and agree in detail about what they saw; some UFOs behave like material objects, show up on film and radar screens, and have apparently left physical traces behind. These cannot be classed as apparitions without using the same sort of circular logic criticized elsewhere in this book. They represent the other side of the UFO puzzle, the physical basis around which so much imagery and mythology has gathered over the years.

In all probability, that physical basis is highly diverse. One part of it consists of unusual natural phenomena well understood by science such as parhelia, meteors, and ball lightning, and another is clearly due to conventional aircraft and spacecraft misinterpreted in various ways. Still, at least two other things need to be added to the list.

The first almost certainly consists of a natural phenomenon not yet known to science, possibly associated with tectonic stress in earth faults, that produces glowing blobs of light that can be photographed and seen by multiple witnesses. Researchers into the geophysical hypothesis such as Michael Persinger and Paul Devereux, working on a shoestring budget with very little help from the wider scientific community, have gathered an impressive body of evidence that needs to be taken into account in any explanation of the UFO phenomenon. Whatever the lights turn out to be, there's every reason to think that a well-funded research program into them might turn up results of significant scientific interest, and could also provide a solid explanation to one set of sightings identified with the UFO phenomenon.

The second thing that needs to go onto the list has much less to teach from a scientific point of view, though it could redefine some parts of the last sixty years or so of history, and it is only a secret because most people on all sides of the UFO controversy have been looking the other way. It broke out into plain sight in 1997, with the publication of a declassified internal study of the CIA's involvement in the UFO controversy by National Reconnaissance Office historian Gerald K. Haines.

Behind the Veil of Secrecy

Most of Haines' study covered ground familiar to those who knew the history of U.S. government involvement in the phenomenon. In the midst of the article, however, Haines dropped a bombshell:

> *According to later estimates from CIA officials who worked on the U-2 project and the OXCART (A-12/SR-71 Blackbird) project, over half of all UFO reports from the late 1950s through the 1960s were accounted for by manned reconnaissance flights (namely, the U-2) over the United States. This led the Air Force to make misleading and deceptive statements to the public in order to allay public fears and protect an extraordinarily sensitive national security project.[170]*

A detailed study of the U-2 program published the following year repeated these claims and included more details.[171] The Lockheed U-2 was a high-tech spyplane with a cruising altitude above 60,000 feet. Commercial airliners in the 1950s flew between 10,000 and 20,000 feet, and publicly admitted military aircraft in those years reached maximum altitude well below 50,000 feet; nobody, except those informed of the top-secret U-2 program, knew that any aircraft existed that could fly more than 10,000 feet higher. Thus one of the first results of the U-2 program was an upsurge in the number of UFO sightings.

Today's U.S. reconnaissance craft are painted black, but the original U-2s were unpainted, and their aluminum wings and bodies reflected sunlight strongly. Thus hundreds of commercial airline crews flying from west to east before dawn, or from east to west after sunset, were treated to the sight of bright sunlight reflecting off something 40,000 feet or more above them. Many of them reported the sightings as unidentified flying objects—which, of course, is exactly what they were, to anybody outside

---

170. Haines 1997, 73.

171. Pendlow and Welzenbach 1998.

the U-2 program. When those sightings were reported to the Air Force, according to the CIA sources, Project Blue Book staff contacted the CIA to check the sightings against U-2 flight logs. Since the U-2 program was, in Haines' words, "an extraordinarily sensitive national security project," the Air Force then came up with false explanations for the sightings to cover up what was actually going on.

What makes this even more interesting is that these were not the only UFO sightings that clearly involved a secret military program and a coverup to protect it. At least one of the classic UFO sightings, the Mantell case of 1948, falls into the same category. The UFO chased by Mantell, shaped like an ice cream cone with a red upper end, was a Skyhook balloon, at the time a secret technology being tested for espionage and aerial reconnaissance purposes.[172] The Air Force's initial claim in the Mantell case was that the pilot had been chasing the planet Venus. Not until several years later, when the Skyhook program was declassified, was the actual nature of the craft that caused Mantell's death revealed.

Nor was the United States the only participant in these schemes. A useful article by space scientist and null hypothesis supporter James Oberg documents the use of the same stratagem by the former Soviet Union.[173] On more than ten occasions in 1976, witnesses across a large swath of the southwestern USSR watched a huge unknown craft, shaped like a luminous crescent half a mile wide, moving across the sky from west to east. These sightings were listed as definite unknowns in a 1979 report on UFOs issued with the official sanction of the Soviet Academy of Sciences.

In point of fact, as Oberg documents, these "UFOs" correlated exactly to tests of the Fractional Orbital Bombardment System (FOBS), a secret Soviet nuclear weapons program meant to drop warheads on targets from low Earth orbit. The crescent shape, it turned out, was caused by the shockwave generated when the FOBS reentered Earth's atmosphere, and the Soviet government labeled them

---

172. See Stehling and Beller 1962 for the Skyhook program.

173. Oberg 1982.

UFO sightings in an attempt to distract attention from them. It was a clever ploy, and one used on both sides of the Cold War.

"Something is seen, but one doesn't know what."[174] With these words, Jung defined the UFO phenomenon in his time, and the definition still holds. A point that has too often been missed, however, is that there can be more than one reason for something unknown to remain unknown. Some truths are hidden because they are naturally difficult to get at, others because the tools and ideas used to get at them prove inadequate to the task. Still others, though, are hidden intentionally. UFO researcher Jacques Vallee has pointed out at length that the UFO phenomenon is deliberately deceptive, and in such a case the obvious conclusions may be far from the truth.[175]

Yet the strategy of secrecy that underlies such campaigns of disinformation remains poorly understood by all sides in the UFO debate, and without a sense of how that strategy works, the phenomenon remains an insoluble puzzle. Since the earliest days of the phenomenon, accusations that the Air Force or some other official body knew more about the UFO mystery than they were telling have filled the popular press. Now, after six decades of speculation, the contemporary UFO myth is at least as much about government secrecy as it is about spacecraft from other worlds.

It's hard to dispute the suggestion that there was indeed a campaign of government secrecy surrounding the UFO phenomenon. The evidence amassed by numerous researchers in a half century's worth of books, notably Richard Dolan's admirably documented if biased *UFOs and the National Security State*, present compelling evidence that the Air Force and the U.S. intelligence community had a continuing involvement in the phenomenon from its earliest days, and deliberately shaped public opinion on the subject. The question that has too rarely been asked, though, is whether something other than alien spacecraft might have been concealed by that coverup. Many things

---

174. Jung 1978, 6.

175. Vallee 1979, 196–201.

can be hidden beneath a blanket of secrecy—a lesson taught by one of military history's classic campaigns of secrecy and deception.

Bodyguard of Lies

In 1943, as the tide of the Second World War turned against the Axis, all eyes—not least those of the German high command—focused on the inevitable Allied invasion of Nazi-occupied Europe. Northern France, just across the English Channel from the massed British and American armies in England, was the logical target. Still, the Wehrmacht lacked the resources to fortify every inch of the Channel coast. If the Germans could anticipate the site of the Allied landing, the commanders of both sides knew, the invasion attempt would likely fail and Germany could win a dramatic reprieve. If the Allies managed a landing in some unexpected place, on the other hand, the invasion would almost certainly win a foothold, and the Wehrmacht faced disaster, caught between the Anglo-American armies and the Russian juggernaut slowly advancing from the east. The huge and capable German espionage machine thus turned every available resource to figuring out the invasion plan in advance.

The Allied commanders knew this perfectly well. They also realized that no matter how good their security might be, information was bound to leak out. Their response was Operation Bodyguard, one of the most audacious campaigns of trickery in the history of warfare.[176]

Under the command of General George Patton, a massive military force—the First U.S. Army Group—was stationed in the southeastern counties of England, just across the narrowest point in the Channel from Calais in northern France. Dozens of new camps rose in the area to hold the invasion force, complete with massed tanks, artillery, trucks, and munitions dumps. All this took place under the tight secrecy befitting preparations for the greatest amphibious assault of the war. Meanwhile, Allied reconnaissance aircraft buzzed around the beaches near Calais like inquisitive bees, agents of the French Resis-

---

176. The following account of Operation Bodyguard is based on Brown 1976.

tance scoped out German emplacements in the same area, and all the other preparations for the coming invasion took place.

The remarkable thing about all these preparations is that the First U.S. Army Group did not, in fact, exist. Patton's headquarters was a minor division headquarters reworked to look much more important than it was. The camps allegedly holding his troops were staffed with small teams of actors instructed to make themselves look as busy and numerous as possible; the tanks, artillery, and trucks were dummies specially manufactured to look convincing at a distance or from the air; the munitions bunkers were empty. The whole campaign of lies was orchestrated by a special task force reporting directly to the Allied high command and veiled in the same total secrecy that shrouded the Allies' atomic-bomb program at the same time.

What made the deception perfect was that Patton's phantom army was only the most plausible of a series of false stories spread whole-sale through every available channel. Bits and pieces of fake intelligence suggesting landings all along the coasts of occupied Europe made their way to German ears. Operation Fortitude created an imaginary British Fourth Army in Scotland, preparing for an invasion of Norway, while Operation Zeppelin conjured up equally fictional forces in North Africa preparing for an invasion of the Balkans. Meanwhile, the real invasion force filtered into dispersed camps more than a hundred miles farther west, across from the invasion's real target—the beaches of Normandy.

As history shows, Operation Bodyguard succeeded brilliantly. The German high command assembled the data available to them, sifted the apparent wheat from the chaff, and drew the logical conclusion that the invasion would land near Calais. They correctly dismissed the rumors of planned landings in Norway, the Balkans, and elsewhere because all the evidence supported an invasion of France, but it never occurred to them that the evidence pointing to Calais as the invasion target might have been faked as well. Even after reports of landings in Normandy reached Berlin, the German high command assumed that these were a feint, intended to draw forces away from a real landing near Calais, and sent no reinforcements. Their fatal misjudgment made D-Day a tremendous Allied victory and sealed Germany's defeat.

Operation Bodyguard has been cited now and again in the UFO literature, but very rarely has anyone paid attention to the central lesson it teaches: that an effective campaign of deception requires *two stories* below the public one. In the case of Operation Bodyguard, the public story was "No comment," the tight security normal for any important military operation. Below that was the cover story embodied by Patton's First United States Army Group, with its dummy tanks and empty bunkers. The cover story would not have worked if it had been public; it had to be kept secret, so that German spies had to work hard to get information about it, and it had to be guarded by a haze of misinformation the enemy had to sort through. This made it look like a real secret, and convinced the German high command that it had pieced together the Allied plan.

Beneath the cover story, in turn, is the real story, similar enough to the cover story that any evidence that points to it can easily be mistaken as evidence pointing to the cover story. Operation Bodyguard would never have worked if the cover story had denied plans for any invasion at all, or focused on claims that the invasion would land somewhere far away from northern France. It worked because the Germans could be allowed to learn almost everything about the invasion except the exact location of the landing beaches. Every bit of evidence their spies turned up, pointing toward an imminent invasion of northern France, thus reinforced the German high command's belief that the assault would land near Calais. As Jacques Vallee points out, they had 95 percent of the information they needed to figure out the Allied invasion plans—but it was the wrong 95 percent.[177]

An Alien Bodyguard?
A similar project to distract attention from another set of important military secrets would have made perfect sense in the context of the Cold War. The years following the end of the Second World War saw the secrecy that guarded the Normandy invasion and the genesis of the atom bomb ramped up to new heights as the campaigns against Nazi

---

177. Vallee 1979, 68.

Germany and imperial Japan gave way to the long struggle against the Soviet Union. As the Cold War took shape, an entire secret economy centered on aerospace technology sprang up in the United States and its allies, shielded from public oversight by the same safeguards that kept it out of sight of Soviet intelligence agents.[178]

Most of the significant advances in American aerospace technology during this period were birthed in this hidden economy, and only emerged from secrecy years or decades later. The Bell X-1, the first aircraft to fly faster than the speed of sound, is a timely example, since it first flew in 1947, as the UFO phenomenon was getting under way. When it was first tested, the X-1 was a secret project, and Chuck Yeager's pioneering supersonic flight on October 14, 1947, took place under strict secrecy. When *Aviation Week* published a story on the flight two months later, the Air Force considered legal charges against the magazine on national security grounds.[179]

Many other programs sheltered under the same blanket of secrecy. Beginning in 1946, the U.S. tested high-altitude balloons as a way of carrying out reconnaissance missions into the upper atmosphere. Projects Helios and Skyhook tested manned gondolas meant to reach 100,000-foot altitudes, while Project Mogul used unmanned balloons to spy on Soviet nuclear testing. Also beginning in 1946, the United States flew "ferret" planes packed with electronic gear on secret missions over foreign territory to snoop on the communications and radar of its enemies and allies alike. The U-2 entered the spyplane field in 1955 and the A-12/SR-71 Blackbird first flew in 1962. Around this same time the first U.S. pilotless drones went into service, and secret tactical reconnaissance planes such as the Lockheed YO-3A, a nearly silent single-seat observation plane, went into service later in the same decade. The decades that followed had their own secret aircraft, and all the evidence suggests that similar secret programs continue today.

Nor were U-2 flights and Skyhook balloon tests the only secret projects known to have generated UFO reports during this period. In

---

178. See Burrows 2001 and Taubman 2003, among other sources, for discussions of secret U.S. aerospace activities during the Cold War.

179. Miller 2001, 28–29.

1954, for example, the Air Force conducted drop tests of the bomb case for the EC-14 hydrogen warhead—the first thermonuclear weapon in the U.S. arsenal—over the Nellis Air Force test range in Nevada, not far from Groom Lake. The cases, covered with bright multicolored lights for tracking purposes, were dropped from a B-36 bomber flying at 45,000 feet over the Nevada desert at 4:00 AM. The predictable result was a flurry of UFO reports from the Las Vegas area, which were dismissed by the Air Force and debunkers alike in the usual terms.[180]

It's thus a matter of record that the UFO phenomenon served as a cover for secret U.S. aerospace activities. The possibility that has too rarely been pointed out is that this could well have been deliberate policy. Put the UFO phenomenon side by side with Operation Bodyguard, and parallels stand out at once. The public story would have been a flat denial that anything out of the ordinary was happening in America's skies, equivalent to the normal operational secrecy around the D-Day invasion. This public story would have been backed up by a covert campaign of disinformation that filled the media with claims that any unusual aircraft was actually a sighting of stars, swamp gas, or some other natural phenomenon.

The cover story beneath the public story would have been the claim that extraterrestrial spacecraft were visiting the earth. The Air Force rejected this forcefully in public. At the same time, its actions encouraged many people to believe that the cover story must be true, just as the Allied high command did everything in its power to convince the German high command that the invasion force would hit the beaches near Calais. It's entirely possible that the Air Force or CIA deliberately faked some of the most spectacular sightings to help spread the cover story, creating fake UFOs and landings in the same way that Operation Bodyguard's managers created fake tanks, munitions dumps, and army units.

Alongside this primary cover story would be alternative theories about the nature of the UFO phenomenon, parallel to the alternative landings in Norway, the Balkans, and elsewhere that Operation Bodyguard generated as additional publicity. Below this flurry of

---

180. Peebles 1994, 322.

cover stories, finally, was the real story, the secret aircraft and spy missions that had to be concealed from Soviet espionage, the equivalent of the Normandy landing beaches that had to be kept secret from the Wehrmacht.

Reconsider the original 1947 UFO flap in this light and a startling possibility emerges. In the days immediately after Kenneth Arnold's sighting, many witnesses in the Pacific Northwest spotted what looked like silver dots, disks, or spheres high in the air. These were not simply apparitions; they were photographed, as mentioned in chapter 2, and sighted by large numbers of witnesses at the same time. The sightings spread across the country over the days that followed, and then gradually slowed to a halt. Meanwhile, rumors buzzed through the country that the mysterious craft were a secret weapon of some kind.

Strip away the later mythologizing, and this sounds like a good description of a test launch of multiple high-altitude balloons over American territory. The technology certainly existed in 1947 to do this. During the Second World War, the Japanese launched several thousand bomb-carrying balloons at the forests of western North America in a project named Operation Fugo. This had enough success that the U.S. had to clamp down a lid of press secrecy and maintain battalions of firefighters in constant readiness during the summers of 1944 and 1945. The American occupation of Japan after the war put all the records and technology of Operation Fugo in American hands, and the possibility of doing something similar to the Soviet Union—possibly with something much more lethal than incendiary bombs attached—cannot have been far from the minds of U.S. military planners.

If a secret balloon test took place in the summer of 1947, the balloons would have been launched either in the Pacific Northwest or from ships in the Pacific, and drifted eastward across the United States, following the prevailing high-altitude winds. The United States used much the same approach in a 1955 project, Operation Genetrix, that sent more than five hundred observation balloons over the Soviet Union, so the possibility that the same technology was tested earlier in American airspace is hard to dismiss. At least one solidly documented book on U.S. Cold War intelligence claims, on the basis of confidential interviews, that balloon tests in 1947 caused the UFO wave that year.[181] If this was what happened, it would certainly explain multiple sightings of unusual, silvery objects in the skies whose existence was flatly denied by the U.S. Air Force and government officials.

The 1947 sightings were forerunners, but the birth of "Operation Alien Bodyguard" seems to have happened later, in response to a different set of unmentionable realities in American skies. The huge 1952 UFO flap was most likely the crucible for the project, and it deserves notice that its causes remain unexplained by the 1997 CIA disclosures. In its historical context, however, 1952 was a good year for secret plans. Effective intercontinental ballistic missiles were still years away, but many American military leaders, notably Strategic Air Command head Curtis LeMay, believed that the Soviet Union had a large enough advantage in bombers that a Russian nuclear first strike was a real possibility.

Did the United States prepare and test some emergency weapon so risky, or so morally repellent, that the tests remain classified to this day? Or does the weapon itself still remain on a Pentagon shelf, a last-ditch emergency option protected by tight secrecy?

By 1952 the idea of using the UFO phenomenon as protective camouflage would hardly have required a stroke of genius. The belief that UFOs were alien spacecraft had rooted in the American popular imagination; the first wave of contactees were proclaiming the imminent arrival of the Space Brothers, and the pervasive 1947 rumors that UFOs were a secret military project had long been forgotten. Meanwhile, America's military and intelligence agencies were still staffed with hundreds of men who had played some role in Operation Bodyguard during the war, and knew how deception could be used as a military weapon.

Many secret projects from the 1950s have been declassified since that time, of course, and it's reasonable to ask why "Operation Alien Bodyguard" would still be secret today. The answer lies in the way the same stratagem came to be used for many different secret projects. Whatever was tested in 1952 was only the first of many programs hidden behind the convenient camouflage of the UFO phenomenon.

---

181. Volkman 1985, 140–41.

From 1954 to 1960, when a U-2 flight was shot down over Soviet airspace, the U-2 was America's most secret reconnaissance technology. In 1962 the SR-71 began its flight tests, and continued in service into the 1980s. The United States launched its first successful spy satellite in 1960, but it was not until 1974, when a new generation of spy satellites went into service, that orbital reconnaissance became central to U.S. strategic reconnaissance. That detail may have more relevance to the history of UFOs than most researchers suspect, because the time when aircraft were central to U.S. strategic reconnaissance, and spy satellites were a new technology prone to fall out of orbit, was also the period during which UFOs were sighted by large numbers of witnesses in American skies.

By the time spy satellites took the lead, however, the ruse of blaming any unusual aerial sightings on aliens would have found many other uses in the labyrinths of American intelligence activities and aerospace technology testing. The long campaign of secrecy would also have had a potent impact on the unfolding UFO mythology, convincing countless people of its correctness while driving believers in the extraterrestrial hypothesis into repeated confrontations with the U.S. government. When government agencies began leaking information relevant to the history behind the UFO phenomenon during the relative openness of the 1990s, they found that neither the true believers in the extraterrestrial hypothesis nor their opposite numbers in the null-hypothesis camp wanted to hear about it.

The resurgence of the American national security state at the beginning of the new century put an end to these initiatives, but they were probably doomed from the start. The myth of the UFO had developed a momentum of its own, and among those who accepted it, it had long since become unfalsifiable. Half a century after the dawn of the UFO age, nothing that anyone could do or say could break its grip on the popular imagination or weaken the conviction among ETH believers that they were on the track of spaceships from other worlds.

Sourcing the Disinformation

Like a stage conjurer's trick, disinformation relies on drawing the viewer's attention to something irrelevant while the real action takes place elsewhere. If you look at the hand that holds the wand, you see what the conjurer wants you to see. If you look at his other hand, you have a chance to see through the deception and understand what's really going on.

One of the more interesting ironies about campaigns of disinformation and deception is that while they exist to protect a secret, they manifest in public actions. If the evidence pointing to an invasion near Calais had not come to the attention of Nazi spies, after all, the efforts of Operation Bodyguard would have gone for nothing. In the same way, if a program of deception meant to conceal some of the most important Cold War military secrets played a large role in shaping the UFO phenomenon, the misleading stories and deceptive clues churned out by the disinformation machine had to find their way to their audience. Look for the points where deception enters the public sphere and you have the equivalent of the conjurer's other hand, a point of access to what is going on behind the scenes.

In the case of the UFO phenomenon, the places to look are the organizations and individuals who had a central role in leading serious civilian investigations onto the false path of the extraterrestrial hypothesis, and one essential starting point is to check for people in these contexts who had close connections to the U.S. intelligence community. Ironically, much of this work has already been done by researchers convinced that concealing the extraterrestrial origin of UFOs was the point of the coverup. Look at the same data with Operation Bodyguard in mind, though, and one thing stands out: a very large share of the groups and individuals most active in promoting the idea that the U.S. military was concealing evidence of alien landings had close connections with the very military and intelligence bodies they claimed to be challenging.

NICAP, the civilian UFO body that had more responsibility than anyone else for promoting the idea of a government coverup of alien spacecraft, is a case in point. Throughout its history, many of its key players were intelligence assets. NICAP board members with intelligence backgrounds included Admiral Roscoe Hillenkoetter, the first director of the CIA; Colonel Joseph J. Bryan III and Nicholas de Rochefort, respectively the head of the CIA psychological warfare staff and one of his assistants; and CIA briefing officer Karl Pflock.

Richard Hall, NICAP's acting director through the 1960s, was an Air Force veteran who had a CIA security clearance, and is on record as having funnelled NICAP data to the CIA. When Donald Keyhoe was forced to resign in December 1969, Bryan, who led Keyhoe's ouster, replaced Keyhoe with John L. Acuff, who had previously headed a scientific body closely associated with the CIA, and NICAP assistant director Gordon Lore, Jr., with G. Stuart Nixon, whose close liaison with CIA officials in the following years are a matter of public record.[182]

Another important figure in the UFO community whose connections with the U.S. intelligence community have been much discussed is J. Allen Hynek. In many ways Hynek was America's most influential UFO researcher, and his pilgrimage from Project Blue Book researcher to the guiding spirit of CUFOS tracked the shift in the UFO phenomenon from fringe preoccupation to popular icon during the second half of the twentieth century. It is less well known that Hynek's contracts with the Air Force came through the USAF's Foreign Technology Division by way of a third-party cutout—standard practice in the intelligence field—and focused on evaluating UFO sightings for intelligence purposes. UFO researcher Richard Dolan has argued that Hynek's connections and activities through the Blue Book years suggest a close connection with the intelligence community.[183]

The promoters of the more recent mythology of underground bases and imminent alien takeover of the earth have their own connections to the intelligence community. All the people who played key roles in propagating these stories—M. William Cooper, Richard Doty, William English, John Lear, and William Moore—were either former employees of intelligence agencies or, in the case of Moore, admitted working as an informant for Air Force intelligence while distributing the MJ-12

---

182. For these details, see Dolan 2002, 191, 279–80, and 364–65.

183. See Dolan 2002, 221–24.

documents. Turn to the 1990s and the refocusing of the same stories on Groom Lake, Nevada, and the key figures—Robert Lazar and William Uhouse—both openly admitted their involvement in a range of secret research projects with ties to the intelligence community.[184] The possibility that they were working for intelligence agencies in a somewhat different capacity has too rarely been taken into account in assessing the improbable claims they brought to the UFO controversy.

Nor was there any shortage of intelligence connections on the other side of the UFO controversy, among proponents of the null hypothesis. Donald Menzel, the Harvard astronomer who became the first professional UFO debunker, was also a consummate insider in the U.S. intelligence community with a Top Secret/Ultra security clearance. Menzel cracked Japanese codes for the Office of Naval Intelligence during the Second World War, and worked as a contractor for the NSA and CIA later in his career. All through the 1950s and 1960s, as he made his reputation as the chief proponent of the null hypothesis, he was a contract employee for the CIA and discussed UFO matters regularly with Air Force intelligence personnel.[185]

Philip Klass, who took over Menzel's mantle and became America's UFO debunker-in-chief for more than three decades, was less directly linked to the intelligence scene than Menzel but spent most of his working career as senior editor for *Aviation Week and Space Technology*, a magazine so often used as a conduit for U.S. disinformation projects that its nickname in the aviation trade is *Aviation Leak and Space Mythology*. Klass was also the author of one of the first books ever published on spy satellites, a project that involved close liaisons with some of the most secret American intelligence programs of the time.[186]

Yet these direct connections are only part of the puzzle. Look through any detailed account of the UFO phenomenon that gives sources for its data, and notice how many of the more colorful claims come directly from the military itself. This in itself poses an interest-

---

184. See Darlington 1997; Patton 1998, 157–58; Bishop 2005, 108; and Vallee 1991, 166, for the intelligence backgrounds of major figures in the UFO community.

185. Westrum 2000, 36.

186. Klass 1971.

ing paradox. From December 1953 on, under the terms of JANAP 146, making a public report of a UFO sighting was a federal crime under the Espionage Act for military personnel, commercial airline pilots, and a few other classes of civilians. This regulation, it may be worth pointing out, finds a ready explanation if "UFO sightings" were in fact sightings of secret military aircraft, and in fact the whole apparatus of the U.S. coverup surrounding the UFO phenomenon makes a good deal more sense as an attempt to hide military secrets than it does as a response to a supposed extraterrestrial invasion. If all the UFO reports from 1953 to 1974 that came from military personnel, commercial airline pilots, and others covered by JANAP 146 were dropped from the body of UFO evidence, that body would be a very modest fraction of the size it is.

A crucial clue has been missed by researchers into the UFO coverup, however: *none of the military personnel or airline pilots whose reports helped feed the UFO movement ever faced prosecution under JANAP 146.* All through the peak years of the UFO phenomenon, reports of UFO sightings from witnesses subject to JANAP 146's draconian rules kept reaching the media and the UFO research organizations, without legal charges apparently ever being filed. If the illusion of alien spacecraft was simply a cover story for a succession of secret U.S. aerospace projects, such "leaks" would have been an essential part of the camouflage. Like the planted evidence for Allied landings anywhere but in Normandy, they would have helped maintain a thick fog of confusion around the entire subject and make it difficult for anyone to pick out accurate details from misinformation.

The work of the Air Force disinformation mill left visible traces all through the case of Paul Bennewitz, an American physicist and UFO buff whose role in spreading some of the core modern UFO legends was referred to briefly in chapter 4.[187] Bennewitz, a member of APRO, operated an electronics firm in Albuquerque, New Mexico, just outside Kirtland Air Force Base. Beginning in 1979, he noticed moving lights in the sky above the base. Thinking they might be alien spacecraft, he began using his technical skills to observe the skies over Kirtland.

---

187.   I have drawn extensively on Bishop 2005 and Vallee 1991 for the following discussion.

What Bennewitz did not know was that he was snooping on some of the most secret technological initiatives of the American defense industry. Kirtland was the home of Sandia National Laboratories, one of the nation's primary centers for secret research; the NSA also had a presence there, as did some 160 other government agencies. According to one account of the case, Bennewitz's radios began picking up tests of a new NSA system for transmitting multiple cipher messages in a single radio message, and his cameras caught traces of laser devices used to jam Soviet reconnaissance satellites. While Bennewitz believed that all these things had to do with UFOs, others were not so gullible, and channeled information from his work to those who wanted to know Kirtland's secrets.

It was apparently when NSA intercepts of Soviet communications started pulling in material that came through Bennewitz that the U.S. intelligence community intervened. According to several accounts, officers from the Air Force's Office of Special Investigations (AFOSI) contacted Bennewitz. These officers passed on "secret information" to Bennewitz that diverted his attention away from Kirtland to the area of Dulce, New Mexico, two hundred miles north of Albuquerque, where the officers claimed the aliens had an underground base. With AFOSI help, and that of a highly respected UFO researcher who was also an Air Force intelligence asset,[188] Bennewitz figured out how to program a computer to "translate" the NSA signals, turning them into alien-themed gibberish. As the material passed on to Bennewitz grew steadily more paranoid, so did Bennewitz himself, and in 1987 he was admitted to a mental institution.

During this same period, OSI officers recruited another member of the UFO community, William Moore, to keep watch on Bennewitz. Moore helped write *The Roswell Incident* (1980), the book that put claims about a Roswell UFO crash back into circulation in the UFO research community, and was widely considered a rising star among UFO researchers in the 1980s. According to Moore's own 1989 confession, the Air Force officers who contacted him claimed to represent a group within the Air Force opposed to UFO secrecy, and offered him

---

188. According to Bill Moore, this was J. Allen Hynek. See Bishop 2005, 95.

access to secret information on UFOs in exchange for regular updates on what Bennewitz was doing. Moore swallowed the bait, and for most of a decade AFOSI counterintelligence officers fed him forged UFO documents that supported the material they were feeding to Bennewitz.

None of this stopped the disinformation passed on to Bennewitz and Moore from turning into accepted beliefs in large parts of the UFO movement during the 1990s. The MJ-12 documents and much of the material now in circulation about an underground alien base near Dulce, secret treaties between the U.S. government and extraterrestrials, and alien involvement in cattle mutilation and human abductions can all be traced straight back to this source. All of this points to the possibility that much of the other information circulating in the UFO scene today has similar origins.

The Rendlesham Secret

Examine other elements of the UFO phenomenon with an eye to their role in military disinformation campaigns and similar patterns emerge. A solid example is the Rendlesham incident of 1980, one of the most famous close encounter cases in the history of the phenomenon, and the subject of several books.[189]

Rendlesham Forest is in East Anglia, the round bulge near the middle of England's eastern coastline, and lies between two British air bases leased to the U.S. Air Force. Among the units based there, according to British UFO researchers, is the 78th Aerospace Recovery and Rescue Squadron, which is trained to rescue American astronauts and spacecraft that might have to make an emergency landing anywhere on Earth.

In the early morning hours of December 27, 1980, civilian radar operators reportedly tracked an unidentified aircraft as it flew inland from the North Sea coast to the vicinity of Rendlesham Forest. Several witnesses on the two air bases reported that bright lights were seen in the forest, and a civilian electrician stated that he was brought in to repair landing lights that seemed to have been destroyed by an aircraft

---

189. See Randles, Street, and Butler 1984; Warren and Robbins 1997; and Vallee 1991, 153–65, for details of the Rendlesham affair.

making an emergency landing. One witness at the base and one of the civilian radar operators claimed that Air Force officers admitted that a UFO had landed at Rendlesham. Another witness, an Air Force security guard named Larry Warren, claimed that he and some forty other people had been sent to a prearranged spot in the forest, and witnessed a UFO "shaped like an arrowhead" that landed and disgorged three alien creatures, who talked to the base commander before taking off again.

Believers in the extraterrestrial hypothesis have promoted this case as a well-documented crash landing of an alien spacecraft. Believers in the null hypothesis have insisted that the beam of the Orford Ness lighthouse four miles away, and a few bright stars, were mistaken for UFOs on that December night. Yet the evidence would be explained much more concisely by an emergency landing of a secret aircraft, followed by a coverup in which the manufactured story of a UFO landing was deployed as a cover story to distract attention from the actual events. The scene described in Larry Warren's testimony, as Jacques Vallee has pointed out,[190] has all the hallmarks of a staged event in which witnesses saw what they were supposed to see.

The claim that the UFO was shaped like an arrowhead is in many ways the clinching detail. Since the late 1970s, reports and sightings of black triangular aircraft with U.S. markings have been in circulation. Two of them—the F-117 stealth fighter and the B-2 stealth bomber—came out of the closet of government secrecy later in the decade, but others apparently remain out of sight. One is a blunt triangle larger than the F-117 but smaller than the B-2; rumors in the aviation industry label it the TR-3 Black Manta—TR stands for "tactical reconnaissance"—and it derives from a slightly earlier experimental stealth plane, code-named ARTICHOKE.

Another—a larger, sharper triangle—has been identified as the SR-91 Aurora, a strategic reconnaissance aircraft capable of flying five times the speed of sound, built to replace the aging SR-71 Blackbird. When engineers on a North Sea oil platform in 1989 spotted an unknown delta-shaped aircraft refueling in flight from a U.S. Air

---

190. Vallee 1991, 158–60.

Force KC-135 Stratotanker, while two F-111 fighters flew protectively nearby, their reports convinced the respected aviation periodical *Jane's Defence Weekly* that the rumors about Aurora were correct.[191] The United States still denies the existence of either plane, but such denials are a common factor in the world of "black budget" aircraft; after all, U.S. authorities formerly denied the existence of the SR-71, F-117, and B-2, among many other advanced aircraft.

Bring this data together with the Rendlesham case, and the repeated sightings of black triangular UFOs in American skies all through the 1980s, and a plausible pattern emerges. The U-2 had its first test flight in 1955, and its successor, the SR-71 Blackbird, first took off in 1962. By 1980 they were old technology, but official sources insist that, because of budget cuts, nothing new has been brought into service since the 1960s. Perhaps I am overly suspicious, but this seems about as likely as claiming that the CIA contracts out its reconnaissance program to Santa Claus' flying sleigh; satellites form the mainstay of U.S. reconnaissance, but their orbits can be tracked and they can be shot down by antisatellite weapons. A strategic reconnaissance plane using stealth technology would be a crucial backup, and in the huge U.S. defense buildup of the 1980s something of the sort will have been pretty much inevitable.

The first U.S. stealth aircraft, the experimental testbed HAVE BLUE, first flew in 1977. Back then, speculation about stealth technology—and there was plenty of that in the press at that time—focused on the concept of radar-absorbing paints or panels; among the pieces of disinformation put into circulation through Paul Bennewitz, for example, was the claim that the Air Force had developed a secret aluminum-titanium alloy that absorbed radar.[192] What made HAVE BLUE slip past radar screens, though, was something different: a revolutionary faceted design that reflected radar waves uselessly away from the aircraft. That design became the basis for the F-117 Nighthawk, the first U.S. stealth fighter.

---

191.   Patton 1998, 39–40.

192.   Patton 1998, 145, and Bishop 2005, 193–94.

Yet the Nighthawk did not fly for the first time until 1982. For Lockheed Aircraft's legendary Skunk Works—the secret aircraft design center that created the U-2, SR-71, HAVE BLUE, F-117, and many other classified projects—that was absurdly slow. The Skunk Works put the first U-2 in the air eight months after signing the contract, and the far more demanding SR-71 took only two years.[193] Once HAVE BLUE proved that the faceted design would work, building the first F-117s on the same plan should have taken a matter of months. One plausible explanation for the delay was that the Skunk Works team was building something else using the same technology first. ARTICHOKE, the prototype of the TR-3 reconnaissance plane, or the prototype of the SR-91 Aurora would have been a logical "something else."

As the stealth program moved to completion, though, it was arguably the most sensitive secret in the American arsenal, and that secret could be blown by a single photograph: the workings of the stealth technology could easily have been reverse-engineered from a good look at the faceted design. A smokescreen of total secrecy was absolutely necessary, and the UFO phenomenon, which had been entangled with spyplane flights at least since the first days of the U-2 program, would have offered a perfect tool for applying that smokescreen.

This may have been the driving force behind the sudden flurry of triangular UFOs that burst into American airspace in the very early 1980s. Just as U-2 and SR-71 flights had hidden behind the double protection of the UFO mythology and the Air Force's strident denials of the myth, flights of the secret stealth planes would have benefited from the same treatment. The campaign of secrecy could readily have extended to a modern equivalent of Patton's inflatable tanks, with a triangular "UFO" that paraded over the Hudson River valley and other locales at night to confuse the issue, leaving foreign intelligence services baffled about the meaning of other reports of black triangular aircraft that didn't show up on radar.

The "boomerang" might have been something as simple as a big triangular balloon with a rack underneath for lights, and an ultra-

---

193. Patton 1998, 108–19 and 128–31.

light airplane towing it. It might, however, have been something more interesting. One of the stranger stories in the aviation industry at the beginning of the 1970s was the case of the Aereon 7, a radically new triangular dirigible that was invented and flight-tested by a network of lighter-than-air buffs.[194] The Aereon was an intriguing technology with many potential uses, not least in the antisubmarine work for which the U.S. Navy used blimps all through the Second World War. The possibility that something based on the Aereon was behind the "Westchester boomerang" deserves much more attention than it has received from researchers obsessed with the extraterrestrial hypothesis.

All this forms the context for the Rendlesham incident. In 1980, the emergency landing of a secret prototype reconnaissance plane at one of the air bases near Rendlesham, accompanied in the usual way by a U.S. Air Force "chaser plane" that would have been detected by civilian radars, could have potentially jeopardized the entire stealth program. If Soviet agents realized that something out of the ordinary was afoot, they could have deployed all their resources and quite possibly gotten enough information to crack open the secret of the stealth technology.

The UFO mythology provided a perfect cover story to throw them off the track. Like static drowning out a radio signal, the deliberate manufacture of rumors of alien contact—bolstered by staged events like the one reported by Larry Warren—confused the issue thoroughly enough that foreign agents and intelligence analysts could never quite be sure what they were looking at, thereby missing their chance to break the biggest secret of the Cold War's last decade. Similar scenes may well have been played over and over again from 1952 on by military and intelligence units who had learned to put an alien mask over their own operations.

Scrimmages in Darkness

These glimpses of disinformation at work in the UFO phenomenon are crucial pieces of the puzzle, but it's just as crucial to keep in mind that the American military intelligence community has no monopoly

---

194.   See McPhee 1973 for more information about the Aereon project.

on the use of disinformation. The concealment of Soviet FOBS tests under the same capacious cloak of "unexplained UFO sightings" is a useful reminder that more than one side could play the same game. Any number of nations could have used the same convenient excuse to cover up their efforts to spy on their neighbors and develop military technologies in secret.

It is by no means impossible, for example, that some of the balloons and aircraft behind UFO sightings between 1947 and 1974 were Russian rather than American. For that matter, the original 1947 flap that launched the UFO phenomenon on its way could have been a Russian program of balloon reconnaissance inspired by the Japanese Fugo balloon bombs. That could explain the fact that whatever came down at Roswell was quickly flown to Wright Field (now Wright-Patterson Air Force Base) near Dayton, Ohio, where the Army Air Corps in 1947 had a special unit that studied foreign aviation technology.

Nor were all these operations necessarily structured by the demands of the Cold War. During the same years the United States was carrying out secret overflights of Soviet territory, for example, it was also engaged in aerial reconnaissance of its own allies. During the 1956 Suez crisis, for example, U-2 flights tracked the activities of British, French, and Israeli military units, and found out that the latter two governments had lied to the United States about the number of French Mirage jet fighters that had been shipped to Israel.[195] Even close allies have divergent interests, and espionage forms a time-honored way of pursuing those interests.

The flurry of UFO sightings around the world in the 1960s and 1970s takes on a different meaning when the global reach of American espionage during those same years is kept in mind. The Soviet Union had high-altitude spyplanes of its own during those years—a U-2 clone with the NATO code name Mandrake entered Soviet service in 1963—and other nations likely pursued their own secret programs at the same time. In this context it's once again worth noticing how

---

195. Patton 1998, 120.

many of the classic UFO sightings around the world were reported by military personnel, with the approval of their commanding officers.

During the heyday of the UFO phenomenon, after all, any nation that wanted to carry out aerial reconnaissance on its neighbors, parachute supplies to insurgents in a neighboring country, trade technology across Cold War borders, or smuggle drugs by air—just to name a few of the possibilities—could readily have used a flurry of manufactured UFO sightings as protective camouflage. The major UFO flaps in Latin America during the 1960s and 1970s, among many others, take on a noticeably different shape when this possibility is considered. It's entirely possible, along the same lines, that the "ghost planes" and "ghost rockets" of 1930s and 1940s Scandinavia were early moves in the same game; they would have made a plausible cover story, for example, for Swedish aerial reconnaissance along the borders of the Soviet Union.

All this inevitably spilled over into other dimensions of the UFO phenomenon, not least because claiming to be a UFO buff provided a nearly perfect cover story for spies interested in a target nation's aerospace industry, offering a watertight justification for cameras, high-powered binoculars, and long hours spent watching the skies near military bases. The Paul Bennewitz affair provides a rare glimpse into this underground dimension of the phenomenon. While there is no reason to doubt Bennewitz's own loyalty, it's worth remembering that information from his lab apparently found its way into NSA intercepts of Soviet intelligence communications. The channel could have been as simple as a trusted fellow UFO researcher who was paid to forward information to an anonymous post office box in another state, and had no idea that the person picking up the mail on the other end was a Soviet agent.

It might have been much more complex than that, however. UFO researcher Jacques Vallee noted in the 1990s that the French authorities were investigating the possibility that the UMMO hoax, one of the most audacious pieces of fakery in the history of the phenomenon, had been launched by an Eastern European intelligence service for the purpose of scientific and industrial espionage.[196] The possibility that UFO research

---

196.   Vallee 1991, 115.

organizations might be infiltrated and systematically used for espionage purposes was raised in then-classified U.S. government reports back in the 1950s. This goes far to explain the presence of so many people with connections to U.S. intelligence services in those same organizations, and raises the question of just how much of the UFO phenomenon was simply a side effect of Cold War espionage—a haze of false stories and manufactured reports meant to confuse the opposition or communicate secret information in some carefully encoded form.

The result might be compared to a football game in pitch darkness in which every player belongs to a different team, wears an unmarked jersey, and is trying to get the ball into an end zone none of the other players can identify for certain. Where the scrimmage was thickest—around high-tech reconnaissance planes in the 1950s and 1960s, for example, or around the first stealth planes in the 1980s—every player had a different agenda, and the confusion must have reached dizzying levels. Since the game revolved around hiding, controlling, falsifying, and disseminating information, the result was a cloud of half-truths and untruths that would have done much to make the UFO phenomenon the murky mess it is today.

Governments and their intelligence services dominated this no-holds-barred scramble, but they were not necessarily the only players, and may not have been first on the field. Another set of players belonged to the American occult scene. George Hunt Williamson, George Van Tassel, and many other occultists of the early 1950s clearly set out to use the UFO controversy as a vehicle to bring the teachings of occult tradition to the attention of a wider audience. The rise of the New Age movement in the years since then shows that their efforts had some success.

The possibility also exists that members of the occult community played a role in launching the UFO narrative in the first place. Occult secret societies in the Western world have a long track record of trying to influence popular opinion by deliberately placing evocative images into the collective imagination. In the first years of the seventeenth century, for example, as an earlier European cold war moved toward the catastrophic explosion of the Thirty Years' War, a circle of German occultists launched an audacious project of this kind, circulating claims that a hidden fraternity of wise men possessed all the secrets of nature and would share them with the worthy.[197] The continent-wide furor that erupted around the original Rosicrucian manifestoes had a remarkable impact on European intellectual life, putting ideas into circulation that came to flower with the founding of the Royal Society—the Western world's first scientific research society—in Britain half a century later.

I have argued elsewhere, similarly, that the revival and popularization of the Atlantis legend in the late nineteenth century might have been a deliberate attempt on the part of occultists associated with the early Theosophical Society to shape their culture's dialogue about technology and the future.[198] A good deal less speculative is the project launched by Dion Fortune, one of the leading occultists in Britain at the outbreak of the Second World War, to form a network of occult lodges that worked to boost British morale in the face of Nazi propaganda and military pressure.[199] For that matter, the activities of Wilhelm Landig's circle in Vienna after the Second World War, discussed in chapter 5, fall into the same category.

Attempts to shape the consciousness of a culture or an age using powerful symbolic patterns, in other words, are among the things occultists do. The possibility exists that something of the sort lies behind the remarkable involvement of the American occult community in the first days of the UFO phenomenon. While it's certainly possible that figures such as Meade Layne and Harold Sherman, who predicted the arrival of the flying saucers in advance, were simply reporting visions and dreams that would shortly burst out in a flurry of apparitions across America's skies, the possibility has to be considered that these highly publicized reports were meant to help *cause* such an event.

Such a project would make perfect sense in the context of its time. The fireballs over Hiroshima and Nagasaki that brought the Second World War to its cataclysmic finale brought home the possibility that

---

197.   See Yates 1972.

198.   Greer 2007.

199.   Fortune 1993.

the next war might well bring an end to human history. As the Cold War divided the world into two nuclear-armed camps, people around the world responded in desperate ways—digging backyard shelters, hunting for scapegoats, flinging themselves into strange ideologies that promised safety. Thus it's at least possible that somewhere in the broad overlap between the American occult community and the science fiction scene, a group of occultists driven by the same sense of desperation set out to deliberately create the belief that extraterrestrial beings were about to intervene on Earth.

They may have hoped simply to slow the march toward a Third World War, to inject just that moment of hesitation into the minds of politicians and generals that could keep them from plunging over the edge into a nuclear abyss. They may have had other aims. If they existed—and it's only fair to admit that at this point, the suggestion that they did is sheer speculation—they covered their tracks well, and I have not been able to find anything more solid than rumors and hints in the occult literature of the time. Still, it's clear where luckier or more painstaking researchers might best begin looking for them: in the Chicago occult and science fiction scene where Raymond Palmer, Harold Sherman, and some of the first generation of contactees rubbed elbows right at the end of the Second World War.

Summing Up the Phenomenon

Whether or not this last suggestion turns out to be correct, the conclusions suggested above offer an ironic commentary on the claims made by the contenders in the UFO controversy. If half of the apparent UFO sightings in the phenomenon's busiest decades were the product of U-2 flights, and other secret aviation technologies take up their own portion of the remaining sightings, the foundation under claims that UFOs must be craft from other worlds becomes very hard to prop up. At the same time, a surprisingly large number of the other claims made by proponents of the extraterrestrial hypothesis have turned out to be entirely justified. There was, in fact, a coverup; the Air Force was deliberately lying about what was behind UFO sightings, and handing out bogus explanations to the public; UFO researchers even caught the close relationship between UFOs and the Groom Lake base in Nevada, for many years the home of America's spyplane fleet. It's just that what was being covered up had nothing to do with aliens from outer space.

The debunkers' side of the conflict comes off rather less impressively. Defenders of the null hypothesis such as Philip Klass insisted that all UFO sightings are adequately explained by known aerial phenomena, witness error, and fraud. Klass himself participated with fellow debunkers Robert Sheaffer and James Oberg in a research effort that claimed to explain all the "unknowns" listed in the Condon Report.[200] Secret U.S. aerospace technologies had no part in their explanations, though. If a large proportion of UFO sightings were actual sightings of secret aircraft, then the same proportion of the explanations proposed by Klass, Sheaffer, and Oberg were dead wrong, and the reasoning used to justify those identifications was every bit as dubious as defenders of the extraterrestrial hypothesis claimed all along. The witnesses to many UFO sightings did, in fact, see something genuinely strange, even though the source was much closer to earth than anyone realized at the time. The only thing the proponents of the null hypothesis consistently got right was the fact that UFOs are not spacecraft from other planets—and, by and large, they reached that correct conclusion for the wrong reasons.

The key to understanding the UFO phenomenon, then, is the realization that it is a single phenomenon only in a social and cultural sense. The only factor that unites the disparate experiences lumped together as UFOs is a set of cultural narratives that took shape in America in the early twentieth century—narratives that splashed contemporary ideas about progress across outer space, and envisioned every detail reported by UFO witnesses decades in advance. Spread through the American subconscious by the science fiction pulp magazines, those narratives took on new force and meaning with the coming of the Cold War— when global confrontation between the United States and the Soviet Union, backed by the threat of nuclear holocaust, made the narratives a lightning rod for the hopes and fears of a troubled epoch.

---

200. Sheaffer 1981, 15.

The framework provided by the narratives gave context and meaning to the unfolding UFO phenomenon, but the reports of UFOs themselves came from at least three other sources. First, like any other rumor panic, the belief in flying saucers as alien spacecraft shaped the way people interpreted countless less exotic phenomena, so that any light or unusual object in the sky could readily be mistaken for spacecraft from another world. Among the phenomena that were pressed into service in the unfolding UFO narratives was one not yet understood by science, an unusual natural process that causes visible balls of light to form in the air under rare conditions.

Many of the phenomena that found places in the narrative, however, had a more mundane origin. From the dawn of the Cold War, American military and intelligence interests found the mask of alien visitation a convenient source of camouflage for projects they wanted to conceal from Soviet intelligence and civilian oversight alike. By 1952, if not before, the exploitation of the unfolding UFO phenomenon for military and intelligence purposes had turned into deliberate management of the phenomenon, using methods perfected in the Second World War. While the United States pioneered the use of UFO-related disinformation as a cover for its activities, the same convenient habit was taken up by other nations thereafter, and remains in active use in some parts of the world today.

A third source of UFO experiences comes from the normal human gift for experiencing apparitions while in altered states of consciousness, and filling those apparitions with powerful imagery from contemporary culture. Just as other cultures' beliefs in gods, spirits, saints, and angels were reflected back in the mirror of visionary experience, beliefs concerning UFOs took shape as apparitions experienced by countless people. The materialistic biases of modern industrial culture gave these visionaries few options for interpreting their experiences, and so most of the resulting visions were interpreted as eyewitness accounts of material spacecraft from other worlds.

Ultimately, the secret of the UFO phenomenon was hidden in plain sight. The actual sources of UFO sightings remained invisible because they did not match the solution that most of the participants in the UFO controversy thought they were looking for. The conviction that a single solution had to account for every truly unidentified UFO sighting was the most important factor that kept the mystery fixed in place, and made attempts at a solution so difficult for so many years.

Considered on their own terms, after all, the great majority of the UFO sightings recounted in the first part of this book can be accounted for by straightforward and distinctly falsifiable hypotheses. Secret aerospace projects already discussed provide the most likely explanations for the 1947 high-altitude balloon flap and its most famous sighting, the Roswell crash; the high moving lights that made up such a large proportion of UFO sightings starting in 1954, when the U-2 began testing; the worldwide expansion of the same phenomenon that began in the late 1950s, as the U-2 and its successor, the SR-71, along with equivalent aircraft from the Soviet Union and elsewhere, carried out reconnaissance programs around the world; and the profusion of black triangular UFOs, from the Rendlesham mystery craft to the Westchester Boomerang, that provided protective camouflage for the first U.S. stealth aircraft in the early 1980s.

As we have already seen, these were by no means the only secret technologies hidden beneath a cloak of UFO disinformation. Two famous 1965 sightings mentioned in chapter 2 point to the role of secret space technology in helping to feed the UFO narrative. The brilliant lights in the sky tracked by thousands of witnesses over the Great Plains on the night of August 2–3, 1965, correspond in every detail to the fiery re-entry and breakup of a satellite in a low polar orbit—whether it was American or Russian is anyone's guess. Similarly, the Kecksburg crash on December 9 of the same year is best accounted for as the crash landing of a satellite that survived its return to earth, leaving an acorn-shaped re-entry vehicle to be seen by witnesses and recovered by the U.S. Air Force.

The busiest flap of all, the great 1952 wave of saucer sightings, cannot be accounted for by secret spyplanes or black budget satellites, since neither one existed at that time. Such dramatic accounts as the Nash-Fortenberry sighting and the great Washington, D.C., mass sightings demand an explanation. Pay careful attention to the chronology of the flap, though, and an unexpected possibility emerges at once. The wave began shortly after the publication of a widely read *Life* article, "Have We Visitors From Space?"—an article that was prepared with the active cooperation of the Air Force's Project Blue Book. Thereafter, as reports poured in, most of the truly dramatic reports came from military sources, or from people such as commercial aircraft pilots who were subject to some military regulations.

The possibility that seems never to have been considered is that the U.S. Air Force, with the cooperation of other military branches and intelligence agencies, *could well have faked the entire 1952 flap.* Those reports that involved a few observers, such as the Nash-Fortenberry sighting, could have been invented out of whole cloth and presented to the media by "witnesses" whose patriotism could easily have induced them to cooperate. Those that involved many witnesses, such as the Washington, D.C., sightings, could have been faked just as easily by simple methods: for example, a handful of high-altitude balloons carrying powerful lights and radar reflectors, shrouded in an aura of undeserved mystery with the help of doctored press releases that lied shamelessly about the Air Force's response. The sudden emergence of the contactee movement right on cue in the midst of the flap raises additional questions—might this also have been deliberate disinformation, or were the occultists who played so large a role in launching the contactees into public notoriety attempting to ride the wave of UFO publicity for purposes of their own? Barring a serious breach in the U.S. government's culture of secrecy, a definitive answer will be hard to reach, but the possibility of deliberate fakery deserves to be considered as a viable explanation for this largest of UFO flaps.

Deliberate fakery also offers the most likely explanation for the Zamora close encounter in 1964 and the MJ-12 furor of the late 1980s, and the UMMO sightings of 1966 have already been revealed as an intentional fraud. The social and psychological impact of the unfolding UFO phenomenon, though, would have given rise to UFO apparitions from an early stage. The "Flatwoods Monster" close encounter of 1952, with its close echoes of traditional Southern folklore, belongs in this category. So, of course, does the Hill abduction of 1961, and those of its successors that were not simply manufactured by incompetent hypnotherapists or the very real financial incentives available in the 1980s for those who publicized abduction narratives.

Another set of narratives that clearly derives from apparitional experience centers on the phantom airship sightings of 1896 and 1897, and its later equivalents. The crucial detail missed by most researchers into the subject is that the airships described by witnesses could not have flown even if they had been built. Their flapping wings, paddle-wheels, electric engines, and the like copied late-nineteenth-century speculations of what airships of the future would be like, rather than anticipating the effective airship technologies of the next century.

Alongside all these are the floating blobs of light that have been sighted by human beings in every culture and age—the physical basis, whatever it turns out to be, of the "flying witches" reported by East African tribes such as the Gusii and Azande, the Will o' the Wisp and foxfire of English and American folklore, and their countless equivalents. The Michigan sightings in March 1966 that gave Allen Hynek a lifelong aversion to the words *swamp gas* involved a glowing blob of light; at the time, nearly everyone who admitted its existence at all seems to have assumed that it had to be an extraterrestrial spacecraft, but this hardly follows.

The "foo fighters," flying blobs of light from a few inches to a few feet across that appeared off the wingtips of aircraft belonging to all sides in the Second World War, may be another form of the same phenomenon. The military aircraft of the 1940s were a distinct form of aviation technology, as different from the airplanes of previous decades as they were from the high-speed jets that followed, and careful study of the materials and technologies most often associated with appearances of "foo fighters" could well yield crucial clues to the exotic physical process that brought them into being. This is one of many avenues of research that might have been pursued long ago if the UFO narrative had not confused the issue.

Two sightings discussed in this book remain. The first of them is the Leary, Georgia, sighting in 1969 examined in the introduction to this book. Jimmy Carter and his fellow Lions Club members saw a glowing sphere in the sky that appeared to change color and come closer to them. It may have been exactly that, but another possibility is worth discussing. When observing distant objects against the sky, it's notoriously hard to tell the difference between an object that is coming closer and one that is growing larger. Thus one potential source for the Leary sighting is a fireball from an aerial explosion. Antimissile and antisatellite weapons systems have been developed and tested in the United States for many decades, and the Leary Lions Club may simply have become inadvertent witnesses to a secret test of some such system. Research into activities at nearby military bases on that night in 1969 might well be worth pursuing.

There remains the most famous UFO sighting of them all, Kenneth Arnold's encounter with nine silvery crescents in the skies near Mount Rainier. None of the explanations offered here provide a straightforward solution to what Arnold saw, and other proposed explanations all have their problems. What is more, nobody else seems to have seen anything like them before that memorable June day, and nobody seems to have seen them again. They might have been an unusual natural phenomenon, or an apparition; they might even have been craft from another world—though it has to be said that not one scrap of evidence supports this latter view.

Shorn of the vast penumbra of legend, disinformation, and visionary experience that grew up around it, the Arnold sighting remains a mystery. Still, as serious researchers in every branch of science know well, there are many mysteries in the world, and some of them never will be solved. If the Arnold sighting never finds a conclusive answer, certainly Charles Fort would hardly have been surprised.

nine

The End of the Dream

L ook up at the stars on a clear night and it's easy to understand why so many people down the centuries have tried to find ultimate meaning among those brilliant, distant lights. To the people of the Middle Ages, the stars were windows in the outermost sphere of the sky, through which the splendor of God's heaven blazed down like a promise on the sinful world below. A few centuries later, during the glory years of Newton's worldview, the stars in their courses gave proof of a universe ruled by rational laws that the human mind could discover. Today, in an age that worships technology and splashes its dreams and nightmares of the future across the galaxies in the form of science fiction, the stars have transformed themselves in popular imagination into the suns of countless unknown worlds inhabited by alien life.

As we saw back in chapter 1, the intuition that the cosmos is full of intelligent life goes back well before the dawn of the modern world, but it was not until 1961 that someone put that intuition into the formal language of science. At the Green Bank Conference on Extraterrestrial Intelligent Life that year, Frank Drake, a professor of astronomy and astrophysics from the University of California, Santa Cruz, worked out his much-quoted equation:

$$N = (R \times f_p \times n_e \times f_l \times f_i \times f_c \times L)$$

in which:

N = the number of intelligent species that could be contacted at any given time;

R = the number of stars born in an average year;

f_p = the fraction of those stars that have planets around them;

n_e = the number of those planets at the right distance from the star to support life;

f_l = the fraction of those planets on which life evolves;

f_i = the fraction of those planets in which intelligent life evolves;

f_c = the fraction of those planets on which intelligent life evolves a technology capable of interstellar communication, and uses it for that purpose; and

L = the average lifespan of a technological civilization.

The Drake equation appears fairly often in books supporting the extraterrestrial hypothesis, and with good reason. Most of the people who have proposed answers to it have settled on numbers in the thousands or millions—science writer Michael Kurland's figure of around four million extraterrestrial civilizations in the Milky Way galaxy alone[201] is far from the most optimistic—and if these figures are right, the possibility that at least some UFO sightings might involve visitors from other worlds looks a good deal more plausible.

Here, as so often, the devil is in the details, for it's one thing to have an equation and quite another to solve it. Some of the numbers in the Drake equation are easy enough to estimate—within our own galaxy, the Milky Way, something like ten stars are born in an average year, and recent research on exoplanets (planets orbiting stars other than our own) suggests that a very large percentage of stars, possibly as many as 90 percent, have planets. Other numbers are harder

---

201.   Kurland 1999, 228–32.

to guess—nobody knows whether organisms could thrive on worlds much closer in or farther out from their stars than Earth is from the sun—and still others are a matter of blind guessing; nobody has any idea how common life is on alien worlds, much less intelligent life with a talent for technology and an interest in saying "Here we are!" to the rest of the universe.

Fermi's Paradox

One of the problems with high-end estimates, though, is that the universe around us shows no evidence that any alien civilizations exist at all. This is the basis of the famous Fermi paradox, first proposed by physicist Enrico Fermi in 1950.[202] Fermi pointed out that the Milky Way galaxy is thirteen billion years old and has some four hundred billion stars in it. Even if intelligent species that create technological civilizations are very rare, given the sheer number of rolls of the dice, if indefinite technological progress and interstellar travel are possible at all, somebody—and most probably many somebodies—would have had the raw luck many millions of years ago to break out of its original solar system, and colonize the galaxy. In that case, where are they?

Quite a range of possible solutions have been proposed for Fermi's paradox. One of the great strengths of the extraterrestrial hypothesis, though, is precisely that it offers an answer that seems to make perfect sense: they're here, hovering in Earth's skies in their silvery disk-shaped craft. The logic of Fermi's paradox has long played a central role in arguments for the ETH. Even people who have no direct connection with the UFO community at all commonly respond to skepticism about the extraterrestrial origin of UFOs by pointing out that it's absurd to think we're the only intelligent species in the universe, or the most technologically advanced. On that basis, evidence that spacecraft from a more advanced alien civilization are visiting Earth deserves to be taken seriously.

Though it's been denounced in heated terms by defenders of the null hypothesis, there's nothing inherently irrational about this argument.

---

202.   See Webb 2002 for a readable discussion.

The problem, once again, is in the details. Since the evidence for an alien presence in Earth's skies turns out on closer examination to be a projection of our own fantasies and fears about alien life, manipulated by a variety of entirely terrestrial institutions for their own reasons, the UFO solution to Fermi's paradox doesn't hold up to serious scrutiny. That leaves us once again facing an apparently empty galaxy, and wondering where everybody else is.

What makes this so uncomfortable for many people nowadays is that Fermi's paradox can be restated in another, far more threatening way. The logic of the paradox depends on the assumption that unlimited technological progress is possible, and it can be turned without too much difficulty into a logical disproof of that assumption. If unlimited technological progress is possible, then there should be clear evidence of technologically advanced species in the cosmos; there is no such evidence; therefore unlimited technological progress is impossible. This is a crashingly unpopular suggestion just now, in a society that invests progress with much the same aura of inevitability and goodness older civilizations gave to their gods. Still, it may offer a crucial clue to the shape of our own future.

Let's start with the obvious. Interstellar flight involves distances on a scale the human mind has never evolved the capacity to grasp. If the earth were the size of the letter o on this page, for example, the moon would be a little over an inch and three quarters away from it; the sun about sixty feet away; and Neptune, the outermost planet of our solar system now that Pluto has been officially demoted to "dwarf planet" status, a bit more than a third of a mile off. On the same scale, though, Proxima Centauri—the closest star to our solar system—would be more than three thousand miles away, which is roughly the distance from Florida to the Alaska panhandle. Epsilon Eridani, thought by many astronomers to be the closest star enough like our sun to have a good chance of inhabitable planets orbiting it, would be more than 7,500 miles away, which is roughly the distance across the Pacific Ocean from the west coast of America to the east coast of China.

The difference between going to the moon and going to the stars, in other words, isn't simply a difference in scale. It's a difference in kind. It takes literally unimaginable amounts of energy either to accelerate a spacecraft to the relativistic speeds needed to make an interstellar trip take less than centuries, or to keep a manned (or alienned) spacecraft viable for the long trip through deep space. Thus the Saturn V rocket that put Apollo 11 on the moon, the mightiest human spacecraft to date, doesn't even begin to approach the first baby steps toward interstellar travel. This deserves attention, because the most powerful and technologically advanced nation on Earth, riding the crest of the greatest economic boom in history and fueling that boom by burning through a half-billion years' worth of fossil fuels in a few short centuries, had to divert a noticeable fraction of its total resources to the task of getting a handful of spacecraft across what, in galactic terms, is a whisker-thin gap between neighboring worlds.

The Limits to Progress

It's been an article of faith for years now, and not just among science fiction fans, that progress will inevitably take care of the difference. This belief ties into some of the deepest and most rarely questioned assumptions of the modern world, but in the real world, progress isn't simply a matter of ingenuity or science. It depends on energy sources, and that was the factor that restricted the advancement of human technology to the starkly limited power provided by biomass, wind, water, and muscle until technical breakthroughs opened the treasure chest of the earth's carbon reserves in the eighteenth century.[203]

The central importance of those fossil fuel reserves to the last three hundred years of progress has too rarely been appreciated. If the biosphere had found some less flammable way than coal to stash carbon in the late Paleozoic, the industrial revolution of the eighteenth and nineteenth centuries wouldn't have happened. If nature had turned the sea life of the Mesozoic into some inert compound rather than petroleum, the transportation revolution of the twentieth century would never have gotten off the ground. Each step in the last three

---

203. See, among many other books on this theme, Catton 1980.

hundred years of progress has depended on access to some highly concentrated energy resource that could be put to human use.

The modern faith in progress assumes that this process can continue indefinitely. Such an assertion, however, flies in the face of the laws of thermodynamics, among the most unshakable of all the laws of physics. According to those laws, energy can neither be created nor destroyed, and left to itself, it always flows from higher concentrations to lower; this latter principle is the much-discussed law of entropy. A system that has energy flowing through it from some outside source—physicists call this a dissipative system—can develop eddies in the flow that concentrate energy in various ways. Thermodynamically speaking, living things are entropy eddies; each living thing takes energy from the flow of sunlight through the dissipative system of the earth in various ways, directly or indirectly, and stores some of that energy in concentrated form as living tissue. Since it takes energy to concentrate energy, though, the larger and richer a concentration of energy is, the less common it is. This is why big animals are rarer than smaller ones, and why bacteria outnumber and outweigh all other living things on Earth put together.

It's also why big deposits of oil and coal are much less common than small ones, and why oil and coal are much less common than inert substances in Earth's crust. Fossil fuels don't just happen at random; they exist because huge masses of living things, with their stored energy nearly intact, were buried under sediments and then concentrated into fuel by millions of years of heat and pressure within the earth. Petroleum is the most concentrated of the fossil fuels and thus the least common, and the biggest crude oil deposits—Ghawar in Saudi Arabia, Cantarell in Mexico, the West Texas fields, a handful of others—were the largest concentrations of free energy on Earth at the dawn of the industrial age. They are mostly gone now, along with hundreds of smaller deposits, and decades of increasingly frantic searching has failed to turn up anything on the same scale. Nor is there any sign of another, even more concentrated energy resource waiting in the wings.[204]

Thus the answer to Fermi's paradox may well lie in a factor Drake left out of his famous equation: e_c, the average amount of concentrated energy resources available on a planet capable of supporting intelligent, technologically gifted life forms. If it turns out that the amount of energy stored on Earth in fossil fuels and the like is around average—and in the absence of other evidence, this is probably a fair guess—there may simply not be enough energy at the disposal of any intelligent life form in the galaxy to progress to the point of interstellar travel, much less carry out a program of galactic expansion.

All this impacts the final factor in Drake's equation, too: L, the average lifespan of a technological civilization. As far as the available evidence reveals, our planet first produced a civilization capable of interstellar communication by radio around 1900. It's popular to assume that a human civilization at least as advanced as the one we have today will be around for thousands or even millions of years to come, but the jury's still out on that question, and a growing number of scientists have begun to suggest that technological civilizations may turn out to be very short-term phenomena.[205] Despite common media stereotypes, too, it wouldn't take nuclear war or the collapse of Earth's biosphere to bring our technological civilization to a screeching halt. If it turns out that the fossil fuels now being used so lavishly can't be effectively replaced by other energy resources, for example, another century or so could see our current high technology become a thing of the past forever.

In terms of the kind of progress we have known for the last three centuries, then, we may have reached the end of our rope. Once we've finished burning through the nearly free energy of fossil fuels that was concentrated for us by half a billion years of geology, concentrating energy beyond a certain fairly modest point will rapidly become a losing game in thermodynamic terms. At that point, progress in the modern sense—the sort of progress that could conceivably cross interstellar

---

204. Heinberg 2007 and Greer 2008 discuss these problems in detail.

205. See, for example, Duncan 1993.

space—will be over, and the challenge facing the human societies of the future will be the very different one of learning to build a humane and creative civilization here on Earth, using the very modest energy provided by sun, wind, water, and other renewable sources.

We can apply this logic to Fermi's paradox and reach a conclusion that makes sense of the data. Since life forms create localized concentrations of energy, each planet inhabited by life forms will develop concentrated energy resources. Odds are that our planet is somewhere near the average, so we can postulate that some worlds will have more stored energy than ours, and some will have less. A certain fraction of planets will doubtless evolve intelligent, tool-using species that figure out how to use their planet's stored energy reserves. Some species will have more energy to work with and some less; some will use their reserves quickly and some slowly, but all of them will eventually reach the point our own species is reaching today—the point at which it becomes painfully clear that the biosphere of a planet can only store up a finite amount of concentrated energy, and when it's gone, it's gone.

Chances are that a certain number of the intelligent species in our galaxy have used these stored energy reserves to attempt short-distance spaceflight, as we have done. Some species with a great deal of energy resources may be able to establish colonies on other worlds in their own systems, at least until the energy runs out. The difference between the tabletop and football-field distances within a solar system, and the continental distances between the stars, though, can't be ignored. Given the fantastic energies and technological revolutions that would be required for interstellar travel, the chance that any intelligent species will have access to a vast enough supply of concentrated energy resources to keep an industrial society progressing long enough to evolve starflight technology, and then accomplish the feat of reaching another star, is so close to zero that the lack of alien spacecraft in Earth's skies makes perfect sense.

The Spiritualist Parallel

None of the points just made about the limits to progress have seen much discussion in the mainstream media or the popular culture of the modern world, but all of them have had a shadowy presence in our collective imagination for decades now. They occupy, in fact, much the same position that the science fiction dreams of the pulp era had in their own time, when sensible people dismissed the idea of riding rockets to the moon as impossible Buck Rogers fantasies. Thus it's not the least of the ironies surrounding the UFO phenomenon that a set of beliefs about extraterrestrial visitation that once placed itself in opposition to the accepted worldview of the modern industrial world has gradually become one of the few sources of support that the modern worldview has left.

For this is what the belief in the extraterrestrial origins of UFOs has become in the first decade of the twenty-first century: an act of faith, reinforced by visionary experiences, that serves to bolster the flagging belief that infinite progress is possible, and that humanity's destiny among the stars is something more than a religious idea, an old mythology mistakenly projected onto the inkblot patterns of an increasingly unfamiliar cosmos. If the aliens can soar free of the restrictions imposed by the limited resources of their homeworld, the logic seems to run, the threadbare dream that humanity might do the same need not be wholly surrendered.

For believers in UFO conspiracy theories, the supposed presence of the aliens also offers that very human comfort in difficult times, a scapegoat that can be blamed for the failure of a belief system to conform to reality. For believers in New Age contactee teachings, equally, the anticipated mass arrival of alien starships on a mission of planetary rescue offers the different but equally human comfort of believing that some greater power will save humanity from the consequences of its own mistakes.

All this invites comparison with another phenomenon in American cultural history: the rise, flowering, and fall of Spiritualism. The Spiritualist movement began in 1848, almost exactly a century before Kenneth Arnold's sighting, and like the UFO phenomenon it started with one highly publicized event, the interactions of the three Fox sisters with what they claimed was a ghost who made rapping noises on the floor of the Fox home. Just as Arnold's sighting was followed by a flurry of additional sightings that were assumed to be the same as his, but differed in crucial ways, the media furor that followed the first newspaper articles on the Fox sisters inspired many other people to attempt contact with the dead using completely different means.

Mesmerism, the forerunner of modern hypnosis, provided the toolkit for the nascent movement, and a rich popular mythology of life after death composed of equal parts Protestant folk piety and traditional ghost lore yielded ideas that gave the toolkit its context. Within a short time Spiritualism had evolved into a network of mediums—individuals with a talent for altered states of consciousness that allowed them to apparently speak with the dead—linked by a common ideology and a support system of venues, journals, and supporters. Leading figures in the alternative spiritual scene such as Andrew Jackson Davis, the George Van Tassel of his time, added older spiritual teachings to the mix and gave the movement a veneer of philosophy. Meanwhile, the media of the time threw fuel on the fire with sensationalistic articles praising and denouncing the new movement, guaranteeing it maximum publicity.

The public reaction to the rise of Spiritualism sorted itself out into three main channels, each of which became a social movement of some significance in its time. First and most colorful were those who embraced it as a new religion and founded Spiritualist churches, recycling the popular religious ideas of their time under a new banner. Second were those who wanted to study the phenomenon scientifically, and founded a series of research organizations to gather evidence about mediums and spirits. Third were those who rejected Spiritualism from top to bottom, and launched their own investigations of notable mediums in an attempt to prove that all Spiritualist phenomena were caused by fraud or delusion.

Trace the history of the two movements over their first six decades or so, and the parallels are hard to miss. Through the peak years of the Spiritualist phenomenon, the great quarrel between supporters of "psychical research" and their detractors occupied center stage in the public eye. Psychical researchers set out to collect evidence that mediums could actually contact the dead; in the process, they turned up a great deal of data about the farther shores of human mental and spiritual experience, but no conclusive proof of postmortem contact. Debunkers set out to collect evidence that the entire thing was produced by trickery and delusion, and managed only to prove that some mediums were deliberate frauds who used sleight-of-hand techniques to fake spirit communications. Neither side ever managed to come up with evidence that the other would accept, and both ended up preaching to the converted.

Behind these debates, mentioned only occasionally but providing them with most of their relevance to contemporary culture, lay the great nineteenth-century struggle between Christian theology and scientific materialism. By the middle of that century, many people in America and elsewhere in the Western world found it impossible to believe traditional Christian teachings, but could not abandon their faith in more basic religious ideas such as life after death. The Spiritualist movement, which claimed to move the afterlife out of the realm of faith and make it a matter of experimental evidence, offered a solution to the dilemma.

This cultural crisis played a huge role in boosting Spiritualism in its time, but too much dependence on contemporary issues is rarely an advantage for a religion in the long run. As the nineteenth century ended and the struggles between science and faith shifted to new ground, Spiritualism found itself left behind by its own culture.

In this context, the later history of Spiritualism offers a cautionary tale. As the debate between the psychical researchers and the debunkers unfolded, both sides became so obsessed with the goal of defeating their opponents that the last traces of impartiality and common sense got lost in the scrimmage. In the end, both sides effectively cancelled one another out, and left the field to the true believers. As the cultural forces that boosted Spiritualism faded out, though, the ranks of the believers thinned as well. A century after the Fox sisters, a phenomenon that had once seized the collective imagination of American culture and bid fair to redefine the religious landscape of the modern Western world had dwindled to a tiny network of churches scattered across the country, attended mostly by the elderly, where a handful of followers went through the motions of a familiar faith that nobody else found relevant. Today, many decades later, the churches and their faithful are even fewer, and most Americans barely remember that the Spiritualist movement ever existed in the first place.

Seven Falsifiable Predictions

It seems more than a little likely that this is the fate waiting for the UFO controversy in the decades to come. To a crucial degree, UFOs were a phenomenon of the Cold War era, profoundly shaped by the fears, fantasies, and unquestioned assumptions of that time. Without the firm belief in inevitable technological progress that the industrial world, and America above all, brought into that era, the popular faith that apparitions sighted in the sky meant the imminent arrival of visitors from other planets would never have emerged. Without the waning of the belief in progress after the cultural crises of the 1960s and 1970s, in turn, that faith would never have traced the tortuous path it did. The twenty-first century will doubtless have its own strange beliefs, but they will draw on the events of a different era and take different shapes.

Still, it's possible, and perhaps necessary, to be more specific in talking about the future of the phenomenon. Earlier in this book, I commented that valid hypotheses—about UFOs or anything else— need to make specific falsifiable predictions if they are to be taken seriously in anything like a scientific context. It thus seems reasonable to offer a set of specific predictions that follow from the hypothesis I've proposed here. If they are solidly disproved in the years to come, my hypothesis falls with them.

> 1. *No definite evidence of extraterrestrial involvement in the UFO phenomenon will ever surface.* Solid evidence for an extraterrestrial presence in Earth's skies need not involve the mass landings or alien invasions that have been predicted so often, and just as often failed to occur. An extraterrestrial wrench or fragment of saucer hull made of a material that cannot be duplicated by human technology would be more than enough; so

would a piece of scientific knowledge received by a contactee or abductee that was unknown to human science but turned out to be true when tested. Such proofs have been expected and promised for six decades and have never materialized; if one does, this book's hypothesis fails.

2. *UFO sightings and closely related phenomena will undergo an overall decrease in the next few decades.* In all probability, people will continue to see strange things in the sky in the future, and the vagaries of popular culture over the next few decades may yet add new wrinkles to the existing flying saucer narrative. Still, if my hypothesis is correct, UFO sightings of the kinds I have identified as apparitions will become less common as the years pass, as other images seize a larger role in the collective imagination. The chance that future secret aerospace programs in the United States and elsewhere will use UFOs as protective camouflage is harder to assess, but the waning of UFOs as a factor in popular culture is likely to make that camouflage less effective and so less likely to be used in the future.

3. *If the "earth lights" phenomenon ever becomes the focus of sustained scientific study, the existence of a natural process generating unusual light effects will be documented.* The glowing spheres of light sighted by anthropologists in Africa, as mentioned in chapter 1, and documented by proponents of the geophysical hypothesis, as shown in chapter 6, have been interpreted in many different ways over the centuries, but behind the interpretation lies an almost certainly natural phenomenon that can be photographed and observed by multiple witnesses. A solidly funded field study in an area where the lights are regularly seen could easily put their existence beyond question, though it may take a great deal of further work to identify the process that causes them.

4. *UFOs of the types identified in this book as probable apparitions will consistently follow trends in media portrayals of extraterrestrial life, with the first media appearances preceding the first*

UFO-related reports by months or years. Just as past UFO sightings and beliefs have closely tracked media imagery since before the beginning of the phenomenon, future manifestations of the UFO narrative will show the same pattern, and surveys of popular media about visitors from outer space in the months and years before the emergence of any new type of UFO-related phenomenon will show exact parallels with the new phenomenon.

5. *UFOs of the types identified in this book as probable secret aerospace projects will consistently follow trends in the underlying technologies, with retrospective studies finding close equivalents in projects that were secret at the time of the sighting.* It takes something around fifteen years on average for a secret aircraft technology to move from the experimental stage, through active deployment, to a level of obsolescence at which its existence can be admitted by the government. If another wave of multiple-witness sightings that describe a specific type of UFO should happen in the future, researchers one to two decades later should be able to point to close parallels to known technologies that were still secret when the sightings took place. The visual similarity between black triangular stealth planes and the black triangles of 1980s multiple-witness sightings is an example of the sort of connection that can be expected.

6. *Should a major breakdown of the national security apparatus in the United States ever occur, leading to large-scale publication of currently secret information, evidence supporting the claim that UFO reports were used to conceal real military and espionage technologies will come to light.* It's impossible to predict whether the twists and turns of history in the decades to come will bring mass releases of currently classified documents, but a fair number of possibilities—anything from a crisis of national confidence of the sort that caused similar releases in the 1970s up to the collapse of the current American system of government and its replacement by a different one—could do just

that. If that happens, my hypothesis predicts that no amount of digging will turn up proof of the crashed saucers and suppressed alien technologies of current UFO conspiracy lore, for the simple reason that these don't exist. Rather, if this happens, material released in this way will back up and expand the revelations discussed in chapter 8 of this book, showing how the United States government used claims and rumors about UFOs to conceal the nature and activities of entirely earthly technologies of various kinds.

7. *Neither the contactee community, the more scientific believers in the extraterrestrial hypothesis, nor the debunking community defending the null hypothesis will alter their positions in response to any of these changes.* The discussion of the barriers to understanding in chapter 5 of this book is a central part of my hypothesis, and outlines the mechanisms that have allowed the controversy to run on as long and unproductively as it has. My hypothesis predicts that those barriers will remain solidly in place in the future. More likely than not, the UFO research community and the debunking community will fade out by sheer attrition as current members die or leave the field, and younger people find less and less interest in a dated and unproductive controversy.

The contactee community, under its present New Age banner or some new label, is likely to survive much longer, and could well contribute to the alternative religious movements of the twenty-first century in much the same way Spiritualism contributed to the contactee movement itself. It's all too easy to imagine the conversations between the Space Brothers and the original contactees of the 1950s embroidered into legend, with the mass landing of the saucers taking on the same mythic role as the Second Coming of Jesus has in more mainstream faiths. It seems unlikely that this would give rise to a major religion in the future, but stranger things have happened.

If the future of the UFO phenomenon turns out to be anything like what I've outlined here, it will mark the close of a strange and, in many ways, a sad history, located somewhere in the poorly defined space between tragedy and farce. It would be all too easy to turn the whole tapestry of the UFO phenomenon, from its origins in the gaudy pages of the 1920s pulps to its twilight among the squabbling personalities and paranoid conspiracy theories of the present day, into nothing more than a target for mockery. Ultimately, though, I'm far from sure that this would be just.

Despite the deceptions, delusions, misunderstandings, and often-shoddy reasoning that created it and kept it going, after all, the UFO phenomenon for much of its sixty-year history served as an anchor for some of the highest aspirations of our species. For a great many people, the image of the flying saucer embodied the dream of contact with other worlds, the passionate quest for knowledge, and the conviction that individuals armed only with a desire to find the truth can overcome all odds and revolutionize humanity's understanding of itself and its world. Even the debunkers who warred against it drew their inspiration from a respect for truth, however poorly that respect expressed itself in the heat of the struggle. It seems only fair to hope that in the future, when the entire controversy has been laid to rest, people will remember that when they think about the time when millions of people convinced themselves that our planet was being visited by flying saucers from another world.

glossary of acronyms

A-12: Single-seat version of the SR-71 Blackbird reconnaissance plane

AFOSI: U.S. Air Force Office of Special Investigations

APRO: Aerial Phenomena Research Organization, a UFO research organization founded by Coral and James Lorenzen in 1952

B-2 Spirit: The first American stealth bomber, made public in 1988

BCE: Before the Christian era, nonsectarian equivalent of BC

CE: Christian era, nonsectarian equivalent of AD

CE-1: Close encounter of the first kind, in Hynek's UFO taxonomy a UFO that approaches within three hundred meters of an observer

CE-2: Close encounter of the second kind, in Hynek's UFO taxonomy a UFO that leaves physical traces

CE-3: Close encounter of the third kind, in Hynek's UFO taxonomy an encounter with UFO occupants

CE-4: Close encounter of the fourth kind, in current UFO parlance the abduction of one or more persons by UFO occupants

CIA: Central Intelligence Agency, U.S. intelligence agency founded in 1947 ·

CUFOS: Center for UFO Studies, a UFO research organization founded by J. Allen Hynek in 1973

DD: Daylight disk, in Hynek's UFO taxonomy any UFO seen at a distance in the air during daylight, whether or not disk-shaped

ETH: Extraterrestrial hypothesis, the theory that some UFO sightings can only be explained as visits by spacecraft from another planet

F-117 Nighthawk: The first American stealth fighter, test-flown for the first time in 1982 and made public in 1988

FOBS: Fractional Orbital Bombardment System, a Soviet military space project that was deliberately labeled a UFO by the Soviet government

GSW: Ground Saucer Watch, a UFO research organization founded in 1957 by William and J. A. Spaulding

IFSB: International Flying Saucer Bureau, a UFO research organization founded in 1952 by Albert K. Bender and dissolved the next year

JANAP 146: Joint Army-Navy-Air Force Publication 146, a regulation issued in 1953 making it a federal felony for military personnel, commercial air pilots, and certain other persons to release a UFO report to the public

MIB: Men in Black, sinister figures who are claimed to harass UFO researchers

MUFON: Mutual UFO Network (formerly Midwest UFO Network), a UFO research organization founded by Walter Andrus in 1969

NH: Null hypothesis, the theory that UFO sightings can all be accounted for by fraud, hallucination, or misperceptions of known objects

NICAP: National Investigations Committee on Aerial Phenomena, a UFO research organization founded in 1956 and headed from 1957 to 1970 by Donald E. Keyhoe

NL: Nocturnal light, in Hynek's UFO taxonomy any luminous UFO seen at night

NSA: National Security Agency, U.S. intelligence agency founded in 1952

ONI: Office of Naval Intelligence, the oldest U.S. intelligence agency, founded in 1888

SR-71 Blackbird: American high-altitude reconnaissance plane, first flown in 1962

SR-91 Aurora: An alleged secret American stealth reconnaissance plane, the successor to the SR-71; its existence is officially denied by the U.S. government

TLE: Temporal-lobe epilepsy

TR-3 Black Manta: An alleged American stealth reconnaissance plane whose existence is officially denied by the U.S. government

U-2: American high-altitude reconnaissance plane, first test-flown in 1954 and still in service; according to published CIA documents the cause of many apparent UFO sightings

UFO: Unidentified flying object

bibliography

Adamski, George. *Inside the Space Ships*. New York: Abelard-Schumann, 1955.

Arnold, Kenneth, and Ray Palmer. *The Coming of the Saucers*. Amherst, WI: privately printed, 1952.

Baker, Robert A. *They Call It Hypnosis*. Buffalo, NY: Prometheus, 1990.

Bamford, James. *The Puzzle Palace*. Boston: Houghton Mifflin, 1982.

Barclay, David, and Therese Marie Barclay. *UFOs: The Final Answer?* London: Blandford, 1993.

Barker, Gray. *They Knew Too Much About Flying Saucers*. New York: University Books, 1956.

Bender, Albert K. *Flying Saucers and the Three Men*. London: Neville Spearman, 1963.

Bethurum, Truman. *Aboard a Flying Saucer*. Los Angeles: DeVorss and Company, 1954.

Bishop, Greg. *Project Beta*. New York: Paraview, 2005.

Blacker, Carmen. *The Catalpa Bow*. London: George Allen and Unwin, 1975.

Bok, Bart, Paul Kurtz, and Lawrence Jerome. "Objections to Astrology." *The Humanist* 35 (September/October 1975), 4–6.

Bord, Janet, and Colin Bord. *Alien Animals*. London: Grafton, 1980.

Brown, Anthony Cave. *Bodyguard of Lies*. New York: Bantam, 1976.

Bryan, C. D. B. *Close Encounters of the Fourth Kind*. New York: Alfred Knopf, 1995.

Bullard, Thomas C. *UFO Abductions: The Measure of a Mystery*. 2 vols. Mt. Rainier, MD: Fund for UFO Research, 1987.

———. "UFOs: Lost in the Myths," in Jacobs 2000, 141–91.

Burrows, William E. *By Any Means Necessary: America's Secret Air War in the Cold War*. New York: Farrar, Straus and Giroux, 2001.

Burton, Robert. *The Anatomy of Melancholy*. New York: New York Review of Books, 2001. (Originally published in 1621.)

Busby, Michael. *Solving the 1897 Airship Mystery*. Gretna, LA: Pelican, 2004.

Cahn, J. P. "The Flying Saucers and the Mysterious Little Men." *True* (September 1952).

———. "Flying Saucer Swindlers." *True* (August 1956).

Carballal, Manuel. "Jordan Peña Habla de UMMO en Radio." *El Ojo Crítico* 52 (January 2006), 4–7.

Catton, William R., Jr. *Overshoot*. Urbana, IL: University of Illinois Press, 1980.

Childress, David Hatcher, and Richard Shaver. *Lost Continents & the Hollow Earth*. Kempton, IL: Adventures Unlimited, 1999.

Clair, Stella. (Illustrated by Edward Andrewes.) *Susie Saucer and Ronnie Rocket*. New York: T. Werner Laurie, 1952.

Clark, Jerome. *Extraordinary Encounters*. Santa Barbara, CA: ABC-Clio, 2000.

Cohn, Norman. *Warrant for Genocide*. New York: Harper & Row, 1967.

Condon, Edward U. *A Scientific Study of Unidentified Flying Objects*. New York: Bantam, 1969.

Conroy, Ed. *Report on Communion*. New York: William Morrow, 1989.

———. "Who Is the Joker in the Gulf Breeze UFO 'Hoax'?" *The Communion Letter* 2:2 (Sumer 1990), 1–16.

Cooper, M. William. *Behold a Pale Horse*. Flagstaff, AZ: Light Technology, 1991.

Couliano, Ioan. *Eros and Magic in the Renaissance*. Chicago: University of Chicago Press, 1984.

Crowe, Michael J. *The Extraterrestrial Life Debate 1750–1900: The Idea of a Plurality of Worlds from Kant to Lowell.* Cambridge: Cambridge University Press, 1986.

Curran, Douglas. *In Advance of the Landing: Folk Concepts of Outer Space.* New York: Abbeville Press, 1985.

Däniken, Erich von. *Chariots of the Gods?* Translated by Michael Heron. London: Corgi, 1971.

Darlington, David. *Area 51: The Dreamland Chronicles.* New York: Henry Holt, 1997.

de Mille, Richard, ed. *The Don Juan Papers.* Santa Barbara, CA: Ross-Erickson, 1980.

Dean, Jodi. *Aliens in America.* Ithaca, NY: Cornell University Press, 1997.

Denzler, Brenda. *The Lure of the Edge.* Berkeley, CA: University of California Press, 2001.

Derr, John S. "Earthquake Lights: A Review of Observations and Present Theories." *Bulletin of the Seismological Society of America* 63 (December 1973), 2177–87.

Devereux, Paul. *Earth Lights.* Wellingborough, UK: Turnstone, 1982.

———. *Earth Lights Revelation.* London: Blandford, 1989.

———, and Peter Brookesmith. *UFOs and Ufology: The First Fifty Years.* London: Blandford, 1997.

Dick, Steven J. *Plurality of Worlds: The Origins of the Extraterrestrial Life Debate from Democritus to Kant.* Cambridge: Cambridge University Press, 1982.

Dickhoff, Robert Ernst. *Homecoming of the Martians.* Ghaziabad, India: Bharti Association Publishers, 1958.

Dohrman, H. T. *California Cult: The Story of "Mankind United."* Boston: Beacon Press, 1958.

Dolan, Richard M. *UFOs and the National Security State.* Charlottesville, VA: Hampton Roads, 2002.

Donderi, Don C. "Science, Law, and War: Alternative Frameworks for the UFO Evidence." In Jacobs 2000, 56–81.

Dorwart, Jeffery M. *The Office of Naval Intelligence.* Annapolis, MD: Naval Institute Press, 1979.

Druffel, Ann. *Firestorm: Dr. James E. McDonald's Fight for UFO Science.* Columbus, NC: Wild Flower Press, 2003.

Duncan, Richard C. "The Life-Expectancy of Industrial Civilization: the Decline to Global Equilibrium." *Population and Environment* 14:4 (1993), 325–57.

Eliade, Mircea. *Shamanism: Archaic Techniques of Ecstasy.* Translated by Willard R. Trask. Princeton, NJ: Princeton University Press, 1964.

Ellis, Bill. *Raising the Devil: Satanism, New Religions, and the Media.* Lexington, KY: University Press of Kentucky, 2000.

Ferguson, Marilyn. *The Aquarian Conspiracy.* New York: J. P. Tarcher, 1980.

Festinger, Leon, Henry W. Riecken, and Stanley Schachter. *When Prophecy Fails.* Minneapolis, MN: University of Minnesota Press, 1956.

Fiore, Edith. *Encounters.* New York: Doubleday, 1989.

Flournoy, Theodore. *From India to the Planet Mars.* New Hyde Park, NY: University Books, 1963.

Fort, Charles. *The Complete Books of Charles Fort.* New York: Dover, 1974.

Fortune, Dion. *Applied Magic and Aspects of Occultism.* Wellingborough, UK: Aquarian, 1987.

———. *The Magical Battle of Britain.* Bradford on Avon, UK: Golden Gates, 1993.

Fuller, John. *Incident at Exeter.* New York: Putnam, 1966.

———. *The Interrupted Journey.* New York: Putnam, 1968.

Gardner, Martin. *Are Universes Thicker Than Blackberries?* New York: W. W. Norton, 2003.

———. *Urantia: The Great Cult Mystery.* Amherst, NY: Prometheus Books, 1995.

George, Llewellyn. *Improved Perpetual Planetary Hour Book.* Portland, OR: Llewellyn, 1906.

Godwin, John. *Occult America.* New York: Doubleday, 1972.

Godwin, Joscelyn. *Arktos: The Polar Myth in Science, Symbolism and Nazi Survival.* Grand Rapids, MI: Phanes, 1993.

Goldberg, Bruce. *Time Travelers from Our Future.* St. Paul, MN: Llewellyn, 1998.

Good, Timothy. *Above Top Secret.* New York: William Morrow, 1988.

Goodrick-Clarke, Nicholas. *Black Sun: Aryan Cults, Esoteric Nazism and the Politics of Identity.* New York: New York University Press, 2002.

———. *The Occult Roots of Nazism.* New York: New York University Press, 1992.

Goulart, Ron. *Cheap Thrills: An Informal History of the Pulp Magazines.* New York: Arlington House, 1972.

Greenbank, Anthony. *The Book of Survival.* New York: Harper & Row, 1967.

Greenler, Robert. *Rainbows, Halos, and Glories.* Cambridge: Cambridge University Press, 1980.

Greer, John Michael. *Atlantis: Ancient Legacy, Hidden Prophecy.* Woodbury, MN: Llewellyn, 2007.

———. *The Long Descent: A User's Guide to the End of the Industrial Age.* Gabriola Island, BC: New Society, 2008.

Haines, Gerald K. "CIA's Role in the Study of UFOs, 1947–90." *Studies in Intelligence* (Summer 1997), 67–84.

Hall, Manly Palmer. "The Case of the Flying Saucers" (1950); reprinted in Grey Lodge Occult Review vol. 1 (Autumn 2002), http://www.greylodge.org.

Harpur, Patrick. *Daimonic Reality.* New York: Viking, 1994.

Hay, David. *Exploring Inner Space.* London: Mowbray, 1987.

Heard, Gerald. *Is Another World Watching?* New York: Harper & Row, 1950.

Heinberg, Richard. *Peak Everything.* Gabriola Island, BC: New Society, 2007.

Hendry, Allan. *The UFO Handbook.* Garden City, NY: Doubleday, 1979.

Herbert, Frank. *Hellstrom's Hive.* New York: Bantam, 1972.

Hopkins, Budd. "Hypnosis and the Investigation of UFO Abduction Accounts." In Jacobs 2000, 215–40.

———. *Intruders: The Incredible Visitations at Copley Woods.* New York: Random House, 1987.

———. *Missing Time.* New York: Marek, 1981.

———. *Witnessed: The True Story of the Brooklyn Bridge Abductions.* New York: Pocket Books, 1996.

———, and Carol Rainey. *Sight Unseen.* New York: Atria, 2003.

Hori, Ichiro. *Folk Religion in Japan*. Chicago: University of Chicago Press, 1968.

Howe, Linda Moulton. *An Alien Harvest*. Littleton, CO: Linda Moulton Howe Productions, 1989.

Hurley, Matthew. *The Alien Chronicles*. Chester, UK: Quester, 2003.

Hynek, J. Allen. *The Hynek UFO Report*. New York: Dell, 1977.

———. *The UFO Experience*. Chicago: Henry Regnery, 1972.

———, Philip J. Imbrogno, and Bob Pratt. *Night Siege: The Hudson Valley UFO Sightings*. St. Paul, MN: Llewellyn Publications, 1998.

Icke, David. *. . . And The Truth Shall Set You Free*. Wildwood, MO: Bridge of Love, 1995.

———. *The Biggest Secret*. Wildwood, MO: Bridge of Love, 1999.

———. *Children of the Matrix*. Wildwood, MO: Bridge of Love, 2001.

Jacobs, David M. *Secret Life*. New York: Simon & Schuster, 1992.

———. *The Threat*. New York: Simon & Schuster, 1998.

———. *The UFO Controversy in America*. Bloomington, IN: Indiana University Press, 1975.

———. "UFOs and the Search for Scientific Legitimacy." In Kerr and Crow 1983, 218–32.

———, ed. *UFOs and Abductions: Challenging the Borders of Knowledge*. Lawrence, KS: University Press of Kansas, 2000.

James, Trevor. *They Live in the Sky!* Los Angeles: New Age Publishing Company, 1958.

Jansma, Sidney J., Sr. *UFOs, Satan and Evolution*. San Diego: Institute for Creation Research, 1980.

Jung, Carl. *Flying Saucers: A Modern Myth of Things Seen in the Sky*. Princeton, NJ: Princeton University Press, 1978.

Kafton-Minkel, Walter. *Subterranean Worlds*. Port Townsend, WA: Loompanics, 1989.

Kagan, Daniel, and Ian Summers. *Mute Evidence*. New York: Bantam, 1983.

Kamann, Richard. "The True Disbelievers." *Zetetic Scholar* 10 (December 1982), 50–65.

Keel, John. *The Complete Guide to Mysterious Beings*. New York: Tor, 2002.

———. "The Man Who Invented Flying Saucers." In Ted Schultz, ed., *The Fringes of Reason*. New York: Harmony Books, 1989, 138–45.

———. *The Mothman Prophecies*. New York: Tor, 1991.

———. *UFOs: Operation Trojan Horse*. New York: Manor Books, 1976.

Kerr, Howard, and Charles L. Crow. *The Occult in America: New Historical Perspectives*. Urbana, IL: University of Illinois Press, 1983.

Keyhoe, Donald E. *Aliens from Space*. Garden City, NY: Doubleday, 1973.

———. *Flying Saucers Are Real*. New York: Fawcett Publications, 1950.

———. *Flying Saucers from Outer Space*. New York: Henry Holt, 1953.

———. *Flying Saucers—Top Secret*. New York: Putnam, 1960.

Kinder, Gary. *Light Years* New York: Pocket Books, 1987.

Klass, Philip J. *Secret Sentries in Space*. New York: Random House, 1971.

———. *UFO Abductions: A Dangerous Game*. Buffalo, NY: Prometheus, 1989.

———. *UFOs Explained*. New York: Random House, 1974.

———. *UFOs: The Public Deceived*. Buffalo, NY: Prometheus, 1983.

Korff, Kal K. *Spaceships of the Pleiades: The Billy Meier Story*. Amherst, NY: Prometheus Books, 1996.

Kuhn, Thomas. *The Structure of Scientific Revolutions*. Chicago: University of Chicago Press, 1970.

Kurland, Michael. *The Complete Idiot's Guide to Extraterrestrial Intelligence*. New York: Alpha Books, 1999.

Kusche, Lawrence David. *The Bermuda Triangle Mystery—Solved*. Buffalo, NY: Prometheus Books, 1975.

Lamy, Philip. *Millennium Rage*. New York: Plenum Press, 1998.

Laumer, Keith. *The Invaders*. New York: Pyramid Books, 1967.

Lawson, Alvin H. "Hypnosis of Imaginary UFO 'Abductees.'" In Curtis G. Fuller, ed., *Proceedings of the First International UFO Congress*. New York: Warner Books, 1980.

Layne, Meade. *The Ether Ship Mystery and its Solution*. Bayside, CA: Borderland Sciences, 1950.

Le Poer Trench, Brinsley. *The Flying Saucer Story*. London: Neville Spearman, 1966.

Lear, John. "The Grand Deception: How the Gray EBEs Tricked MJ-12 into an Agreement." *CUFORN Bulletin*, March/April 1989, 2–8.

Leslie, Desmond, and George Adamski. *Flying Saucers Have Landed*. New York: British Book Center, 1953.

Lewis, James R., ed. *Odd Gods: New Religions and the Cult Controversy*. Amherst, NY: Prometheus Books, 2001.

———. *UFOs and Popular Culture: An Encyclopedia of Contemporary Myth*. Santa Barbara, CA: ABC-Clio, 2000.

Long, Greg. *Examining the Earthlight Theory*. Chicago: Center for UFO Studies, 1990.

Lorenzen, Coral. *Flying Saucers: The Startling Evidence of the Invasion from Outer Space*. New York: New American Library, 1966.

———. *UFOs Over the Americas*. New York: New American Library, 1968.

Lovejoy, Arthur O. *The Great Chain of Being*. New York: Harper, 1936.

Mack, John E. *Abduction: Human Encounters with Aliens*. New York: Charles Scribner's Sons, 1994.

———. *Passport to the Cosmos*. New York: Crown, 1999.

Magee, Judith. "Maureen Puddy's Third Encounter." *Flying Saucer Review* 24:3 (November 1978), 12–13 and 15.

McClenon, James. *Deviant Science: The Case of Parapsychology*. Philadelphia: University of Pennsylvania Press, 1984.

McPhee, John. *The Deltoid Pumpkin Seed*. New York: Farrar, Straus and Giroux, 1973.

Menzel, Donald H. *Flying Saucers*. Cambridge, MA: Harvard University Press, 1953.

———, and Ernest H. Taves. *The UFO Enigma*. Garden City, NY: Doubleday, 1977.

Miall, Robert. *UFO-1: Flesh Hunters*. New York: Warner, 1973.

———. *UFO-2: Sporting Blood*. New York: Warner, 1973.

Michael, Cecil. *Round Trip to Hell in a Flying Saucer*. Bakersfield, CA: Roofhopper Enterprises, 1971.

Miller, Jay. *The X-Planes: X-1 to X-45*. Hinckley, UK: Midland Publishing, 2001.

Nash, William B., and William H. Fortenberry. "We Flew Above Flying Saucers." *True* (October 1952), 65 and 110–12.

Neihardt, John G. *Black Elk Speaks*. Lincoln, NE: University of Nebraska Press, 1988.

Newbrough, John Ballou. *Oahspe, A New Bible in the Words of Jehovih and His Angel Ambassadors*. Los Angeles: Essenes of Kosmon, 1950.

Nickell, Joe, with John F. Fischer. *Mysterious Realms*. Buffalo, NY: Prometheus Press, 1992.

Oberg, James. "The Great Soviet UFO Coverup." *MUFON UFO Journal* (October 1982).

———. *UFOs and Outer Space Mysteries: A Sympathetic Skeptic's Report*. Norfolk, VA: Donning, 1982.

Oreskes, Naomi. *The Rejection of Continental Drift*. Oxford: Oxford University Press, 1999.

Orne, Martin T., W. G. Whitehouse, D. F. Dinges, and E. C. Orne. "Reconstructing Memory through Hypnosis." In Helen M. Pettinati, ed. *Hypnosis and Memory*. New York: Guilford Press, 1988.

Overall, Zan. *Gulf Breeze Double Exposed*. Chicago: CUFOS, 1990.

Patton, Phil. *Dreamland*. New York: Villard, 1998.

Peebles, Curtis. *Watch the Skies! A Chronicle of the Flying Saucer Myth*. New York: Smithsonian Institution, 1994.

Pendlow, Gregory W., and Donald E. Welzenbach. *The CIA and the U-2 Program, 1954–1974*. Washington, DC: Central Intelligence Agency, 1998.

Persinger, Michael A. "The UFO Experience: A Normal Correlate of Human Brain Function." In Jacobs 2000, 262–302.

———, and Gyslaine F. Lafreniere. *Space-Time Transients and Unusual Events*. Chicago: Nelson-Hall, 1977.

Pfeiffer, Bruce Brooks, and Gerald Nordland, eds. *Frank Lloyd Wright in the Realm of Ideas*. Carbondale, IL: Southern Illinois University Press, 1988.

Picknett, Lynn, and Clive Prince. *The Stargate Conspiracy*. London: Little, Brown and Co., 1999.

Pottenger, Doris M. *UFOs: Aliens or Demons?* Middleton, OH: CHJ Publishing, 1990.

Randles, Jenny. *UFO Reality*. London: Robert Hale, 1983.

———, Dot Street, and Brenda Butler. *Sky Crash*. London: Neville Spearman, 1984.

Rawlins, Dennis. "sTARBABY." *FATE* 34 (October 1981).

Reeve, Bryant, and Helen Reeve. *Flying Saucer Pilgrimage*. Amherst, WI: Amherst Press, 1957.

Regardie, Israel. *The Golden Dawn*. St. Paul, MN: Llewellyn, 1971.

Renterghem, Tony van. *When Santa Was a Shaman*. St. Paul, MN: Llewellyn, 1995.

Richelson, Jeffrey T. *The Wizards of Langley*. Boulder, CO: Westview Press, 2001.

Ring, Kenneth. *The Omega Project: Near-Death Experiences, UFO Encounters, and Mind at Large*. New York: William Morrow, 1992.

Ross, Hugh, Kenneth Samples, and Mark Clark. *Lights in the Sky and Little Green Men*. Colorado Springs, CO: NavPress, 2002.

Roszak, Theodore. *Person/Planet*. New York: Anchor Press, 1978.

Sagan, Carl. *Broca's Brain*. New York: Random House, 1972.

———. *The Demon-Haunted World*. New York: Random House, 1995.

———, and Thornton Page, ed. *UFO's—A Scientific Debate*. Ithaca, NY: Cornell University Press, 1972.

Saler, Benson, Charles A. Ziegler, and Charles B. Moore. *UFO Crash at Roswell: The Making of a Modern Myth*. Washington, DC: Smithsonian Institution Press, 1997.

Sanderson, Ivan. *Invisible Residents*. New York: World Publishing, 1970.

———. *Uninvited Visitors*. London: Neville Spearman, 1969.

Schnabel, Jim. *Dark White: Aliens, Abductions, and the UFO Obsession*. London: Hamish Hamilton, 1994.

Sheaffer, Robert. "The New Hampshire Abduction Explained." *Official UFO*, August 1976.

———. *The UFO Verdict: Examining the Evidence*. Buffalo, NY: Prometheus, 1981.

Sladek, John. *The New Apocrypha*. New York: Stein and Day, 1974.

Slobodkin, Louis. *The Space Ship Under the Apple Tree*. New York: Macmillan, 1952.

Sparks, Brad, and Barry Greenwood. "The Secret Pratt Tapes and the Origins of MJ-12." *MUFON 2007 International UFO Symposium Proceedings*. Edited by James Carrion (Bellvue, CO: MUFON, 2007), 95–126.

Spengler, Oswald. *The Decline of the West*. Translated by Charles Francis Atkinson. New York: Alfred A. Knopf, 1962.

Stehling, Kurt R., and William Beller. *Skyhooks*. Garden City, NY: Doubleday, 1962.

Stenhoff, Mark. *Ball Lightning: An Unsolved Problem in Atmospheric Physics*. New York: Kluwer Academic Publishers, 1999.

Stevens, Wendelle, Brit Elders, and Lee Elders. *UFO . . . Contact from the Pleiades*. Munds Park, AZ: Genesis III Publications, 1979.

Story, Ronald. *Guardians of the Universe?* New York: St. Martin's Press, 1980.

Sturrock, Peter A. *The UFO Enigma: A New Review of the Physical Evidence*. New York: Warner, 1999.

Stutley, Margaret. *Shamanism: An Introduction*. London: Routledge, 2003.

Sweetman, Bill. *Aurora: The Pentagon's Secret Hypersonic Spyplane*. Osceola, WI: Motorbooks, 1993.

Taubman, Philip. *Secret Empire: Eisenhower, the CIA, and the Hidden Story of America's Space Espionage*. New York: Simon & Schuster, 2003.

Temple, Robert K. G. *The Sirius Mystery*. London: Sidgwick and Jackson, 1976.

Thompson, Keith. *Angels and Aliens: UFOs and the Mythic Imagination*. New York: Addison Wesley, 1991.

Thompson, William Irwin. *At the Edge of History*. New York: Harper, 1971.

Tulien, Thomas. "Revisiting One of the Classics: The 1952 Nash/Fortenberry Sighting." *International UFO Observer* 27:1 (Spring 2002).

Udolf, Roy. *Handbook of Hypnosis for Professionals*. New York: Van Nostrand Reinhold, 1981.

Vallee, Jacques. *Confrontations: A Scientist's Search for Alien Contact*. New York: Ballantine, 1990.

———. *Dimensions: A Casebook of Alien Contact*. Chicago: Contemporary Books, 1988.

———. "Five Arguments against the Extraterrestrial Origin of Unidentified Flying Objects." *Journal of Scientific Exploration* 4 (1990), 105–17.

———. *Messengers of Deception: UFO Contacts and Cults*. Berkeley, CA: And/Or Press, 1979.

———. *Passport to Magonia*. Chicago: Henry Regnery, 1969.

———. *Revelations: Alien Contact and Human Deception.* New York: Ballantine, 1991.

Vesco, Renato, and David Hatcher Childress. *Man-Made UFOs, 1944–1994.* Stelle, IL: Adventures Unlimited, 1994.

Victor, Jeffrey S. *Satanic Panic.* Chicago: Open Court, 1993.

Volkman, Ernest. *Warriors of the Night.* New York: William Morrow, 1985.

Walker, Jearl, ed. *Light from the Sky: Readings from Scientific American.* San Francisco: W. H. Freeman, 1980.

Walters, Ed, and Frances Walters. *The Gulf Breeze Sightings.* New York: William Morrow, 1990.

Warren, Larry, and Peter Robbins. *Left at East Gate.* New York: Marlow & Co., 1997.

Webb, Stephen. *If the Universe is Teeming With Life . . . Where Is Everybody?* New York: Copernicus Books, 2002.

Westrum, Ron. "Limited Access: Six Natural Scientists and the UFO Phenomenon." In Jacobs 2000, 24–56.

White, Andrew Dickson. *A History of the Warfare between Science and Theology.* New York: D. Applegate, 1896.

Williamson, George Hunt. *Other Tongues—Other Flesh.* Amherst, WI: Amherst Press, 1953.

——— (as "Brother Philip"). *The Secret of the Andes.* London: Neville Spearman, 1961.

Wilson, Colin. *Alien Dawn: An Investigation into the Contact Experience.* New York: Fromm International, 1998.

Wright, Susan. *UFO Headquarters.* New York: St. Martin's Press, 1998.

Yates, Francis. *The Rosicrucian Enlightenment.* Chicago: University of Chicago Press, 1972.

Zaleski, Carol. *Otherworld Journeys.* New York: Oxford University Press, 1987.

Zelazny, Roger. "A Rose for Ecclesiastes." *Fantasy and Science Fiction,* November 1963.

index

Blue Island, 132
Boaistuau, Pierre, 4
Browne, Howard, 20–21
Bullard, Thomas, xv, 166

C

Carter, Jimmy, xii–xiv, 120–121, 130, 209
cattle mutilations, 64–68, 79, 86, 90, 92, 96, 142, 195
Center for UFO Studies (CUFOS), xi, 59, 84, 191
Central Intelligence Agency (CIA), 46, 70–71, 91, 179–180, 186, 188, 191–192, 197
Chen Tao, 101
CIA. *See* Central Intelligence Agency
Clarion (planet), 43
Close Encounters of the Third Kind (movie), 78–79, 84, 86, 167
Cold War, 45, 131, 181, 184–185, 187, 190, 199–206, 222. *See also* Russia
Committee for Scientific Investigation of Claims of the Paranormal (CSICOP), xiii, 74–76, 82, 120
Communion (book), 85, 87
Condon, Edward, 55–60, 122, 205
Condon Report, 57–60, 205
confirmation bias, 117–120
contactees, 32, 39–44, 46, 50, 55, 69–72, 81, 101–102, 105–106, 109, 114, 142–144, 146, 170, 173–174, 188, 204, 208, 219, 223, 225
continental drift, 124–125
Cooper, Milton William, 96–99, 191
Copernican revolution, 12, 107–110
Couliano, Ioan, 176
Creighton, Gordon, 141
cryptoterrestrial hypothesis, 136–138, 148, 151

d

Däniken, Erich von, 69
Davis, Andrew Jackson, 220
Day the Earth Stood Still, The (movie), 33, 39, 77
demonic hypothesis, 141–144, 148, 151
deros, 20–21, 26, 99
Devereux, Paul, 140, 178
dirigibles, 7–9, 150, 156, 199
disinformation, 181, 186, 190, 192–193, 195, 197, 199–200, 206–208, 210
Dolan, Richard, 181, 191
Doty, Richard, 90, 191
Drake, Frank, 211–212, 217
Drake equation, 212
Dreamland, 92–94. *See also* Area 51
Durante, Jimmy, 81, 167

e

E Yada da Shi'ite, 26
earthquake lights, 139
ETH. *See* extraterrestrial hypothesis
Evans-Pritchard, E.E., 6
extraterrestrial hypothesis (ETH), xv–xvi, 3, 5, 33, 37, 44–45, 49, 55–56, 59–60, 63, 66, 68, 74, 76–78, 81, 84, 90, 96, 106, 108–109, 111–113, 115–120, 122–123, 125–126, 128–130, 135–138, 140, 146, 151–152, 155, 158, 160, 166, 169, 171, 173, 177, 189–190, 196, 199, 204–205, 212–213, 225

f

Fantastic Adventures (magazine), 19, 32
FATE (magazine), 32, 42, 61, 135
federal hypothesis, 133–134